I
Aches,

"I highly recommend this excellent book. *Aches, Pains, and Love* is chock-full of candid and down-to-earth advice, all of it liberally spiced with wisdom coming from the author's many years of experience living with chronic pain and illness. I particularly appreciated the crucial distinction she makes between a partner being educated about your condition (a necessity) and your partner being able to actually feel what life is like for you (highly unlikely). The good news is that the latter isn't necessary in order for a relationship to thrive, so long as respect and compassion are present. I hope that everyone who is chronically ill and is either in a relationship or wishes to be in one will read this book."

TONI BERNHARD, author of *How to Be Sick and How to Live Well with Chronic Pain and Illness*

"Clear your calendar because once you start this book you will want to read it from cover to cover! At turns laugh-out-loud funny and poignant, Kira Lynne teaches you how to be your best self so you can have the relationship you deserve. She makes clear that self-improvement is a choice; choose this book, and you won't be disappointed."

SUSAN MILSTREY WELLS, author of *A Delicate Balance: Living Successfully With Chronic Illness*

"Kira Lynne candidly shares her experience of what she has learned through dating and marriage while suffering from a chronic illness. Communication is key, and this book delivers insight and communication tactics to educate the reader on how to best build open, loving relationships. Kira's witty style makes this an easy to read. This may be the most thorough book on dating and chronic illness ever written, and I wish it had been available when I was navigating the dating circles. Bravo!"

LORI HARTWELL, author of *Chronically Happy: Joyful Living in Spite of Chronic Illness*

"Brilliant and long overdue. A must-read for anyone living with pain or chronic illness and for those who love them. Bringing refreshing insights from her own personal experience, Kira Lynne guides you, step by step, on a path to meaningful, loving, happy, and healthy relationships, starting with yourself."

DENISE STROUDE, RPC, MPCC, Vice President of Rhodes Wellness College

"Kudos to Kira Lynne for her efforts to help herself and so many others in dealing with chronic, often debilitating pain and illness. With a wisdom few of us can muster, she brings hope to people living with these conditions, a genuine hope for loving and nurturing relationships".

PAUL STEINBERG, MD, author of *A Salamander's Tale*

"Kira Lynne invites the reader to share her journey through decades of aches, pains, and love with a degree of unvarnished frankness rarely seen in non-fiction. She utilizes her often painful experiences to formulate a practical, useful guide for any reader who lives with chronic illness and pain. The topic is sensitive, but Kira lays out a welcome mat for readers to join her and step through the door to a healthier life and better relationships. Beyond the central topic of managing relationships while ill, Kira shares a path to a fuller and more meaningful life with illness, whether one is in a romantic relationship or not."

JOY H. SELAK, PhD

"Kira has written an accessible, humorous, moving, and honest account of the very real impact chronic health conditions can have on romantic life. Packed full of useful tips learned through her own experience, as well as wise counsel, this book is a valuable resource for anyone seeking a relationship whilst living with a chronic health condition of any kind. I could have saved myself a lot of heartache if this book had been available many years ago, when I was a young woman first living with a spinal injury— daunted and shy about how to find intimacy and love through a sexual relationship. Intimacy and chronic health conditions is an area that is rarely discussed or written about, which makes this book all the more important."

VIDYALAMA BURCH, author of *Living Well with Pain and Illness: The Mindful Way to Free Yourself from Suffering*

"A comforting and helpful guide to navigating relationships while dealing with chronic pain. Kira Lynne walks you through a healing and hope-filled process to create safe and loving relationships!"

ABIGAIL STEIDLEY, Mind-Body Coach

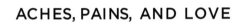

ACHES, PAINS, AND LOVE

ACHES, PAINS, AND LOVE

A GUIDE TO DATING AND
RELATIONSHIPS FOR THOSE WITH
CHRONIC PAIN AND ILLNESS

KIRA LYNNE

Aches, Pains, and Love: A Guide to Dating and Relationships
for Those with Chronic Pain and Illness
Copyright @ 2016 by Kira Lynne
All Rights Reserved

Library and Archives Canada Cataloguing in Publication
Lynne, Kira, author
        Aches, pains, and love : a guide to dating and relationships
for those with chronic pain and illness / Kira Lynne.

Issued in print and electronic formats.
ISBN 978-0-9949935-0-2 (paperback).
ISBN 978-0-9949935-1-9 (ebook)

1. Dating (Social customs). 2. Chronically ill.
3. Chronic pain—Patients. I. Title.

HQ801.L955 2016   646.7'7   C2016-900124-5
C2016-900125-3

Cover and Interior Design: Naomi MacDougall
Published in Canada by Moppet Press

10 9 8 7 6 5 4 3 2 1

For all my fellow spoonies

CONTENTS

Foreword

IT IS A TRUE privilege to write the foreword for this remarkable book. While reading *Aches, Pains, and Love*, I was struck
by Kira Lynne's honesty and clarity of thought, and I was
amazed by the transformation she has undergone since I
first met her. I was also reminded of one of my patients, a
man I will refer to as John.

John uses humour to deal with his *de-identification*, the
process by which someone with chronic illness lets go of
their old identity and accepts a new reality for themselves.
John, a very funny man, now refers to himself as "John-lite."
Recently, when a friend called him to go out for a beer, he
quipped, "John would love that. But John-lite would prefer
if you came over and brought some tea so we could chat for
a half-hour."

I share this story because John's method of dealing with
and ultimately surmounting some of the social challenges
related to chronic illness demonstrates many of the core
messages of *Aches, Pains, and Love*. This is an important

book that focuses on dating and relationship advice for those with chronic pain and illness but is also filled with wisdom for anyone struggling with the social side of life.

John's decision to refer to himself as "John-lite" reveals many things: it shows us the incredible power of thought, the ability we all have to reframe our conception of ourselves through language and ideas; it shows us how compassion for oneself is the vital first step to engaging with the outside world, as John's nickname indicates an endearing tenderness towards his own circumstance; and it shows us that acceptance is a process, not a decision, and certainly not the same as giving up—a message that lies at the heart of this wonderful book.

Patients with chronic conditions often have an unarticulated agreement with themselves: their life is on hold until they get better. But what if they don't get better? What if this is now their life? Most people think of chronic illness and happiness as two mutually exclusive things. Kira is here to tell you that yes, the relationship between illness and happiness is indeed complicated, but happiness does not have to be contingent on getting better.

"Invisible" illnesses, such as myalgic encephalomyelitis/chronic fatigue syndrome (ME/CFS), have their own special challenges. Patients are often subjected to unsolicited advice from well-meaning people—the dreaded if only's: if only you exercised more, if only you cut out wheat and dairy from your diet, and a host of other suggestions. Dealing with people who have misperceptions about your illness or unrealistic expectations can be terribly stressful. Sometimes it can seem that even friends and family need constant reminding of your limitations. So what should you decide to disclose about your illness? And what is the best way to do that? Kira has some good suggestions.

Avoiding isolation and disconnection is another challenge. We are social animals; we all long to belong and connect. Too often, patients turn to mood-regulating substances (e.g., food or alcohol) and behaviours (e.g., gambling or spending money they don't have) to fill the social void. Some patients chafe at the idea of seeking professional help (from psychiatrists, psychologists, counsellors, therapists, social workers, ministers, rabbis, or other trained professionals). But there is great value in working with healthcare professionals who listen to and support you. Connecting with others can absolutely help, but here's the key: self-management is vital. You need to be in charge. Kira offers important insights on the ins and outs of self-management, including the crucial role of journaling.

Throughout this book, Kira provides examples of the power of thought, both positive and negative. She shows you how to leverage cognitive behavioural therapy—something she calls a "thought-wrangling tool"—to deal with negative thoughts that often lead to self-defeating and paralyzing behaviours. Kira also calls attention to the idea of identity, and the importance of avoiding the sick role, the victim role, and the resultant burden of blame; each of these can lead to learned helplessness.

The social lives of some patients are further complicated by a history of abuse or trauma. The consequences of trauma can include challenges with trust, intimacy, shame, and communication, all of which get in the way of healthy relationships. Kira reminds you to beware of the "rescuer" and explains how to avoid the hazard of co-dependency, which often develops in relationships when one partner is ill.

This book also reviews the importance of boundaries and provides simple yet effective strategies for setting them. I tell patients to think of boundaries as "superpowers." With great power comes great responsibility. You have two goals when setting boundaries: to maintain them, but to also maintain your close relationships.

Aches, Pains, and Love offers more than just ideas and concepts. Kira provides a plethora of concrete planning ideas and tools. Early on, she notes that she used to read self-help books from cover to cover but skimmed the exercises. She understood the advice on offer but then did nothing to actually implement it in her life. When I suggest workbooks for patients, I say that I don't want them to "read" the books, I want them to "do" the books. The old saying that knowledge is power is incorrect. Knowledge acted upon is power. So take Kira's advice here, and "do" some of her ideas.

The Serenity Prayer has an important place in my life. I try to instil its principles within all of my patients, including John (and John-lite):

> *Grant me the serenity to accept the things I cannot change,*
> *the courage to change the things that I can, and*
> *the wisdom to know the difference.*

The last sentence is the most difficult to put into practice—you need to avoid "all-or-nothing" thinking and learn to embrace shades of grey. Kira covers the importance of creative thinking in accepting uncertainty and adapting to change. Transformation can be slow. One needs to cultivate patience and an attitude of gratitude.

Congratulate yourself and celebrate the small victories.

This book is about many things. But most of all, it's about living your best life and not putting everything on hold until you get better. A patient recently sent me a card with an aphorism inside that captures the essence of this idea beautifully:

Life isn't about waiting for the storm to pass,
it's about learning to dance in the rain.

Read this book. Absorb its important messages. And then go dig out those dancing shoes.

Ric Arseneau, MD FRCPC MA(Ed) MBA FACP CGP
Clinical Associate Professor
Division of General Internal Medicine
St. Paul's Hospital
Director of Program Planning
Complex Chronic Disease Program
Women's Hospital
University of British Columbia

Introduction

WHEN I WAS 20, my doctor sent me to a specialist who told me that, due to my recently diagnosed chronic pain condittion, I would never be able to have a successful marriage or intimate relationship.

Wham! Imagine hearing that at 20, with your whole life ahead of you, when endless possibilities and opportunities seem to be on the horizon, and one of the most important things in your life is meeting a life partner. It's unthinkable.

Yet when it's coming from a doctor—a specialist, no less—an impressionable young woman tends to believe what she's told. I believed, and I was devastated. This physician's words greatly affected my life from that moment on, even after I realized she was not necessarily correct. I mean, who was she to say I would never be able to have a successful relationship?

I am writing this book for my twenty-year-old self, for the girl who gave up hope based simply on what one doctor told her. And I'm writing this for everyone else who may have given up hope on relationships due to their health conditions. I now know there *is* hope. I have spent two decades disproving that doctor's message, and maybe I can save others some time by sharing my experiences.

Let's rewind a little bit.

When I was about 15 or 16, I began experiencing almost constant pelvic pain. Pain when I rode a bike, pain when I rode my horses, pain when I walked, pain when I wore tight pants, and, most upsetting, pain during sex. It also meant pain that lasted after all of these activities, often for days or weeks. After several years of enduring the pain in secret and with great shame, I went to see my doctor, which started the chain of events leading up to my visit with the specialist.

The specialist gave me a diagnosis, explained the condition and presented me with my options. She told me that the condition would likely be lifelong and chronic. Then she broke the news about my romantic relationship prospects.

After the initial shock wore off, I started getting used to the idea of having a chronic condition (although not without a huge helping of self-pity). I figured this pain would be the worst I'd have to endure. It was uncomfortable but manageable. Being in denial helped me through much of this initial phase, especially when it came to the doom-laden prediction about future relationships.

Unfortunately, when I hit my 30s, I was blindsided by a shitstorm of additional, more serious and more severe conditions and illnesses, and a lot more pain. Several other doctors and specialists also told me that my condition was chronic and likely lifelong, and only if I was very lucky would it not get worse. According to many of those doctors, intimate relationships weren't even an option anymore—not to be addressed or discussed, not on the menu.

I often wondered: Could this really be true? Was I never going to have the relationship I had always dreamed of? I felt that I had been robbed not only of a pain-free life, a life where I could be physically active and work full-time (or at all), but also of a life with a boyfriend, partner, husband, whatever you want to call him. I had been robbed of romance and love and affection. I felt like so much had been taken away from me.

In my 30s, I met other women with similar conditions who were a little older and had been dealing with their illnesses for even longer than I. When I asked for their thoughts on relationships, they gave similar answers: "I don't have the energy. Who would want me? How can I possibly meet someone? It's the last thing on my mind."

Well, let me tell you, it's never been the last thing on my mind. It's often the first thing on my mind. In the past, I'd feel sorry for myself. A lot. Like, all the time. Especially when I saw a couple walk by holding hands or looking happy. But lately, I've become determined to prove that specialist wrong. I lived through my 20s and most of my 30s believing that a successful and happy relationship would never be possible for me, which is a long time to hold onto a misguided belief. This isn't to say that I didn't have relationships. I did. I had several and was even married for a short time. My marriage split up in large part due to my pain issues. Ta-da! The doctor must have been right. But was she really? After all, I did have actual relationships, some of which lasted up to six years. And they were certainly happy at times. The only piece missing was the "successful" part.

I'm going to pause briefly and consider what a "success-ful relationship" means to me, since it likely takes on vari-ous meanings, depending on who you are. For the purpose of this book, a successful relationship is a long-lasting, lov-ing, caring, interdependent relationship devoid of abuse. The definition of long-lasting again depends on your per-spective; I would love to meet someone to be with for the rest of my life, so since this is my dream and my book, we'll go with that.

There is very little information out there on dating and relationships for people with chronic pain and illness. And yet thousands (if not millions) of people in North America alone suffer from chronic pain and illness. Why are there not more resources on this topic? Likely because writing is not a priority when you are in pain day in, day out, when just getting through the tasks of the day can be a victory. But why, just because we have a medical condition, should we not be able to have companionship, love, intimacy, and partnership? Sure, finding these may be harder than if we were healthy, but is it really impossible?

I don't believe it is. I know it's possible to live joyfully with illness and pain. I know it's possible to laugh, find pur-pose, and feel fulfilled. I know it's possible to make new friends, deepen connections, and live in a more rewarding way than even before the pain began. I know it's possible to see life with a sense of humour, even when you can barely get out of bed some days. I know this because I have expe-rienced it. It hasn't been easy, I won't kid you, and I've had to work extremely hard to get here—but it's possible, and it's worth the work. And if I made all of these things happen despite the pain and illness, I believe there is a way for me, and you, to find lasting love and companionship in an intimate relationship.

It may require thinking outside the box, considering options I may not have been open to before, changing my expectations or just becoming more flexible, creative, and imaginative. There are billions of people on this planet. No one can tell me that not one of them is right for me (or you).

This book is going to explore all the ideas I've touched on here and many more. In each chapter I'll share some stories of my own dating experiences. My dear friend Paula has been after me for years to write a book about my adventures in dating, so those parts of the book are dedicated to her; hopefully you will enjoy them as well. We'll also look at some of the issues facing people with chronic pain and illness who are wanting to date or improve their relationships (that's probably you, if you're reading this). At the end of each chapter, I've included a "Take Action!" section to help you start taking the steps towards finding and creating the relationship you want. The points in these sections come from my own experiences, education, research, and, occasionally, other people's advice.

Just a note on these points: I used to read self-help books from cover to cover but skimmed through the exercises—understanding what I was advised to do but not doing it. I felt that simply understanding the message of the book would help me. But nothing was changing in my life. One day, it finally clicked: for the book to help me change my life, I actually had to *do* the exercises and *implement* the tools that the book provided. The same goes for this book. You can read through it and understand it, but unless you actually take action, you're just going to stay where you are. So I'm challenging you to take action. The great thing is that when you do begin to take steps in a certain direction, things can't help but start to change because *you* are changing.

We are all in various places in our lives, and our pains and illnesses are similar but also different. Not everything I talk about will click with everyone. Take what you like from this book and leave the rest. Some chapters are aimed more specifically at single people, while others are written for those already in relationships, but there is something useful for everyone in each chapter. If you're in a relationship, I still recommend you read the chapters on dating as well. There are little tidbits throughout the book that you might find helpful.

I'm writing from my perspective as a white, sexually active, heterosexual female with a certain set of health conditions (which you'll learn about shortly), and my perspective only reaches so far. I would like for this book to be as accessible to as many people as possible, but there will be limitations. If you're a heterosexual man reading this, in most cases the "he" that I use in reference to a partner can just as easily be flipped to "she," so please don't feel as though this book isn't for you. This book can also just as equally apply to readers who are gay, lesbian, transgendered, polyamorous, celibate, you name it.

Throughout the book I often rely on the phrase "chronic pain and illness" because that is my experience. You may have chronic pain, you may have chronic illness, or you may have both. The phrase is simply meant to be inclusive and representative of an often complex health condition.

Finally, I'm not a doctor, I'm a counsellor and life coach.

A lot of my theories and hypotheses are based on my life experience, research, training, and information obtained from various doctors, combined with my spiritual experiences and intuition. I'm not claiming to have any definitive medical answers or solutions. My explanations are based on personal beliefs that I have developed over the years. I'm not aiming to write a scientific book; so, while I do make certain statements and draw conclusions, I haven't included footnotes or references, although there is a Resources section at the end. My wish is that this book be a conversation rather than a lesson.

So let's start talking.

PART I
CREATING YOUR FOUNDATION

CHAPTER 1

The Beginning

MY STORY

ALL OF THE stories and anecdotes in this book are true. Names have been changed to protect, not the innocent, but the many men I've dated (and in one case married). This first story is difficult and painful to recount, but it is mine, and I would like to share it.

One of the reasons I think it is important to tell you about this particular event is that many medical experts, including my current internist, believe that physical, mental, and emotional trauma can lead to chronic pain conditions. I also want to tell you because life is sometimes messy and painful and scary. I lived in shame over this for so long and only recently discovered that I didn't have to. So yes, I know I'm starting out on a heavy note, but it gets lighter from here.

Picture me, if you will, at 15. Average looking, average

build, brown hair, brown eyes, bigger than average nose, and on the tall side. I was an only child with strict parents and had been in a private all-girls school since kindergarten. Guys, let me stop you before you get too excited. It was essentially like being locked in a prison from 8:40am to 3:20pm every day. I was a sensitive child who loved creativity and freedom and found herself stifled in an unnatural, and unnaturally authoritarian, environment.

As teenagers often do, I decided that I should have a boyfriend, so I went out and found one. His name was Jamie, and he was the son of one of my father's colleagues. He had a mullet, wore a trench coat and smoked. I could tell my parents weren't too thrilled that I was dating him, because they changed my curfew from midnight to 10pm. I mean, everyone knows that nothing bad ever happens before 10pm, right?

Jamie and I spent all our free time in his basement rec room on his ratty black-leather couch, watching movies and kissing. For a long time, things never got past second base and all clothes stayed on. Thanks to my strict upbringing, I was very sheltered and clueless about relationships, much less about the male anatomy or the inner workings of a teenage boy's mind. One day, after a couple of months of dating, Jamie told me about a conversation he had had with his mother.

"My mom said I'd better not be trying to get into your pants," he said, "And I told her, 'What else would I be trying to do?'"

I was shocked. It hadn't even crossed my mind that sex was an option. I really didn't know what it was or what it involved. We had practiced putting condoms on bananas at school and had some very basic and vague sex-ed classes, but that was it. And when it came right down to it, I didn't want to have sex. At 15, I didn't yet know what a "red flag" was, but looking back, I would say that this was the first of many that would flap in front of my face and I would willingly ignore.

After this big reveal, Jamie started trying a variety of plots, ploys, tricks, and schemes to get into my pants. As things got heated, he would tell me he loved me. He took me to different and (in his mind) seductive venues, encouraged me to drink beer, and persistently attempted to take off as many of my clothes as I would allow.

I finally relented. My parents had gone away for the weekend, and I was staying at a friend's house. On the pretence of going home to do some homework, I went back to my parents' house and met Jamie there. The plan was unspoken but clear: we were going to have sex. I don't remember much about the actual attempt. We were in the downstairs guest room. It was dark and musty. Unfamiliar. I remember the scratchy comforter, the narrow single bed, the brown colour scheme, and the small window up high in the corner of the room. I remember him, condom-free, pushing himself into me. I was tense and afraid.

"Is it in yet?" I asked.

"No, not even close," Jamie said. Not even close?

How could that be? What more had to happen? I had no idea what was going on down there, what was meant to happen, or why it wasn't happening the way it was supposed to. "Try to relax," he said.

I couldn't relax, no matter how hard I tried. My body was so tense and tight with fear, nothing was making its way into my vagina that day. I doubt even a pencil would have succeeded. My muscles contracted completely, telling me that this wasn't right and telling him no. I wasn't ready for this, at all.

I felt ashamed. Inadequate. Embarrassed. There was obviously something wrong with me. I told no one.

After that, Jamie backed off, and sex wasn't mentioned for a few months. A glorious reprieve! Then, one night in late spring, we went to the park with a friend of his. Jamie had brought beer and we were all drinking. I think I might have had one beer, at the most; I was a supreme lightweight and also very suspicious and untrusting of Jamie and his present intentions. He and his friend talked about sex and I remember Jamie saying, "It had better happen tonight. I've been waiting long enough." He sounded bitter. I just laughed. I didn't believe he was serious. And I had no interest in trying to have sex with him again. By now I had buried the failed experience and had no desire to revisit it. Besides, he was only 16. Since when does six months of dating constitute "long enough" at that age? (Or any age for that matter?)

I don't remember how we got from the park back to his house, or when his friend left, but here's what I do remember. Us in his basement rec room. Naked together in a sleeping bag on the floor. Short, dark, damp carpet surrounding us. Darkness everywhere. Him on top of me. Kissing me. His rough, coarse, mulleted hair in my hands. His rubbery erection. Him just about to enter me. My panic. Although my memory of that night's events has always been patchy at best, I can still remember that moment of unbridled fear when the adrenaline pumped into me. No! I needed to escape!

"No, wait, stop!" I said. He didn't stop, but rather pushed forward, and this time there were no contracted muscles to stop him. I lay there. I didn't fight. I don't even know whether I could think. I don't remember much else, other than trying to seem like I was enjoying the sex, because he had told me that he hated it when girls would "just lie there like a dead fish." I didn't want to be a dead fish. What I remember most is that it didn't hurt. That was one of the only times that sex has not hurt for me.

Afterwards, I felt ashamed. I felt so completely and thoroughly dirty. I went home and ran a bath. It was late for me to have a bath, and I thought my parents would know for sure that something was wrong. I crouched in the tub, crying as quietly as possible. I scrubbed, trying to clean off the humiliation. The bath didn't help. My parents said nothing. I assumed that this was what it was like for all girls when they lost their virginity (and believed it for another 20 years). I told no one.

Twenty-five years later, I am writing this book. My life has changed a lot, and I have developed a significant list of medical conditions. Whether these are related to being date-raped or not, I'll never know, but I do sense that that night in Jamie's basement played a role in determining my future health.

WHEN I READ books or articles about people who are dealing with illnesses, they often don't mention what it is they are suffering from. I'm a very curious person. I want to know! Give me the details! Spill it! For some, not naming their condition is a way of maintaining privacy. But for me, it creates a sense of separation, of disconnectedness.

So, on the one hand, I don't like to identify myself by my conditions, and I don't introduce myself as a "sick person." Some people in my life are completely unaware that there is anything wrong with me and that I receive disability benefits. Yet I also believe in fairness, so, to get it out of the way, here is a list of my officially diagnosed conditions, in order of appearance (take a bow, all of you):

Migraines
Vulvodynia
Post-Traumatic Stress Disorder
Anxiety and Panic Attacks
Depression
Interstitial Cystitis
Myalgic Encephalomyelitis
Fibromyalgia
Postural Orthostatic Tachycardia

First of all, let me say that it's not as bad as it sounds. Well, that's not entirely true. My nervous system has essentially gone haywire. There have been times where the pain, depression, and anxiety felt so terrible I wanted to be dead, but those were just moments in the long movie of my life. All of these conditions are non-fatal, and they come and go, and for that I am grateful. I have bad days, good days, really bad days, and really good days.

I don't function nearly as well as a "healthy person," but I manage quite well. I'm independent. I have a great support system, including friends, family, co-workers, and health professionals. My life has purpose, and I am happy (most of the time). I am actually happier now than I have been in a long time, perhaps ever. It's taken a lot of work to get here, but I've made it, and I keep working on it every day. I am not my illness. There is illness, but I am not sick. I am Kira.

You may have some of these conditions; you may not. Even if you have different medical conditions and sources of pain, this book is still for you. Pain and suffering are pain and suffering, whatever form they take. What matters is finding a way to live a fulfilling and happy life despite them.

Before moving to the next section, I'd like to offer a quick word on trauma. Many medical professionals assert that most, if not all, of the above conditions may result from traumatic events that occur in childhood. While I don't think my experience with date rape was the only factor in the development of my conditions, I do think it was one factor. There were other contributors as well: my mother developing cancer in my teens and dying when I was 21; my many falls from horses, including one onto my helmet-less head that resulted in a concussion; and growing up in a household where I was encouraged (read: forced) to suppress my emotions. Being a sensitive child, I had a lot of emotions, and they were often very big and difficult ones. In our house, anger was not ok, crying was not ok. Only happiness was ok, so all the anger, fear, hurt, and pain got stuffed back down inside me. Where did it go? I'm not sure, but I'm pretty sure I know how it eventually came out (see the above list of medical conditions).

LET'S DISCUSS

Starting Out

We need to have a stable mental, emotional, physical, and spiritual foundation before we start dating. Well, we don't *need* to, but having one greatly increases our odds of being in a successful relationship. This is particularly important for people with chronic pain and illness because we must ensure that we know how to take especially good care of ourselves.

Throughout this book I'll be talking a lot about creating a solid foundation. To create that foundation, we can't dive straight into the topics of dating and mating. Before we even begin to talk about dating, we need to look at ourselves. Who are we? Where are we in our lives? What are our biggest emotional wounds? How can we heal them? What are our attitudes and beliefs towards dating and relationships? Towards the opposite sex (or the same sex, whatever the case may be)?

We've all traveled different paths to our conditions and illnesses. No two people's experiences are the same, yet we have all wound up in this place of physical pain. If you have physical pain, you're most likely also experiencing some degree of emotional pain. That emotional pain may be due to dealing with the constant physical pain and illness on a daily basis or to past unhealed emotional hurts, or both. That's a lot of pain! The key is to unravel and then reduce as much of your emotional pain as possible before bringing it into a relationship, for your benefit and your partner's. If you can also reduce your physical pain before you start a relationship, even better!

You may be thinking that you're going to skip the part where you work on yourself and dive straight into the dating section because, more than anything, you want someone in your life. Hey, I get it. And if that's what you really want to do, don't let me stop you. But know that we are each responsible for ourselves and need to take care of our own issues.

No one else is going to do it for us. Finding an amazing partner will not solve our emotional problems. In fact, our emotional problems may end up ruining an amazing partnership. It is worth your time to work on yourself before you start dating. *You* are worth it.

Semantics

Since I'm going to be referring regularly to illness, sickness, disease, and syndromes, I would like to clarify how I'm employing these words. I have chosen to use "condition" rather than "sickness" or "illness" because "condition" sounds a little more neutral and less daunting. Less sick. Don't get me wrong, I'm not saying that you're not sick. What I'm saying is that words are powerful, and the more we refer to ourselves as "sick" day in and day out—in our conversations and in our thoughts—the more we start to believe we are sick, maybe even sicker than we are, and the more we identify ourselves, first and foremost, as "sick."

"So what?" you may ask. "I *am* sick." And yes, you are, but is that what you want to lead with? Let me explain.

Last winter I was in Hawaii with my friend, Stephanie, and we were driving down the highway, looking at all the license plates on the cars we were passing. One plate, which we saw a few times, said "Disabled Veteran." I remember asking Stephanie why someone would want to lead with that, for the first thing someone to know about them was that they were disabled.

"But he's a veteran, and that's something to be proud of," Stephanie said. And she's absolutely right. But I still wanted to know, why would you want to be so clearly identified as disabled, right off the bat?

Let me explain further. The more we tell ourselves we

are sick (or disabled), the more we reinforce that in our brains and the more that becomes part of our identity, who we are. It may also lead us to give into the sickness and become more ill. Or we might use it as an excuse not to do something that might help us heal or give us relief. In my case, my doctor refers to my condition as a disease and an illness. I've accepted that I have a serious medical condition. But I still call it a condition. My identity is not "sick person," it's "Kira." I lead with who I am, not with the conditions I'm facing. I am Kira, and I have some extraordinary challenges in my life, but they are not who I am.

We can start to re-wire our brains into a more positive way of thinking and living by being careful about how we label ourselves. This doesn't mean that we are denying our illness or are going to miraculously heal (like some people may wish you to believe), but it will help us maintain our identity and show ourselves and others that we aren't our illness.

Start with the Emotional Stuff

Most of us carry our pasts around with us, pasts that may have included dysfunction, abuse, and/or trauma. By bringing our past into our present, we let things that are no longer happening to us affect our current relationships, unless we do the work to heal what is still hurting. We all struggle with this, healthy, disabled, or otherwise. If you want to have a successful intimate relationship, it's a good idea to confront and deal with at least some of your emotional issues so they don't follow you into the future. For example, I found that until I was able to forgive myself for being date raped, I treated all men like opponents, which isn't useful when you're trying to build a loving relationship.

Sometimes, you might find your past emotional issues are closely connected to your health condition, and in other cases they might seem quite separate. Either way, before you start to date it's a good idea to take a good, long look at your past and what needs to be healed. It's also useful to take a look at how you feel about yourself as a person and at your attitude towards your health condition. What do you want to lead with?

As you might imagine, there are numerous steps in emotional healing. If you're interested in diving deeply into your healing, I encourage you wholeheartedly. It's certainly one of the most rewarding journeys I've ever taken. You may find that you would like the help and support of a counsellor or psychologist. On the other hand, you might wish to keep it on the down-low and start with a book. Included at the end of this book is a list of my favourite books and other resources, which, along with my counsellor, helped me clear out a lot of past issues and create a solid foundation.

Since this is a book on dating, and not on healing the past, I'm not going to delve too deeply into the subject. However, two key points are worth discussing: awareness and acceptance.

Awareness

With the increased popularity of meditation, yoga, and new-age philosophies, the word "awareness" seems in danger of overuse. It's being bandied about fairly casually in conversations, blog posts, and articles. The mainstreaming of "awareness," however, doesn't decrease its importance. The truth is, increasing your awareness of yourself is the first step to cleaning up your emotional stuff and improving your self-care. Being aware of your thought patterns, emotions, behaviours, habits, values, and fears can enrich your life in so many ways. Awareness allows you to take responsibility for what is happening in your life, to stop taking things personally, and to feel like you do have the power to change what makes you unhappy.

The Blame Game

When you increase your awareness, you will be able to more clearly see other people and how they affect you. How often have you heard someone say, "He makes me so angry!" or, "She always does this to me, and then she makes me go and ruin everything I was working on!"? How often have you heard others blaming people for what is happening to them? What I'm describing is an epidemic of blame. So many of us walk around blaming others for what is going on in our own lives, thinking that all these negative things are happening "to us" and that there is an external force creating problems for us—whether that force is an individual, an institution, or the universe itself.

Here's the good news: the only person creating problems for you is you.

There are a few reasons why we attract situations and people that we don't want:

1. **Our beliefs and attitudes.** If we believe the world is against us, that people intend to wrong others, that we always get the short end of the stick, then that's what we are going to experience. If we walk around angry, we can't expect the people we encounter to be kind to us. They're going to pick up on the angry vibes and act accordingly!

What we put out there, we get back. It's useful to take a close look at our negative beliefs because they are often distorted and not entirely accurate. Once we challenge our negative beliefs and see another way, our attitudes may shift considerably.

2. How we interpret events. Two people can interpret the same event completely differently. Let's say Sue had promised Mark a ticket to a concert. Mark was really excited about going to the concert (I mean, who doesn't love Elton John?). At the last minute, Sue got a date, so she told Mark she would not be giving him the ticket after all.

Mark number one gets really upset. How could Sue do this to him? It's totally uncool, and she's always so unreliable, especially when there's a new man in her life. This is the last straw, she always makes him so angry, he's done with the friendship. He sits on his deck smoking all evening, steaming with resentment.

Mark number two is upset. He hasn't seen Sue for a while and misses her. He's also disappointed that he won't be getting to see Elton perform live. He feels bummed out and wanders aimlessly around his apartment for a while. Then he remembers that there is a football game on tonight, Green Bay Packers vs. New England Patriots, so he knows it's going to be a good one. And if he doesn't go to the concert, he'll also be able to call his mom, which he's been meaning to do for a couple of weeks. He'll catch up with Sue another night.

Which Mark would you rather be? Mark number one, seething over a perceived slight, or Mark number two, who went on to have a great night even though he didn't go to see

Elton John? Which Mark is going to be a happier person? Which one has a better chance of finding his life partner?

3. Repeating and recreating past events. This is something we do unconsciously. We tend to recreate the negative situations and unrewarding relationships that we experienced earlier in our lives, then we blame the event or person for having shown up. But it is we, in fact, who allowed them into our world. By creating awareness around your patterns, you can start to change who and what you invite into your life.

Taking Responsibility for Ourselves

It can be really challenging to start taking responsibility and stop laying blame on others. It can also be very empowering. We end up having more control over what happens in our lives when we are aware of how we live, think, and behave, and when we stop blaming others for things that are not going well.

In my case, I used to be so incredibly angry about my medical condition. I wanted to blame someone for it, and I needed to direct my anger somewhere other than at myself. I blamed Jamie, my parents, and my doctors. I found all sorts of reasons to blame my pain on others. I could justify anything.

Fast forward through many years of personal growth work. I finally gained a good sense of self-awareness, which led to a greater sense of understanding around what had happened to me. I learned to view my condition as a gift rather than a curse. Yes, believe it or not, I really do see it that way! It has given me the means and opportunity to quit a job I didn't like and to have a career I love. It has also allowed me to stop doing things that I didn't want to be doing in the first place and to end unhealthy relationships. Now, I am doing what I enjoy and have a much more confident, calm, and happy life than before I became ill. And this is all thanks to the perspective change I experienced when I started to work on myself.

Sound easy? Not really. I first had to become very aware of my beliefs, values, and attitudes, as well as my negative thoughts (awareness is always the first step!). I had to think about where I was in life, where I wanted to be, and how to close the gap. Closing that gap involved some hard work. I had to work with my negative thoughts on a daily basis, if not hourly. I had cue cards, I listened to webinars, I did an online course on pain reduction (thank you Abigail Steidley—see the appendix for more information on her awesome mind–body pain-management program). I meditated, then I meditated some more.

Meditation was a great way to increase my awareness around what was going on inside my mind. I patrolled my thoughts constantly. I began to see where I had been off track in the past and how that had affected me. Being aware allowed me to see the improvements and rewards I received from doing the work on my thoughts, beliefs, and attitudes. It also helped me catch myself from falling back into negative patterns.

I could have been Mark number one. I could have kept going down the path of self-pity. I could have easily become angry and resentful. I could have given up and become a couch potato. And let me tell you, that path was very tempting, but ultimately, I chose the attitude that would improve my life, not the one that would hold me back. I chose the path of Mark number two. You can choose to hold onto your anger and believe the world is against you, but (a) you'll only be hurting yourself, and (b) you might not be right.

So How Does This Awareness Thing Work, Exactly?
Awareness is the first step in moving forward and making positive change—awareness of what isn't working and awareness that a change needs to happen. It means confronting what is holding you back, facing your light side and your shadow side, and stepping out of denial. When you're in denial, you are definitely not aware. I'm sure you've heard that, "admitting you have a problem is half the battle," and it's true, because when you admit you have a problem, you are stepping into awareness.

Developing awareness means becoming familiar with what is happening around you and, more importantly, inside you—mentally, physically, emotionally, and spiritually. You cannot begin to heal, or to find better relationships, until you become familiar with your own patterns: how you think, what you think, and how your body feels emotionally and physically.

In terms of awareness around dating and relationships, a good place to start is to notice your thoughts. Patrol them! Be your own thought cop! Identify your beliefs, especially around dating. Do you believe you are worthy? Do you believe you are lovable? (You are, even though you may not believe it. And no, you aren't the exception. You. Are. Lovable.)

Sometimes awareness can be difficult because you may discover things about yourself that you don't like or want to acknowledge. Fortunately, when you become more aware of yourself, you have the choice and ability to change what you don't like. The more you move in a positive direction, the more you will like, love, and accept yourself. Acceptance is the next key component in a strong foundation.

Acceptance
A Story About Acceptance

I have an A-type personality. I'm a perfectionist. Things must be done right. In the past, I had to accept all invitations. I took on new projects like they were going out of style. I over-committed myself on a weekly basis. I worked out six days a week religiously. I monitored my food intake down to the half calorie (seriously). I did a lot for other people. What about me? What *about* me? I was fine. I was GREAT. Until I crashed and developed myalgic encephalomyelitis and fibromyalgia (ME/FM). But even that didn't stop me. I didn't understand why I was so tired and in so much pain, so I just kept pushing and pushing. I avoided the doctor, took an iron supplement, and listened to the people who kept telling me there was nothing wrong or that it was all in my head. I kept going. I took handfuls of painkillers. I got more and more tired but kept all my commitments. I started to feel like I was just barely managing to drag myself around, but I kept going. I cried in a bathroom stall at work constantly because I couldn't keep this up, yet I kept it up. Until finally, I couldn't, and I quit my job.

Still, when my body clearly couldn't keep going, my brain did. "I should be doing this," it said. "I should be doing that. I should be doing more." I went back to school because that was easier than returning to work. I drank coffee to keep going. Stopping wasn't an option. Giving up wasn't an option. Go, go, go. Physically, though, I became slow, slower, and then the slowest I'd ever been.

It took me several years to find out what was wrong, but even once I got the ME/FM diagnosis, I wanted to fight it. My friends commended me for being a fighter. It's what you do, fight! I was a shining example to those around me because I wasn't giving up. But all the while, I was becoming more ill and more exhausted. I cried daily and frequently. I felt hopeless and helpless. Finally, I had a massive flare-up that kept me on the couch close to 24 hours a day for almost a year. I was clearly no longer able to keep going.

During that year of living mostly on the couch, I participated in a group led by my internist, the brilliant Dr. Ric Arseneau. It was part class, part mindfulness meditation, and part support group. We learned how to respect our conditions, live with them, take care of ourselves, and even find ways to thrive. This was my turning point. Not only did I receive valuable information and support—I finally opened up to the idea of no longer fighting my condition. When Dr. Arseneau presented the concept of acceptance in class one day, it sunk in.

I finally understood! Accepting my condition didn't mean giving up. It didn't mean I would have to identify myself, first and foremost, as "sick" and "disabled," or that I wasn't going to "fight" anymore. It meant that the fight would be different. By accepting my condition and limitations, I could finally have some compassion for myself. I could stop being so self-critical and setting unrealistic expectations for what I should be able to do, physically and mentally.

Looking after myself had to be my top priority. Whereas previously that had seemed weak, selfish, and completely unglamorous, I now saw its importance. I was putting my health first, no ifs, ands, or buts. I had to do what was necessary to feel my best, and if I wasn't feeling my best, I wouldn't be doing anything except resting. If I didn't feel well, there would be no helping other people or taking on projects until I did.

Acceptance of Your Condition = Compassion = Relief

I felt such relief when the pressure to "do" and to achieve subsided. For the first time, I experienced compassion for myself. When I was exhausted, aching, and sore, I rested and no longer tried to push through it. I really can't explain the amount of relief I felt when I no longer expected myself to function at the same level as a "normal" person. It was huge!

So, acceptance led to compassion which led to relief. This process allowed me the space to rest, and slowly I started to feel better. I also noticed that my self-confidence began to improve. Previously, it had really taken a beating when my condition worsened, and I often felt inferior and worthless. As I began to accept my condition and limitations and see myself as separate from them, my confidence increased. It felt great!

A whole new part of my life opened up. I liked myself again, and then after a while, I realized I loved myself. I especially loved myself for accepting me, taking care of me, and making it ok not to be the high-functioning person I had been for so long. I no longer motivated myself with negative self-talk. I was able to be gentle with myself. Once I allowed myself to follow the acceptance–compassion–relief process, my health finally started to improve and the downward spiral stopped. Hurrah!

Many of you are probably reading this and thinking that you can't give up looking after the people around you, you can't stop working and go on disability, and you are just going to fight through it. I've been there, and I understand. But please don't wait until you crash; don't be like me. It took me a long time to listen to good advice and follow it, but when I finally did, wow, was that ever worth doing.

Acceptance is Part of Your Foundation

When you reject your health condition, you also reject yourself. When you accept your condition, you also accept yourself. Accepting your health condition is essential to creating a good foundation for dating and relationships. If *you* don't accept your condition, how will anyone else? If *you* don't love yourself, how will anyone else love you? How you treat yourself shows others how to treat you. So, treat yourself well— with kindness, compassion, and love—and others will, too.

Accepting the Past

There is another aspect of acceptance that comes into the picture when we start talking about dating and relationships, and that involves acceptance of the past. So many of us bear scars and wounds from what happened to us when we were younger, whether it's from growing up in a dysfunctional family, being bullied in school, experiencing abuse, trauma, or loss, or being in relationships that did not serve us. To my knowledge, I haven't met anyone who doesn't have some sort of old wound.

If we identify strongly with these wounds and carry them with us, holding them out in front of us, showing them to everyone, we are not overcoming them. We are allowing our past to continue to affect us on a daily basis. We are allowing it to lead us through life. If we bring our past wounds into relationships and grant them power, those relationships won't go well. We want to break old patterns of thinking and acting that are no longer helpful. Before we start dating again, we want to deal with the issues that hold us back from living a happy life and from having fulfilling relationships.

What do you want to lead with—your past wounds, or your glorious, loving self?

Don't get me wrong. I'm not telling you to just drop the pain you feel around a parent who was abusive or a partner you lost. That's not realistic. I'm suggesting you become aware (there's that pesky awareness again) of the role this pain plays in your life and how it prevents you from moving in a more positive direction. We must accept that our pasts may have made us who we are, but they don't have to determine what we become. Acceptance, forgiveness, and letting go are important. We want to be the best we can be, right? And we want to be the best partner or girlfriend or boyfriend we can be, right? And to do that, we need to clean out our emotional closets and let go of the things that aren't serving us anymore.

A Note on Forgiveness

Some things may take longer than others to accept, let go of, and forgive. Is forgiveness the goal? Many people would say so. I think it is to the extent that by forgiving someone for a wrong, the memory of that harm will no longer be eating away at your insides or causing ongoing stress and anger— stress and anger that may worsen your physical health. But sometimes, forgiveness seems impossible. Hey, there are things that I'm not ready to forgive. I've found that forgiveness isn't something you force; it just happens when you are working on understanding and compassion. I have never been able to make a purely intellectual decision to forgive someone and then just do it. I need to feel the forgiveness emotionally, too, in my heart, and if I can't feel the forgiveness, I know it's not there. You'll know you've reached forgiveness when you think it *and* feel it. If you can't get there, then maybe it's not meant to happen.

It's About Who You Are

Accepting your condition and your past will allow you to experience life without them getting in the way. I realize that your condition may "get in the way" if you have physical pain or limitations, but it doesn't have to get in the way of who you are. You are *not* your condition or your past.

"Hi, I'm Kira. I love to coach people, write, read, travel, spend time with friends, and play with my dog, Molly. And, oh yeah, I have a condition, but it's not who I am."

In her book *How to Be Sick: A Buddhist-Inspired Guide for the Chronically Ill and Their Caregivers*, Toni Bernhard writes: "There is sickness in the body, but I am not sick!" I love this statement! We are not our bodies. We are not our minds. We are not our illnesses. We are that spark, spirit, soul, essence that has chosen this body for this life. The body may not be 100%, but we are still 100% us.

You may notice that, when you accept your condition, you will have more energy to focus on who you are, on taking care of yourself properly, and (let's not forget) on having a relationship. Accept your condition. Accept it boldly and confidently. Focus on who you are, on all your wonderful

24

qualities, and on how much love you have to bring into a relationship.

Speaking of Love...

Do you feel unlovable because of your condition? I certainly used to. I mean, who would want me if *I* didn't even want me? Well, that's a good question.

How we treat ourselves teaches others how to treat us. If we don't love, want, or respect ourselves, who will? You may think you can cover up your self-loathing and low self-worth with smiles and deflection, but trust me, people will pick up on it.

What I have learned is that we are all lovable and worthy of love, no matter who we are, where we are, or what our condition. I once had a chiropractor who, when I said that I felt utterly unworthy of love, asked: "Who do you think is worthy of love?"

"Pretty much everyone is worthy of love," I replied.

"Would you agree that as human beings, when it comes down to it, we are all the same?"

"Yes, absolutely."

"If we are all the same, and we are all worthy of love, out of the billions of people on this planet, what makes you the exception?" he asked.

He had me there. I could come up with all sorts of excuses and reasons but none that really stood up to his question. Sure, I had done things I wasn't proud of, I'd made mistakes and acted spitefully, but who hasn't?

I've thought about this conversation many times over the years, and he made a good point. If humans are intrinsically worthy of love, how am I different? I'm not. And if *I'm* not, *you're* not. It's just that simple.

TAKE ACTION!

ARE YOU READY to get started on creating awareness and on accepting and loving yourself? Great! Let's begin with some simple exercises and suggestions to get you on your way to making peace with the past and your condition. It's up to you how much work you want to put into yourself before you start dating. If you'd like to go deeper than what I'm offering here, go for it! Find a counsellor or psychologist to work with, start a meditation practice, or read some self-help books specific to your concerns. Do what you need to do.

Quick note: The key to reading self-help books is to not just read them but to actually do the exercises in the books. I learned this the hard way. When you complete the exercises, you get real results! If you simply read over them, you may gain an understanding, but you won't experience change in your life. You get out of the process what you put in, and the more you do, the bigger result you'll get. So, I encourage you to do the exercises, even just to try them once.

Here are some ways to get yourself started on cleaning out your past and getting date-ready:

1. **Writing exercise.** Before you start dating, close your eyes and envision how you would like to feel about yourself, your circumstances, and your life. What sort of foundation would you like to have in place before meeting that special someone? What will it feel like to be in your ideal relationship?

Hold on to this vision and these feelings, then pull out your journal, a sheet of paper or your laptop, and write about it.

Once you've finished writing, notice where you are now compared to where you would like to be. What do you need to do to get there?

- Does your self-confidence need a boost?
- What wounds, attitudes, and beliefs would you like to address before you embark on your dating adventure?
- What negative patterns are you repeating and recreating?
- What are your biggest challenges when it comes to relationships?
- How does your past affect your present?
- What big issues have you been ignoring that you need to confront?
- To what extent have you accepted your condition and physical limitations? Is that something that needs to go on your to-do list?
- Do you feel worthy of love? Of a relationship? If you don't, why not?
- What else do you need to address in order to feel you are truly ready to date?

2. Clean out your emotional closet. Now that you've identified what you want to work on before you start dating, it's time to get to it! The amount of work you do will depend on how much you are willing and able to do. It doesn't have to involve months or years of intense psychotherapy. Some options you might like to consider include:

- Talk to a savvy and trusted friend.
- Enlist the help of a counsellor or psychologist.

- Read self-help books (see the appendix for my suggestions).
- Start a meditation practice. As I've mentioned earlier, this is great for building awareness, and it can be helpful for pain management as well.
- Be more aware of your patterns in relationships, how they came about, and how your old wounds are affecting your current life. This is something you can do lying in bed in quiet contemplation, during meditation, with a counsellor, or at any time when you have a few minutes to yourself to think.
- Accept your condition and physical limitations. How to do this will vary from person to person; there is no one right way. Experiment and see what works for you.
- Connect spiritually. Whether you practice a religion or just enjoy being out in nature, spirituality can be an incredible support and comfort when it comes to coping with pain. It can also help you find ways to love yourself and your life again.

3. Love yourself. Ugh. That was my first reaction when I heard this phrase. It felt woo-woo and touchy-feely and in direct contradiction to how I was raised. But upon closer examination, I discovered that loving yourself can mean a lot of different things. It can mean saying no, setting boundaries, taking a nap, or choosing to spend time with those friends who make you happiest. It means being kind to yourself, because when you are kind and compassionate to yourself, you are loving yourself.

Now would be a good time to make a list of loving acts

you will do for yourself, so pull out a sheet of paper (or your laptop or tablet or smartphone) and get them down, before you second guess yourself.

While part of loving yourself involves performing loving acts for yourself, the other part involves actually feeling the love in your heart. If you have trouble with that, here is a simple technique to get you started. This exercise is most effective when done with your eyes closed:

a. Remember the feeling of unconditional love and joy that you have felt somewhere before. Perhaps it was when you held your friend's baby or you adopted a puppy. Maybe simply the little bird calling outside your window makes you feel that way. Observe the little bird, and contemplate his contribution to the world. Notice the love you feel for him.

b. Now focus on the feeling in your body when you think about the little bird (or puppy or baby). Perhaps your chest feels warm and fuzzy, or maybe it feels expansive. What does unconditional love *feel* like in your body? How about joy? Connect with that feeling, even if it's just for a few seconds.

c. Notice how your love energy is directed towards the bird. Now visualize that energy making a U-turn before reaching the bird, and turn that stream of love directly towards your own heart. What does it feel like to receive your own love? Bask in the feeling of receiving your own unconditional love, and know that you are lovable and worthy of love.

4. Feel grateful. Gratitude is another big one. When we feel gratitude, we attract more things into our lives to be grateful for. I had a gratitude journal in which I wrote down all the things I was grateful for. It took me a long time to really get it, so I had to fake it for a while. At first, it felt like a really cerebral exercise, but eventually, I started to feel it in my heart. I found a greater appreciation for "the little things in life." When you are feeling grateful, there's no room for cynicism, unhappiness, or bitterness in the same moment. Gratitude opens new doors.

Are you ready to get on the gratitude train? If you are (or even if you're not sure but think you *might* like to catch that train) here are a few ways you can start:

- Create a gratitude journal, and write down the things you are grateful for every day, no matter how big or small.
- Before going to sleep at night, think about all the things you are grateful for.
- Tell other people about the things you are grateful for, including them!

5. Be happy. Easier said than done, am I right? The thing is, the best way to attract other happy people (read: potential mates) is to be happy yourself. This can be extremely difficult when you are dealing with chronic pain and illness. But bear with me.

What makes you happy? What can you do, even if really small, to make yourself feel just a little bit happier? I like to listen to birds, play with my dog Molly, watch engaging TV shows, and read crime fiction. It's not about going from zero to 100 on the happiness scale overnight. It's about choosing one thing you can do today, or in this moment, to feel just a little bit happier. What will you choose to do?

————————

HEALING THE PAST and changing patterns that aren't serving you anymore is a lifelong process, and it takes real work. Your life is like an onion. You start by peeling back the top layer and getting rid of some yucky, icky, and painful stuff. You feel great for a while, but eventually you realize there is another layer, so you work and work and manage to peel off the next one. Now you really feel like you're on a roll. You must be close to being "fixed." But uh-oh! There's yet another layer, and another, and another, and they keep on going and going. Please know that this is normal. And healthy. Self-discovery and personal growth are lifelong processes. There is no finish line.

You don't have to pull off numerous layers of the onion before you start dating, but it will make things much easier if you start doing some work on yourself beforehand. Would you build a house without laying a concrete foundation? No, because it would just fall over. The same goes for relationships: the better the foundation we have for ourselves, the better our relationships will be.

CHAPTER 2

"Wait! Let Me Stop You Right There."

MY STORY

THIS IS A chapter about other people. It's about our friends, family, co-workers, healthcare practitioners, and everyone else who wants to give us unsolicited advice. They have lots of opinions, including views on what we need to do in order to get better, and they don't hesitate to share them with us, do they? They really just want to help, but sometimes they end up unintentionally doing the exact opposite. Since developing my condition, I've received a lot of unsolicited advice. *A lot.* Maybe you've had similar experiences.

Here's a taste of what I've heard:

"Have you ever tried juicing?"

"You need to eat kale."

"My friend is selling these amazing supplements, and they completely cured this woman who had [*insert condition of choice*]. You should really try them."

"The raw food diet is amazing. It'll fix any health problem."

"You just need to relax. You're too stressed."

"I sell these magnetic mats, and they heal the body imbalances that lead to illness. They're only $5,000 each. You totally need to get one."

"You need to eat more protein."

"You just need to exercise more. Really push yourself. Fight through the pain; that's what I do."

"I bet if you went back to work, you'd feel a lot better. You just need to keep your mind off the pain."

"It's all in your head."

"But you look great."

So many good intentions, bless their hearts. But boy, don't I just want to strangle each and every one of them!

Sometimes the advice-giving goes a little further. I know a lovely man (let's call him Glen) who considers himself somewhat of an authority on healing because he healed his own painful chronic illness by switching to a raw, vegan diet. This is really incredible, let me just say, and I am truly happy that he found something that worked for him. He deserves to be well.

Glen, referring to his raw, vegan diet: "You should really try it; it works."

Me: "Thanks for the advice, but my digestive system can't deal with raw food, and I'm very anaemic, so it's hard for me to go without meat, especially since I can't tolerate iron supplements."

Glen: "Oh, I had no idea your situation was so complicated."

My inside voice: No shit! Now shut up.

But it didn't end with the raw vegan diet. He told me about a naturopath he had seen. This naturopath, he said, was amazing, a wizard. He could work miracles. Glen shared some of the incredible success stories that the naturopath had brought about, stressing how wonderful, talented, and gifted he was. You get the idea.

And as Glen was talking, I was developing a funny feeling. It was sort of déjà vu crossed with tingling spidey senses.

It turned out that the naturopath he was talking about was the one I had seen for over a year, who had finally told me I was the only client who has baffled him. He said he couldn't help me. True story.

Life is funny sometimes, no?

I don't fault Glen for trying to help. He had achieved a measure of success in his healing and really wanted to help others achieve the same. He was nothing but caring and helpful. And yet I was incredibly triggered by his attempt to help me. I often feel angry and irritated when people make random suggestions or tell me I look good (and, by inference, therefore must not actually be ill or in pain). Why? Because they don't understand, and as a result, they make assumptions about my health and the degree to which I am already helping myself.

If you've got a chronic pain condition or illness, you probably feel that most people don't understand you. They don't get what it's like to live with constant pain. Burning, pinching, sharp, dull, aching, hot, prickly, throbbing, itchy, stabbing, cramping pain.... How do I even begin to describe the vast variety of different kinds of pain that I experience? You know what I mean. There must be at least 20 kinds of pain I feel at various times, all different in quality, intensity, and duration. Not to mention the nausea, dizziness, fatigue, and all the other symptoms.

People forget I'm in pain because I "look fine." They ask me how I am, I tell them, and then they say, "But you look great." Thank you, and fuck you. Yeah, I said it. This, more than anything else, angers me. I am tired of hearing it. If my insides were on my outside, no one would be telling me I looked great, I promise you. The attitude encapsulated in that "but" minimizes and dismisses what I am going through, and it belittles me. Sometimes I think punching them would be easier and more to the point.

I also become angry and frustrated when people are ignorant about my condition yet act as though they are the authority and have *the* solution for me. I want to say to them, "You don't understand. Don't even try." I also sense that they're assuming that because I'm still ill, I'm not doing anything to help myself. I become annoyed because there is no blanket solution for everyone, yet many people still seem to believe one exists. When it comes to helping myself, I've tried it all: general practitioners, specialists, medications, naturopaths, energy healers, shamans, astrologers, mediums, physiotherapy, massage therapy, counselling, Reiki, exercise, acupuncture, nutrition, reflexology, homeopathics, vitamins, herbs, meditation, yoga, qi gong, craniosacral therapy, crystal healing, aromatherapy, mantras, affirmations, art therapy—and that's just what I can remember off the top of my head.

I've done a lot of personal growth work, and I think it shows, and I also have moments when I'm just human and my emotions take over. And yes, I am working on my anger issues. This anger drains me of energy I could be using elsewhere, in a more positive way. I accept that it's up to me to understand that the people around me have good intentions. When they give me advice, I tend to interpret their words as critical, and I realize that this perception is often wrong. Just another layer of my onion that needs to be peeled off!

Since we're on the topic of advice, I'd like to talk a bit about unsolicited and unusable advice offered by health-care professionals. A year or two ago, I was in a very bad place health-wise, in the middle of an extremely painful, year-long flare-up. The pain was so bad that I hadn't slept in a week—literally. I had not been able to fall asleep *at all*. My nervous system consequently had gone haywire. I was extremely depressed and had become suicidal due to both excruciating pain and sleep deprivation. I went to see a psychologist and tearfully explained my situation. During *our first visit*, he said to me, "Have you considered meeting someone? Falling in love increases the dopamine in your brain, and that would help with your depression."

What?!

Wait, what?!

Yeah, not all healthcare professionals should be allowed to practice.

We often look up to healthcare professionals, especially doctors, and trust their opinions and advice over everything else. But they, too, can sometimes give bad advice. It took me a while to wrap my mind around this, especially since I grew up with a physician father, who, in his mind, *always* knew best.

Doctors who aren't family members probably won't offer advice on dating and relationships, but friends often will, whether you want that input or not. I have great friends, a wonderful bunch of girls and guys who are fun, intelligent, caring, and supportive. They really just want the best for me, and I love them for that. Yet no matter how close they are, they can't fully grasp what it's like to live with chronic pain and illness, let alone date with those conditions. What a quagmire! Due to my health, I have so many additional concerns, considerations, and insecurities when it comes to dating that would not even cross a healthy person's mind. When I try to explain these things and express my fears about being endlessly single, my friends often say something like:

"You're totally going to meet someone. You're an amazing person. I know it's going to happen for you."

They mean so well, but in my mind, a response like that negates my struggles. It overlooks my huge dating challenges (pain, fatigue, pain, pain, brain fog, pain), and it dismisses my fears and insecurities. What I really want is for someone to say: "I'd love to see you meet someone, but I guess it can be pretty hard for you to date. I can't imagine what it would be like. I just want you to be happy either way." Validation! Vindication! Victory!

Alas, my anger, frustration, irritation, and sadness over not being understood is *my* baggage. It's not anyone's fault. No one is trying to upset me. Just the opposite, in fact. I'm allowing myself to become upset, and when I do this, I lose my centre and find myself off-kilter.

So this has been *my* story, but if you're reading this book, it's likely that your story is similar. Identifying our frustrations with others' attitudes is the first step. The next section will guide you through the second one.

LET'S DISCUSS

SO WHAT'S THE point of this chapter? By now, we've established that people don't understand our conditions, they give well-intentioned advice, and in turn we may become angry, frustrated, and sometimes even sad. The point of this chapter is to prevent that anger, frustration, and even sadness from coming up in the first place, because it takes a lot of energy that we can't afford to waste. It's energy that we could use for other things, like spending time with friends or going for little walks. The rest of this chapter will look at how the people around you affect your energy levels, and what you can do to maximize your energy stores.

A Word on Emotions

Before we get too far into our discussion, I'd like to clarify my stance on emotions. I believe that we are all entitled to our emotions. Emotions are just fine, even anger. Anger is great when it's expressed responsibly and not directed at others. I like to abuse my couch pillows by screaming into them, punching them, and throwing them on the ground. If anger comes up, the best thing to do is acknowledge it, feel it, express it in a safe way, and then release it. This goes for all difficult emotions, including frustration and sadness.

Here's what else I know about emotions: there are no "silly" emotions that we "shouldn't" be having. Emotions are legitimate for the simple fact that we are experiencing them. There are no wrong emotions or right emotions. There are just emotions. Sure, some are easier to experience than others, but they just are.

A Word on Intuition

You're going to hear me say this a lot throughout this book: trust yourself. Follow your intuition, your gut feeling. So many people are going to have so much advice for you. I've spent thousands of dollars following other people's advice. Did any of it work? Not noticeably. And certainly not in the long term. Not until I followed my intuition and found the right practitioner for me. I'm not going to tell you who that is, because this person is the right fit for *me*. Perhaps Glen's naturopath would be the right fit for you. This is something only you can figure out for yourself, by increasing your awareness around your body and mind and listening to your intuition.

Listen, also, to your intuition when it comes to the people you surround yourself with. You know which friends are energy drainers, which family members feel toxic. You also know that being around certain other people boosts your mood and leaves you feeling happy. Pay attention to this knowledge. It's important.

Friends

How you feel around your friends is important. These are the people you've chosen to surround yourself with.

If your friends have advice about your condition, you know they're going to have advice about dating, too. And their opinions will be based on their own experiences, which very likely won't have involved living with chronic pain or illness. They won't be able to fully understand what you face, no matter how much they would like to or how much you would like them to. Some friends will understand this inability to fully grasp what you are going through, and others will not.

When you're dealing with chronic pain and illness, you have only so much energy. Your energy is valuable. Your time—especially the amount of time you have in a day when you are able to do things—is extremely valuable, so it's important to use it wisely. This means surrounding yourself with the right people, those who boost your energy rather than drain it. The ones who listen. The ones who don't try to fix you. The ones who don't constantly tell you to "stay positive."

Now that's an interesting topic: staying positive. The word "positive" is becoming overused, in my view. And while I'm all for positivity, I'm not for forced positivity. I have read in many sources that forced positivity can actually have a negative effect on us because it's not based on a genuine feeling. It can be stressful and make you feel even worse.

"Being positive" doesn't respect our pain, struggles, or challenges. It's hollow. It ignores our feelings by pushing them back down when it's far more important that all emotions be allowed to come up—ugly, messy, sad, angry—so that once they've been expressed, there will be room for hope, optimism, and empowerment. And have I mentioned that your feelings are ok? Just the way they are? They're not wrong. You should not *not* be feeling this way. They are your feelings, and they are legitimate and real, by virtue of the simple fact that you are having them.

Aside from that, these well-meaning advice-givers have no idea how hard it is to "stay positive" when you are in pain 24 hours a day. Uncomfortable pain. Excruciating pain. Frustrating pain. Accompanied by complete exhaustion and possibly depression. Oh, and right, I must stay positive. Yeeeesh.

We can't just "be positive"; emotions don't work that way. There is a route to positivity, but it's longer and comes from within. It involves awareness, acceptance, forgiveness, compassion, patience, and gratitude. It involves the process of healing, as discussed in Chapter 1. You can get there—you just can't force it. Well, you can, but that won't work long-term. You have to feel the positivity coming from the inside; you can't smash it into yourself from the outside.

Back to talking about surrounding ourselves with good friends. These are the friends who help us feel alive, happy, comforted, and hopeful when we see them. My closest and best friends are spectacular. They don't give me advice, they understand my condition to the best of their abilities, they respect my limitations, and they are willing to accommodate me and help me out when I need it. They let me take the lead when it comes to discussing (or not discussing) my conditions. They treat me like a person, not an illness. Sometimes they do try to help by making suggestions, and I don't get angry. I thank them. I love my friends.

I didn't used to be able to say this about all of my friends. I had to ask myself some hard questions, then end some of my friendships because that was best for me and my health. I invite you to answer the following questions about each friend:

- Does this friend support me?
- Do I feel happy and energized after spending time with this friend?

- Do I feel drained or frustrated after seeing this friend?
- Do I want to kick this friend in the kneecaps after we spend an evening together?

Do you love each of your friends? It's ok if you don't, and it may be time to consider letting some of them go. That's normal. Friends come and go. Relationships change, and you don't have to remain friends with the people you went to high school with if those relationships are no longer serving you. If you have nothing in common with a person, if interactions are awkward or you feel used or drained, it's time to cut that person loose. Remember, you must look after you and create a solid foundation for yourself. Do you want to give your limited energy to someone who takes every last drop? I didn't think so.

Family

I am not an expert on family. I grew up an only child in a small family with extraordinarily dysfunctional communication. My mother died when I was much younger, before most of my health shitstorm occurred. And up until the time he died, my father, the all-knowing physician, refused to believe that there was anything wrong with me (absurd yes, but so was he).

Family are family, though, and we are usually stuck with them, unless we decide to move to the other side of the country. Ideally we would like to feel as good around family as we do around our good friends, but that's not always possible. And it's typically more difficult to end a relationship with a family member than it is with a friend.

Your family may be wonderful, supportive, helpful, and caring, and they may also be infuriating and judgmental. Maybe they think you are being lazy or faking your illness. Perhaps they don't believe things are as bad as they actually are for you. They may have all kinds of advice on what you should be doing, and dole it out freely, because family members don't censor themselves as much as other people. They might want to control you. They might ignore you. They might pressure you to get married and have kids.

To top it off, once you start dating, you may become involved with another family. If the relationship gets serious you are going to have in-laws, and they will also have opinions on your health and relationship.

So how do you make life easier for yourself where family is concerned? While families vary tremendously, there are a few things you can do to help yourself: set boundaries, ask for what you need, and don't take things personally. We're going to talk more about these a bit later in this chapter, so say tuned for the "How To Deal with People" section.

Health Professionals

Over the years, I've had a lot of health professionals, allopathic and alternative, confidently assure me they would be able to remedy my conditions. After various treatments and remedies, most of them said they were baffled by me and unable to help after all. Sometimes they told me that everyone else responded to their treatment method and they didn't understand why I wasn't. Comments such as these led me to feel like there was something even more wrong with me because my body wasn't co-operating and responding to treatment the way it "should" have been. Holistic health practitioners told me that it must be in my karma to be sick in this lifetime. Karma, shmarma. That's an excuse from someone who doesn't have an answer.

What I have discovered is that health practitioners believe in their approaches. Most of them have one main approach they use for a variety of conditions. The problem is that not all approaches work for all people. Perhaps their treatment methods work most of the time, but they won't work for everyone, because we are all so different. This is why it's so important to find the right treatment methods for you, whether allopathic or alternative or both. The downside is that this can take a while—like, years. The upside is that if you persevere, you can create a health team that works really well for you and forms part of your foundation. My health team consists of my family doctor, an internist, a physiotherapist, a counsellor, an acupuncturist, and an energy healer. This team, which took me about 10 years to assemble, has been able to significantly and measurably help me in my recovery and ongoing care. They rock!

I can't stress enough how important it is that you trust yourself: trust your gut and trust your intuition when you are choosing healthcare practitioners. This goes for anything from medical doctors to massage therapists. You need to feel comfortable, and you need to be experiencing results.

Many health practitioners offer hope, especially the alternative ones, who may make unrealistic promises of healing. It happens frequently. If you believe that you just need to find the right therapy and everything will be solved, you raise your hopes and expectations with each new treatment. When that treatment doesn't work, you're likely to endure crushing disappointment. The more you go through this cycle, the more devastating it becomes, and the more desperate you become to find a "cure."

I've been through this myself. For a long time, I felt completely let down and disappointed by alternative medicine and therapies. So many people made so many promises, but no one delivered on them. Each time my false hope was dashed, I became more depressed.

What can you do to stop the hope/expectation/disappointment/depression rollercoaster?

The key is to manage your expectations. Start a new treatment with cautious optimism, not blind hope and trust. Be realistic. Get a second opinion. If you don't like your doctor, switch. Don't accept less than the medical care you deserve.

Now that I know nothing is going to fix me in one shot, I don't expect a new treatment to be the cure-all. I hope that it will help to some degree, but I go in without big expectations. When you have fewer expectations and don't get caught up in all the promises of healing that are out there, you lessen the potential for disappointment and discouragement.

I do what works for me. I've accepted my condition and have reasonable expectations of my body. I know what reduces my symptoms to the point where my life is liveable. I have put together a great health team who are helping me heal, step by step, inch by inch. I am much happier now that I don't have a desperate need to be cured.

Do what works for you. Don't expect miracles, but do believe that they can happen. Some miracles are small—for instance, a day without pain. Small miracles are miracles too. Do expect healing and that life will improve. Change is inevitable: nothing ever stays the same, which means things will change physically for you. If you are doing positive things to help yourself, you may well be rewarded with positive change.

Understanding

Those of us who live with chronic pain and illness often spend a lot of time trying to get others to understand our situation. We can feel frustrated when people don't understand or try to understand, and we may become upset when people seem to forget that we are in pain or struggling with an illness.

I used to need *so badly* for everyone around me to understand my condition. I would regularly update people in my life on my current symptoms and newest meds, as well as my speculations as to why this was happening to me, and my latest theories on the root cause. I really wanted them to know, understand, and FEEL the pain I felt. I wanted them to comprehend how intense and debilitating my condition was. I needed them to know that me lying on the couch and not working, day in and day out, wasn't me being lazy. I was not a lazy person; I had been a go-getter for most of my life, and this was not me giving up. I was afraid of people making assumptions and judgments about me, so getting people to understand was *the* focus in my life for quite a few years.

My friends listened to my speculations with infinite patience (family, not so much), until one day, my internist asked:

"*Why* do you need people to understand your condition?"

"Because! I do! The sole purpose of my life right now is to

get people to understand! They *must* comprehend what I'm going through," I cried.

But the question stuck with me. Did I *really* need others to understand? I knew I was already coming to the realization that the people in my life would never fully grasp what it was like to live with my condition unless they experienced it for themselves (which I would never wish on anyone). And if I was being totally honest with myself, a few people actually did understand: the people in my support group. Through a program at my hospital, I had met a small group of individuals who were dealing with similar conditions. They understood me. It was glorious! I didn't have to explain anything, we just "got" each other, which was such a relief. We had lots of good laughs over our shared struggles—including the "helpful advice" of those around us.

When I finally acknowledged the love and understanding I was receiving from my support group, I found myself thinking that maybe I didn't need everyone to understand my health situation. Perhaps having a few people who understood me really well was plenty. They were able to give me what I needed emotionally, and the rest I could take care of myself by asking others for help when I needed it.

Within a short time I realized this *was* enough. I did not need everyone to understand. I was able to let go of caring about their judgments and assumptions, because I knew they were reacting based on their limited knowledge, and I could forgive them for that. What mattered most was that I could take care of myself and knew how to get my needs met.

I even took it a step further. I discovered that it's easier to be vague about my condition than to provide details.

Details lead to unsolicited suggestions and advice. I no longer need to explain my condition to anyone. Besides, I'm tired of hearing about it myself. People don't need to understand, as long as they respect my limits. Ultimately, my health is none of anyone else's business.

Not needing everyone to understand your condition is important when it comes to dating. Outlining in great detail all of your ailments, medications, and limitations right away is enough to scare away even the bravest dater! In the beginning, being vague is helpful and will protect you. You don't owe anyone an explanation for the state of your health, especially not someone you've only just met.

The Flip Side of Understanding

We spend a lot of time hoping and wishing for others to understand what we are going through, but sometimes it's important to look at the situation from a different perspective. Let's turn this around. Put yourself in the shoes of those close to you. That's right, slip into your partner's runners, your mom's slippers, your sister's heels, your dad's loafers. Imagine what it must be like to live with or be close to someone with chronic pain or illness. You see them in pain and struggling daily. There are things you can't do together anymore. Their mood is erratic—they cry more, they're often irritable, and sometimes they're difficult to be around. And you don't understand because they look healthy. Maybe they even look great!

I know I'm not always the easiest person to be around when things are not going well: I can be sulky, irritable, and sometimes demanding when I'm in constant pain. Yet before I became aware, I just expected people should be making exceptions and considerations for me, visiting and calling me regularly, and waiting on me hand and foot. I never truly considered it from another angle. Sure, I didn't want to be a burden, and I felt bad because some people thought I was lazy, but I never considered what it might be like on the other side.

We can ask people to help and to be supportive. It's also important that we respect *them* and what *they* are going through. Chronic pain and illness don't just affect the sufferer, they affect those around that person as well. This idea took me a long while to accept, but I now see how important it is, especially when I'm thinking about creating an intimate relationship with someone who will have to deal with my health condition on a daily basis.

How to Deal with People

I'd like to share with you three tools for dealing with other people in a productive and non-stressful way, whether they are friends, family, or medical professionals. These skills will help you stay relaxed when you receive unwanted advice or feel judged, and will form an important part of your personal foundation.

1. **Ask for what you need.** Asking for what you need is difficult. Many of us don't want to need help. We may have too much pride. We want to remain independent and do things on our own because we always have in the past. We might think that needing help is weak, that it means we're admitting defeat and are no better than the people we have judged for needing help.

I know a lot of people who have a hard time accepting

help in any form. They believe they don't deserve it. They think they must reciprocate immediately. They feel guilty for asking.

The truth is, asking is actually easy. It's our beliefs and judgments around asking for and receiving help that make it difficult.

Here's the good news: Needing help is not admitting defeat, and it doesn't mean you're weak or losing your independence. It means you are taking care of yourself and delegating the tasks you need help with at this time. Historically, humans have lived in community, and only more recently have we been losing that sense of community. We all used to help each other out. We helped raise each other's children, shared food, pooled resources, and gladly tended to the old and sick. The world has changed, but humans really have not. We would benefit from a stronger community around us in today's world. *You* would benefit. And you know what? You can create your own community around you.

If you consider asking for help a way of delegating, you will still maintain the ability to manage your care and retain some independence and decision-making abilities. You are the manager of your life, and as a manager, you aren't meant to do it all on your own.

There are big requests and small requests. Some may seem big to us but not to a healthy person. Sometimes a little bit of help can go a long way. Something a healthy person would consider a 20-minute breeze might be a half-day chore for someone with chronic pain.

The cool thing is that most people want to help—they just don't know how or what to do. They simply need a little bit of direction. By asking specifically for what you need them to do, you clarify how they can contribute. Ask politely, invite others to help you, and give them the option of saying no. We can't force anyone to do anything; we can simply offer them the opportunity to help us. People like to help, because they feel good about themselves afterwards, so it's a win-win. Plus, if you can channel your advice-giving friends' and family's focus onto something that will actually help you, they will have less time to offer unhelpful advice.

One more point about asking: Try to spread the requests around by not always asking the same person for assistance. Make a list of all the people who have offered their help, and work your way through it. If people have offered in the past, now is the time to take them up on it! Remember: they want to help because they love that great feeling that comes from doing something good for someone else.

Asking and receiving go hand in hand, and many people who have trouble asking also have trouble receiving help. For some, receiving can be as just as hard as asking. If that applies to you, I invite you to ask: How can I open myself up to accepting help?

I love to receive. It feels great to have someone take care of me. I used to be embarrassed about how good it felt to accept help and support. How did I get to the point where I was able to ask for and accept help? I finally realized that I deserve it. I've suffered enough! We humans are built to live in supportive communities, so why would I want to isolate myself and cling so ferociously to my independence?

Another reason why I am happy to receive is because I know that when I am able, I will give back. I may not give back directly to the person who originally helped me, but I will give back to someone in need, thus passing on the kind deed. I may not provide the same kind of help as my friend gave me (for example, bringing me groceries), but I might do something more in my realm (such as editing a friend's blog posts or adopting a rescue dog).

If you're still struggling with the idea of asking for and receiving help, I'm going to provide you with a few more tools in the Take Action! section in this chapter. If those are not enough, you may want to explore the issue a little further with a trusted friend or a counsellor.

2. Set boundaries. Aaah, boundaries. Sometimes it's just so much easier not to have good ones. For many of us, it's much less stressful to just do a task or agree to a dreaded commitment than to say "no" to a friend, family member, or co-worker, am I right? However, having lax boundaries often means instant gratification but long-term suffering.

Consider the following scenario: Your co-worker has a short temper and often leaves early, which means you are left with her work, as well as yours, on a regular basis. It's easier just to do her work because the prospect of having a conversation with her seems too scary. She'd probably freak out, blow up, and turn it around on you, and you would be the one to get in trouble with your boss (as least, that's what you tell yourself). So you suck it up and work overtime yet again, but you feel the resentment building; there's a seething, boiling anger inside of you because the circumstances are just so unfair. The situation may not be one in your life, but do the emotions sound familiar? That's what it feels like when your boundaries are not being respected.

So what are boundaries exactly? Basically, they are the rules of your life that ensure you feel safe, comfortable, relaxed, healthy, happy, and rested. They are an essential part of your personal foundation.

There are all kind of boundaries: physical, mental, emotional, sexual, material, and spiritual. You set them with others as well as with yourself. I have had to set some boundaries with myself to ensure my pain and fatigue are kept to a minimum. Here are a few examples:

"I will be in bed by 10pm every night, no exceptions."

"I will schedule no more than two social activities per week."

"I will sit in a chair for a maximum of one hour at a time."

"When I go for walks, I will sit down for five minutes every 15 minutes."

Not setting clear boundaries—and firmly (yet kindly) enforcing them—may feel better in the short term, but in the long run it feels awful and wears you down, physically and emotionally. Boundaries are important to set in all relationships, and it's especially important to establish right away your boundaries with the people you date. Otherwise, you may realize six months into the relationship that you are feeling resentful because your partner is not respecting your boundaries. Yet, if you haven't delineated those boundaries, he's probably not even aware that he is crossing them. It is imperative that you put your health first, no matter how wonderful your new partner is. If your health suffers, so will your relationship.

Here are some examples of the boundaries you might set with the person you are dating:

"Please call me before 9pm. I don't answer the phone after that."

"I will have sex with you once your STI test results come back negative."

"I can manage one sleepover a week."

"I feel uncomfortable when you swear around me. Would you please not use those words when we're together?"

"If you're more than 20 minutes late for a date, I won't be available when you get to my place."

"I'm sorry, but I don't lend money to friends."

"Your sex swing hurts my back, so I'm not going to be able to use it with you again. Your waterbed is super comfortable, though, so let's get it on between the sheets."

Setting boundaries after the fact is hard. For example, if for the first six months of a new relationship you're ok with staying up until 2am on weekends to see your guy because it's all new and exciting, and in month seven you tell him that you need to be in bed by 10pm every night, that new stipulation is probably not going to go over as well as if you had told him at the outset and stuck to your guns. I've been laughed at for "changing the rules" partway through a relationship. Changing boundaries is much harder than setting the right ones to start with.

Surprisingly, I find that I often have to be stricter with myself than I am with others when it comes to boundaries. And when I'm strict with myself, I respect myself. When others see that I respect myself, they in turn treat me with respect and accept my boundaries. Cool, huh?

3. Don't take things personally. This is a big one! It's human nature to take words and actions personally, even when they are not actually the truth about who you are. You can thank your ego for you taking situations, comments, and even others' circumstances personally. I take it personally when someone cuts me off when I'm driving. My monkey brain thinks that driver did it to irritate or punish me, as though the move was directed at me specifically. Me! Me! Me! In reality, the driver probably didn't see me or thought there was enough space—or maybe generally drives with a blatant disregard for everyone else on the road. One thing is for sure, though: the driver wasn't doing it to piss off me, Kira Lynne. That was simply the side effect.

In *The Four Agreements*, one of my favourite books of all time, Don Miguel Ruiz notes:

> Even when a situation seems so personal, even if others insult you directly, it has nothing to do with you. . . . Nothing others do is because of you. What others say and do is a projection of their own reality. When you are immune to the opinions and actions of others, you won't be the victim of needless suffering.

We're suffering enough! Why suffer more than we need to? People aren't reacting to you, they are reacting to a memory from their past that you have somehow triggered. It's their issue, not yours. Nothing they say or do is because of you, yourself. In fact, most people are so wrapped up in worrying about what others think of them and in taking things personally themselves that they are too busy to be specifically targeting you. This can be a difficult concept to wrap your brain around. You are not as important as your ego may lead you to believe. You are special, and you are ordinary.

Not taking things personally, especially when we start dating, is so important. Dating is a great opportunity for our brain and ego to twist all sorts of things around to be our fault. We're not pretty enough, smart enough, funny enough, fit enough, healthy enough. He didn't call back because you're not rich enough or tall enough or because you're sick. I call bullshit on all of it. You have no idea what's going on in someone else's head, and you're not going to figure it out unless you ask them directly, so stop wasting time speculating. They didn't call you back because you didn't feel like a match for them, for whatever reason. So what, who cares, doesn't matter. You'll save yourself a lot of time, energy, and misery, and be more available to the right person who *will* call you back, when you stop taking things personally.

TAKE ACTION!

THIS CHAPTER HAS been all about the challenges of dealing with people and their advice, reactions, and comments. I'm about to give you some practical tips and tools for handling that advice with ease, setting boundaries, asking for help, and not taking things personally. Please don't try to do it all at once or become frustrated if it doesn't work on the first try. Take it one step at a time, and keep at it. These skills require practice and time. Let's get started!

1. **How to deal with advice gracefully.** After years of explaining to people why their advice wouldn't work for me, or (politely) arguing about why I didn't want to follow their suggestions, I was at the end of my rope. So many suggestions. How could I make people understand that *I* knew what was best for me? Then came an aha! moment. No understanding needed.

This is how I respond to unsolicited advice now:

"I'd never thought of that. What a great suggestion. Thank you," said with no intention of ever following the advice.

"Thank you for the idea."

"Kale smoothies. That sounds delicious!" Not going to happen.

Advice: "Stay positive." Kira: "Stay positive?" I use the repeat technique if I'm tired. And I add a question mark at the end if I'm feeling combative. (I mean, yes, of course I'll stay positive when it feels like my *insides are burning in hell!*)

And my personal favourite: "Thanks so much for the suggestion. I'm super happy with my current health team and health plan. It's been working very well for me." And that's the truth!

The key is to find ways to respond that don't drain you or get you riled up or annoyed. You can start by trying out some of my examples, or come up with your own. Sometimes there might be a little white lie involved, but I figure: they're only trying to help. Why not help them feel good about helping rather than shooting down their ideas?

2. How to ask for what you need. Let me say this: you deserve help. You're in pain. You're feeling unwell. When could possibly be a better time to finally give in and accept some help? I can't think of one. Drop the judgment, accept the help, bask in it, enjoy it. Recognize how many people care about you and are willing to help. Know that one day, you will be able to give back, and you don't have to know right now how you will do that.

When you've accepted that you need help, that it's ok to ask for help, and that you are willing to receive, it's important to think about how you are going to ask.

I have three rules when it comes to asking:

1. Be polite.
2. Be specific.
3. Give the person you are asking the genuine choice to do it or not.

Being polite is a no-brainer. Being specific is important because people can't read your mind. *You* know exactly what you need, so ask for it, whether it's a loaf of flax bread from a certain bakery, a ride to a doctor's appointment at 10am next Friday, or having your kitchen floor washed. Don't be vague.

Instead of asking, "Can you help me out when I'm feeling sick?"—then expecting your friends and family to read your mind as to when exactly you're feeling sick and what exactly you need—try asking like this: "Would you be willing to pick up some kale for me on your way over tomorrow afternoon?" Be specific.

When you ask for help, it's important to give the person a choice. Asking them doesn't mean they are automatically going to say yes; it also doesn't mean they are going to say no. Phrase your question so they have an option:

"Would you be willing to pick me up a loaf of flax bread from Bob's bakery this afternoon?"

"Would you be willing to give me a ride to my doctor's appointment at 10am next Friday?"

"Would you be willing to wash my kitchen floor?"

When you ask someone if they are willing to do something, you give them a choice. People like that, and they will be more likely to say yes than if you demand any of these things. Give it a shot. You might like the results.

And if someone says no, it's important not to take that personally and not to make assumptions about what their "no" means. We're going to talk about that more in the upcoming section on how not to take things personally.

3. How to set boundaries. So, boundaries. What does that look like exactly? When I talk to people about setting boundaries, I've noticed they often seem to equate it with being assertive, aggressive, and demanding. And some people may approach boundary setting in that way, but I prefer the calm, patient, and consistent method.

When you are setting a boundary, it's because something isn't working in your life right now and you need it to change. You may be requesting that someone change their behaviour, or you may be setting the boundary with yourself in order to change your own behaviour.

The ultimate boundary is deciding that you don't want to keep certain people in your life. Unless someone plays an absolutely necessary role, you have the choice of who you want around. You might find the idea of not keeping certain people in your life difficult. You don't have to make any decisions right away, but consider what they are contributing to the relationship. If you feel drained and exhausted after spending time with them, that's a pretty big red flag. Please don't be a martyr; look after yourself in the best way possible. Ask yourself how you would advise a friend who was in the same position as you are, and consider taking your own advice.

Once you feel you are surrounded by the people you want to have in your life, you may find that you need to set some boundaries with them. Maybe your mom calls you to check on you a few nights a week, yet she calls late at night, after you've gone to sleep; and you really need your uninterrupted sleep, otherwise fatigue throws off your whole next day.

There's something called the "feedback formula," which I like to use for communicating boundaries. I learned it during my time at Rhodes Wellness College, and it has stuck with me ever since. It's a good structure to follow when you first start setting boundaries. As you get better at it, you can work with the wording. It goes like this:

When you _____(describe the person's behaviour),
I feel _____(describe the emotion you feel),
The result is _____(describe the effect of that emotion).
Would you be willing to_____(make your request)?

If you were to set a boundary with your mother, it might look like:

When you call me at 11pm at night, I feel upset and frustrated, and the result is my sleep is interrupted, and it throws off my whole day.

Would you be willing to call me at 8pm instead?

People tend to respond well when you use this formula. Sometimes you may need to ask a few times because you are introducing something new—both your behaviour and the boundary. Using this formula will make your life easier, and your life needs to be as easy as possible if you have chronic pain and illness.

Speak up if something in a relationship isn't working for you. It's never going to change unless you do something about it.

The feedback formula is especially useful when you first start dating. It's important to set your boundaries straight off because the longer you wait, the harder it will be. Let your prospective mate know right away what is ok and what isn't. Train them from the very beginning.

Finally, set boundaries with yourself. Here's an example: I've made an agreement with myself that I will be in bed by 10pm every night. I've done this because I know if I don't fall asleep before 11pm, the following day will be a mess for me. I'll be extra, extra tired, be more sore, and I won't be able to accomplish as much as I usually do. Often, I'll have to stay home the whole day. Totally not worth it, no matter how much fun I'm having at 9:59pm. Well… maybe a few times a year I'll stay out late, but I'll go in knowing I'll be a write-off the next day. It's a boundary I set for myself. I respect it, and therefore others respect it.

What boundaries do you want to set for yourself?

4. How not to take things personally. Let's say you've asked your friend if she would be willing to pick up a loaf of bread from the bakery for you, and she says, "Sorry, I can't. I have a date with Bob that night."

What pops into your mind? If you're anything like me, it might be something like:

"A date is more important to her than helping me, a sick friend?!"

"She doesn't care about me, all she cares about is Bob."

"She said she would help before, and when I finally do ask her, she turns me down."

"If she were a good friend, she would bring me the bread."

"That's it. I'm never asking her to do anything for me ever again."

And on and on and on. Whew! That's a lot of taking things personally. Our friend declined to help, and all of a sudden we're getting ready to break up with her. We're making assumptions and judgments all over the place. Over a loaf of bread. Or a ride to the doctor. Or washing the kitchen floor.

In reality, you asked for help, gave her the option of saying yes or no, and she said no. Which she was entitled to do. It doesn't have to *mean* anything. In fact, it doesn't. Her saying no probably has nothing to do with you. Perhaps she's much more focused on her relationship with Bob, and dealing with her own fears and insecurities which have taken over to the point of her not being able to think about anyone other than Bob. Who knows? We can't know unless she tells us.

We take things personally all the time, and not just in the context of asking for help. It's just human nature. Yet, when you take things to heart you give your power away to other people. If you want to keep your power, and keep your energy up, stop taking things personally. This is going to be especially important when you start dating. Things get weird and crazy, and people's baggage starts flying around everywhere. Since you only have so much energy to expend, it's not worth getting upset over what you think someone else did or is trying to do to you. They're not doing anything *to* you, they are reacting to things in their own lives, based on a pattern that was established when they were children.

Ok, so great. You've decided not to take things personally. But how does that work, exactly? I have two tools I like to use:

a. **Remind yourself that this isn't about you.** It's never about you. It's about them and their past.

b. **Get curious.** Instead of getting upset, angry, or indignant, get curious. "I wonder why they reacted that way?" "I wonder what's going on in their lives right now to cause them to react like that...." Just be curious. You don't need to get answers to those questions; it's simply a good way of shifting your perspective. Getting curious may also bring up compassion for them, which is a bonus.

DEALING WITH OTHER people when you are suffering from chronic pain and illness can be a big job. You have less capacity for stress, and emotions tend to rise to the surface much more quickly than when there is no pain to manage. Because the extra stress and emotion of dealing with others can have a negative impact on your health, it's helpful to find ways to reduce as much stress as possible. You probably have a lot more choice and control than you think you do when it comes to interacting with the people around you and asking for what you need. By incorporating the tools in the Take Action! section of this chapter, you will be better able to regulate your stress, emotions, and energy levels.

CHAPTER 3

Your Physical Foundation

MY STORY

SO UP TO this point we've been working on our mental/ emotional selves: cleaning out the closets of our past, working on improving our interactions with others, saying goodbye to energy-drainers, and setting some useful boundaries. Now, it's time to look at our physical selves.

Your physical self is extremely important, no less than your mental/emotional self. I ignored mine for far too long before I was finally forced to pay attention. I was in denial about my various conditions for years, and I didn't understand my state of health because I didn't follow up with doctors, in part because I didn't want to receive any more bad news. I pushed until my body just gave up. My wish is that, by reading this book, you won't push as far as I did before you start taking care of yourself.

It started out simply enough for me; I developed vulvodynia—or, as I like to refer to it, pain in my undercarriage. I was in my late teens and obsessed with horses. I had my own, I rode others, and I worked in the stables doing any and every kind of job available. Now, imagine sitting on horses for several hours a day with pain in your undercarriage. Ow. I did this for years. I ignored the pain because my love of riding was the biggest, most important thing in my life. It got so bad at times I could barely walk from one stable to the next, where the next horse was waiting for me to hop on. I did this for *years*. I didn't listen to my body telling me it was in pain because I was not willing to stop riding—it was my passion. In addition, my first horse, Peanut, helped me through much emotional pain, trauma, and loss during my teens and early 20s. There was no way I was going to part with him.

When I did finally stop riding, it wasn't because of the pain. It was time for a change; my life was moving in a different direction: towards men.

My next ignore-my-body move involved dating. I was 21 and my mother had just died. I was desperately afraid of being abandoned. I was ignoring my undercarriage issues because part of me thought that if I closed my eyes to the problem, it would go away. That's how we dealt with problems in my family, at any rate.

I met a guy and fell in love for the first time, but I didn't tell him about the pain. We had sex, and oh boy did it hurt, and I still didn't tell him. Instead, I found creative ways to avoid sex, and once in a while I would grit my teeth and bear it. We ended up having very little sex during our year-long relationship.

After my first love came my husband-to-be. Same deal. Didn't tell him about the pain. Gritted my teeth through sex at the beginning, and after a while, did my best to avoid it as much as possible. I was 25 when we got married, which was around the time I had a flash of clarity and decided I needed medical help. I went to my doctor, went on medication, started physical therapy, and put together a plan to get rid of the pain. I tried to involve my husband, but he wasn't interested. It was too late. Too much resentment had built up by that time, especially around our lack of a sex life.

For a long time I blamed my undercarriage pain completely for splitting up my marriage. Now I can see that my refusal to respect, listen to, and care for my body earlier on was perhaps more the problem. In hindsight, a number of other issues led to the demise of our marriage, but I know my self-neglect didn't make things any easier for either of us.

Moving right along to the party years; I was 27, newly divorced, and ready to hit the town—get drunk, get crazy, sleep around. Hmmm… slight issue with the last part of the plan, but no matter! I was an empowered woman: I was going to do this differently. My "differently" looked like this: meet a guy, have sex with him (not always immediately), and then tell him about the pain *after* the first or second time we'd had sex. The problem with this method was that I still experienced pain (my previous pain-eradication plan having failed), but since I mentioned it after having sex, the guys often thought it wasn't a big deal. So the expectation was set. More sex through gritted teeth, sexily (or so I thought) encouraging them to orgasm as quickly as possible—to end my agony. Still not listening to my body.

Still thinking that if I acted like a normal person, my body would behave like a normal body.

Sometimes the sex wasn't painful. One of my doctors introduced me to topical Xylocaine, a freezing jelly. I could slather it on my undercarriage, and it would take away the biting pain of sex. So, one day I was getting ready to have sex with a guy I was seeing. I quickly leapt into the bathroom, applied the jelly, and hopped into bed, ready for the main event. Little did I know that he had other things in mind, like oral sex. So down he goes. And I couldn't feel a thing—after all, I was frozen. Nothing. I played along. I faked it. He resurfaced and said, "Do you know why my mouth feels numb and tastes sort of medicinal?" I was totally mortified! I hadn't told him about the pain, let alone about my handy painkiller. I denied everything. Poor guy. To this day, I still wonder what he must have thought.

So there I was, still denying the seriousness of the pain and unable to talk about it because I feared abandonment. This approach was clearly not working for me, although at the time I was desperately hanging on, still wanting to be "normal."

Next up: a long-term relationship. The pain had lessened considerably, partly due to some pro-active experimentation with medications and partly due to reducing the stress in my life. I met a guy. We fell in love. We had sex, and I was doing okay. It was even enjoyable. And then I made the terrible decision of getting an intrauterine device (IUD) for birth control. It was in for three weeks. I was in *agony* for *two years* after the doctor took it out, and I'm still dealing with the consequences 10 years later. The IUD caused a pelvic infection, which triggered interstitial cystitis, my present bladder condition. I can't adequately describe the pain of those first two years, but I'll try. Piercing. Throbbing. Excruciating. Agonizing. Breathtaking. Constant.

At this time in my life, I was a paralegal and worked in a law firm. I remember silently crying at my desk every day because I was in so much pain. I went to the ER, and they told me I had pulled a muscle in my groin (what?!) and wouldn't give me anything for the pain. Pain. *Pain.* And you know what I did while I was in all this pain? I went to work. Every day. And I didn't say anything to anyone there about it. I worked out at the gym, even though that made things worse. I continued to have sex because I believed that if I didn't, my boyfriend would leave.

You know what I didn't do? I didn't continue seeing my doctor. I didn't take medical leave. I didn't stop trying to please my boyfriend. I didn't listen to my body. I kept going and going and going. People like me didn't go on medical leave—that was for wimps or for people who had really serious problems, like cancer.

I kept going for a few more years. After that four-year relationship fell apart, I ended up in a few more shorter ones. My bladder kept calling out for attention, but I didn't listen. I numbed it with painkillers, I numbed my stress with alcohol and exercise, and I didn't listen. Then, one day, my body just stopped. I couldn't walk—I could barely move at all. I couldn't sleep, yet I couldn't get out of bed. I was depressed and cried all the time. The chronic fatigue hit me. After years of pushing through pain, my body had had enough.

Finally, I went to see my doctor, and I went continuously until I got answers and help. I went on medical leave, then disability. I stopped trying to please my partner. In fact, I took a break from intimate relationships altogether. I started listening to my body. It was scary at first. It was telling me it needed a long rest and a lot of care, and this didn't fit in with my life plan. It also flew in the face of many of my beliefs. I had always strived to be "perfect" because I didn't think I was acceptable any other way. Ever since developing the vulvodynia, I had felt inadequate, incomplete, and inferior to other women. They could all offer the one thing that men wanted, and I couldn't, so what man would want me? I hated my body, didn't want it to be mine. And if I didn't want to deal with this body, why would anyone else be willing to take it on?

Wow. When I consider my thoughts back then, no wonder I was scared of facing the pain and illnesses. I had so much fear. My physical foundation was weak and needed to be strengthened. But how was I going to build anything on a weak physical foundation if I was afraid all the time?

I slowly learned that to build a physical foundation you also need to be building your mental, emotional, and spiritual foundations at the same time. They are all connected, and they all support each other. Your body isn't going to heal if you think you are unworthy of healing. I'm not going to lie: it took a lot of work, a lot of challenging my beliefs, and yet here I am. I'm living with these conditions but I'm living well, and I'm happy, possibly the happiest I've been in my life. It's hard to believe, even for me sometimes, but it's true. And this change happened because I listened to my body. I stopped forcing and I faced the fear.

LET'S DISCUSS

TAKE CARE OF your body!

Your body is amazing. It keeps you alive, it fights illness, it creates life. It really is miraculous, and it deserves your respect and love. Do you listen to your body? Or is your story similar to mine?

It can be really hard to listen to our bodies, respect their messages, and then actually respond in a way that honours them.

While I was in denial, I heard so many messages that only fed my denial:

"You just have to fight through the pain."

"Ignore the pain; that's the only way to deal with it."

"Disability is for people who are lazy. They really put a strain on the economy."

"There's nothing wrong with you; you just need to toughen up."

"I have pain in my body, too, but I play soccer, and it's a great way to keep my mind off it. The pain goes away once I start running."

Running. Snort.

Let's go back to the message from the previous chapter for a minute: your intuition. Your intuition is useful when you're dealing with other people. It's also useful when dealing with yourself. You may require a bit of time and quiet to listen, but your intuition will tell you what you need to do. You *know*, on some level, what you need to do. You may not like the idea of taking a break from work. You might think that if you stop "fighting" the pain, this will mean you're giving up or losing the battle, but the opposite is true. When you stop fighting and forcing, you move into acceptance. When you accept that this is what's happening, you're able to have compassion for yourself. And when you have compassion, you will be able to do for your body what it needs you to do. It's important that you establish respect and compassion for your body before you start dating, otherwise you may have similar experiences to mine.

Improving your physical foundation often involves mental/emotional and spiritual work. A healthy outside comes from the inside. You have to do the work. No one else is going to do it for you. Don't kid yourself. *You* are in charge of your own happiness, your own health, your own life. Let me say that again. *You* are responsible for your own happiness (not your partner), your own health (not your doctor), your own life (no one else).

You can't date if your body isn't on board to a certain degree. Well, you can, but I wouldn't recommend it. I'm not saying you need to be 100% in order to date. That's not realistic. Let's say your maximum function is a 6 out of 10 on a good day. It's important that you're hitting 6 as much as reasonably possible before you start dating. If your maximum is a 3, then aim to be at 3 as much as possible. What does it take for you to be at a 3, or a 6? It's about being the best you can be and feel, given your circumstances.

How do you get there, given your circumstances? Only you can know that, but I have some ideas for you.

The Basics

The basics provide a good foundation for pretty much anyone. In my book, the basics are:

Get Enough Good Sleep.

Sleep needs to be your number one priority if you have chronic pain and illness. Most reputable sources agree that people require anywhere from seven to nine hours of sleep per night to be well rested. If you feel best with 10 hours, make sure you get 10. And this doesn't mean lying in bed, it means good quality sleep, with as little interruption and wakefulness as possible, which can be challenging.

You probably know how much sleep works best for you. How often do you get your optimal amount? Is it good quality sleep, or do you toss and turn all night? Perhaps it's time to set some boundaries with yourself so you're able to get the amount of sleep you need. This may become even more challenging once you start dating, since night-time dates are often the most fun, and who wants to go home when you're having fun? *You do!* Your body is your priority, and sleep is at the top of the list.

Drink Enough Water.

Water is important for numerous bodily functions. For example, it helps maintain the balance of body fluids, keeps your skin looking good, energizes muscles, and enables your kidneys to eliminate waste materials from your body. That last point is especially important if you are taking medications.

Get the Right Amount of Exercise.

This means many different things for many different people. In my case, the right amount of exercise is a slow 20–30-minute walk most days of the week, and some extremely light restorative yoga a few times a week. For some, it might mean a light trip to the gym, and for others it might be some arm and leg movements that can be done lying down. Whatever form of exercise is best for you, do it, and keep it up. You might think you're not doing anything, but you are. Just make sure not to overdo it. Know your limits. Consult your doctor before adding in exercise, and consider working with an expert who can help you decide what is best for you, whether that's a kinesiologist, a properly qualified yoga teacher, or a tai chi master. Make sure whoever you choose is reputable, feels like a good fit, and understands your condition before you follow their advice.

Optimize Your Nutrition.

There are endless resources on different diets for different ailments. There are herbs and supplements and remedies, none of which I'm going to get into here since this is a book about dating, relationships, and getting it on. If you are interested in boosting your health through nutrition (which is a really powerful tool), do some research. Pick up some books. See a holistic nutritionist (which I recommend over a dietician because holistic nutritionists consider not just the physical but also the mental, emotional, and spiritual aspects of your life when making recommendations).

Meditate a Little to Give your Intuition a Tune-Up.

Meditation unfortunately isn't glamorous or exciting. It can be difficult to make yourself sit down in quiet contemplation with your thoughts. It can feel impossible to sit down and be with yourself when you are in pain. And it can be immensely valuable. So much of the foundation I recommend is based on intuition. Ultimately, *you* know what's best for you—and that's not what your brain is saying but what your gut is telling you, what you inherently know but have been trying to ignore, that little voice in the back of your head, trying to get your attention. Meditating will help you get in touch with your intuition, so you will be able to hear more clearly what it is telling you. Meditation will also help you be more aware of your body (not just the pain) and more able to acknowledge the messages you are getting from it.

This is about listening. Listen to the messages that come up. Listen to the negative voice in your head, and notice how its messages are not helping you. Would you talk to a friend the way your inner critic talks to you? Your inner critic is not going to help you heal, but your intuition will; that's why it's so important to become more connected to your intuition and more aware of this inner critic, and of how the critic is hurting you. It's crucial to establish this now, because that inner critic can get very *loud* when you're dating or in a relationship.

A note on meditation: When you meditate, your brain-wave frequencies change and you go from the fight-or-flight response paths of the sympathetic nervous system to the happy rest-and-digest place of your parasympathetic nervous system. That's where the healing happens. The more you are in the latter state, the better you will feel. In fact, let's call it the rest, digest, and heal state. It's one of nature's small miracles!

See a Doctor

So you've got the basics in place. Are you seeing a doctor regularly? If you answered yes, wonderful! If you answered no, it's time to see a doctor. Doctors *can* help. A good doctor can be invaluable. It's important you get help for your pain or illness. Doctors are here to provide us with a service, and you are entitled to this service. It might take a try or two to find a doctor who is the right fit, but it's important to have a doctor on your "team." Seeing a doctor isn't a laugh riot, but it's needed.

See Alternative Practitioners

This is totally elective. In most cases, alternative medicine will cost you because it's not covered by government medical plans, as physicians are in Canada. If you are working, some extended medical plans cover a certain number of visits (or amount of fees) to practitioners such as naturopaths, acupuncturists, chiropractors, counsellors, massage therapists, and the like. I encourage you to take advantage of those benefits.

The list of alternative practices is extensive: herbal therapy, Reiki, yoga, quantum touch, Shamanism, Alexander technique, Feldenkrais, physiotherapy, craniosacral therapy, breath work... I could go on for pages. If this is something you are interested in and have the means to do, then go for it! Try some out. I've tried numerous different therapies and techniques, and I've figured out which work best for me. Along with my GP and internist, I also have a counsellor, an acupuncturist, a physiotherapist, and an energy healer on my team. They haven't "cured" me, but they have helped me tremendously.

When you're deciding what sort of practitioner to see, go with your intuition. If a friend is pushing her chiropractor but you're not comfortable with the idea of someone cracking your bones, don't go! Listen to your body. What is it asking for?

THE BASICS (SLEEP, water, exercise, nutrition, and meditation), along with seeing your doctor and possibly consulting an alternative practitioner or two, will all help you create the best physical foundation possible before you start dating. You want to be solid before you bring someone new into your life. You want to feel as good as you can, mentally, emotionally, physically, and spiritually. Having a solid foundation will make a big difference when it comes to weathering the bumps and dips on the dating road and relationship highway. Be solid in yourself. No one else is going to be able to do these things for you, and a relationship won't fix your pain or illness. Be proactive *now*. It will pay off for the rest of your life.

TAKE ACTION!

1. See your family doctor/general practitioner. If you don't have a GP, it's time to find one. It's extremely important to receive basic medical care if you have chronic pain and illness. And it's important to stick with one physician rather than visiting various walk-in clinics and seeing a different doctor each time. Continuity is so important when you have chronic pain and illness as you need a doctor who can get to know you and keep track of your condition.

Finding a GP can be a challenging task because many doctors—especially the good ones—are often not taking new patients. Ask your friends and family for referrals. Bear in mind that you might end up calling many offices before you find an opening. Another option is to call the College of Physicians and Surgeons in your area for a list of doctors who are accepting new patients.

Make sure that when you visit the doctor you clear up any outstanding health concerns or questions. Develop a treatment plan with your doctor. Be persistent and proactive. Since you are about to start dating, it's also a good idea to ask your doctor for a blood test that includes a complete sexually transmitted infection (STI) screen.

I'll say it again, be persistent. Dogged. Get answers. Get help. Get a second (or third) opinion if you're not happy with your doctor.

2. Keep a symptom journal. A symptom journal is very useful, for both you and your doctor. It will allow you to track how you feel each day, and how what you do affects how you feel. You can design the journal any way you like. I buy a medium-sized book with 300 sheets in it—enough for over a year if I use a page a day and write on both sides. At the end of every day, record the following in your journal:

Sleep. How much sleep did you get the night before, and how was it? Restless? Deep? Satisfactory?

Symptoms. What are your physical symptoms? Where is your pain? What feels better today?

Mood. Happy? Sad? Angry? Frustrated? Calm? Take note!

Energy. Describe your energy. Was it high in the morning, low in the afternoon, and better in the evening? How did it change throughout the day?

Energy scale (1–10). Rate your energy on this scale, with 1 being completely lacking in energy and 10 being bursting with it.

Rests. At what time did you rest, and for how long? A rest only counts if you are lying down with your eyes closed. For best results, try for a maximum of twice a day for 15–20 minutes.

Activities. What did you do today? Record everything from exercise to errands to vacuuming to socializing.

Medications. List all the medications and supplements you took today, as well as the dosages.

Overall day (1–10). How would you rate your day? Was it a struggle and therefore a 3 or 4, or did it go so smoothly and enjoyably that you would rate it an 8?

Pain scale (0–10). A day without pain on this scale would be a 0 and you would rate your worst pain day as a 10. This is a great way to keep track of pain and measure progress. It can help a lot to see that not all days are 10s (or 11s!).

You may also wish to track what you eat, as some people find that they have food sensitivities that can drastically increase pain and other symptoms.

If you are tech savvy and want to be more efficient than I am, there are apps available for smartphones and tablets that allow you to track your symptoms. See, for example, sympleapp.com; I've tried it out, and it's pretty good. You can totally customize what you want to track. Since I'm old school, I like my written journal, but for those of you who are more tech inclined, this app is definitely a good choice. There are likely lots more out there, so check out your options.

Having a symptom journal in place is great for when you start dating. You can note exactly how a date affects your energy, mood, sleep, pain, and activities the following day. If you detect a downward trend in your well-being, you can make adjustments accordingly. It's a lot easier to figure out what is worsening your symptoms when you keep track of how you're living your life.

3. Sleep well. Decide how much sleep is optimal for you, and commit to getting that amount. Consider your bedtime routine. It's important to have some time to wind down before bed. Turn down the lights. Read. Relax. Avoid the television, as well as your phone, tablet, or any other electronic device for at least an hour before you sleep. Use eyeshades and earplugs to tune out distractions and light. If you have a lot of trouble sleeping, consult your doctor and your naturopath, if you have one, to find out what your options are. I can't over-emphasize the importance of sleep. If you have pain that keeps you up at night, it is especially important to find out whether there is something that can help you sleep better.

4. Drink water. Drink half your body weight in ounces of water per day. For example, if you weigh 160 lbs (72 kg), drink 80 oz (10 cups; 2.5 L) of water per day. You might find yourself going to the washroom more than usual, but your body will adjust, and soon you won't be wearing down the carpet between the couch and the bathroom as much. And please, don't go from two cups to ten overnight. If you're only drinking a small amount of water right now, build up slowly to the ten cups—for instance, add one cup to your daily intake each week until you're at ten.

5. Exercise. Possibly one of the hardest things to do when you have chronic pain and illness is to exercise, yet it is so important. Be flexible with the word "exercise." Maybe it's stretching. Maybe it's swimming. Maybe, on a bad day, it's range of motion exercises with your neck. Listen to your intuition. Choose something you like to do. But please, don't overdo it. Estimate how much you think you can do, and do half of that, at least until you find your happy place and know how much exercise you can do without aggravating your pain, fatigue, or whatever other symptoms may arise. Getting consistent exercise will help with dating. You may find yourself pushing your body when going on dates or starting a relationship, so it's important to have your body in the best place that you can reach. What is "consistent"? That depends on you. The more, the better, but again, not if it aggravates anything. Consistent for you may be six days a week, it may be three, or it may be one. Figure out what works for you, and keep it up.

6. Eat nutritiously. This alone could be a whole book, so I'm going to provide a small summary. Eat as many fresh foods as possible. Shop from the outside aisles of the grocery store only (fruits, veggies, protein). Try to incorporate as many whole foods as you can—that means foods that aren't processed, don't come in a box or a package, don't contain ingredients you can't pronounce or recognize, and don't list more than five ingredients on the package. Challenging? Yes. But you will feel better for it.

7. Meditate. Are you resisting meditating? I know I did for yeeeaaars! After 15 or so years, the resistance finally dissolved. Hallelujah! What I'm saying is, it wasn't easy, but I did it anyway. And it helped. A lot.

Meditation is an excellent pain management tool. There

are an infinite number of ways to meditate. Maybe you already meditate. Maybe you don't. Either way, I have some suggestions:

a. **Count breaths.** Sit down, preferably cross-legged or with your feet on the floor. If you need to lie down, then that works, too (try not to fall asleep, though). Close your eyes. Notice your thoughts. That's your monkey brain and inner critic! We're going to try and calm those guys with meditation. Start to notice your breathing. Notice how your body feels when you breathe in and out. I always notice, with awe, that this act of breathing keeps this organism that is my body alive. Your breath is powerful. Draw your attention away from your thoughts and to your breathing. Start to count your breaths, aiming to reach 10. Each time a thought comes back into your mind, start again at one. It's a simple and effective technique to calm your brain. I rarely get to 10, but it's not about the goal, it's about the practice.

b. **Use guided imagery.** Sometimes, the monkey brain and inner critic are too loud, and I need some help. At these points, I turn to guided meditations, which give me something to listen to and focus on. My favourite guided meditations can be found in Dr. Andrew Weil and Dr. Martin Rossman's e-book, *Self Healing with Guided Imagery*, which contains three. I do them all, repeatedly, and find them incredibly comforting. I lie down on the couch, put on my eyeshades, plug in my ear buds and go to my happy place for 30 minutes. At the end of each session, I find my sense of calm and peace has increased to an extent that I could not have achieved on my own. If you don't like these specific meditations, there are plenty of them out there, in e-books, on YouTube, or in apps you can easily download on your smartphone. Many of them are free, too!

8. Alternative practitioners. Aside from your doctor, do you see any alternative health practitioners? Let's be honest: it takes a fair amount of time, energy, and money to see acupuncturists, massage therapists, chiropractors, naturopaths, yoga teachers, and others; it may not be possible (or financially feasible) for you to do or access more than the basics at this time. And that's just fine. The most important thing is that you are doing your best to take care of yourself.

If you *do* have the means and ability to get some extra help, I encourage you to find out what can boost your well-being aside from your basic medical plan. Ask friends and colleagues for referrals, and go with your gut. Try some gentle online yoga classes. If you see a practitioner for the first time and it doesn't feel right, yet the person is trying to sell you a package, leave and don't go back! It's got to feel right. A good connection with the practitioner is a great indicator of how effective the treatment will be. Go because it helps you and you feel better afterwards. Don't feel obliged to stick with someone just because they are pushing you to. Experiment with different modalities. Do some research, and find out what works for you.

9. Work on yourself. If you are in pain and would like to do more than just follow the basics and your doctor's advice, and if you are motivated and proactive, I highly recommend Abigail Steidley's website, abigailsteidley.com. She's a wellness coach who has created programs to help others overcome pain and stress. I would suggest her Mind-Body Toolbox for Pain Relief, which you can purchase from her site. She also makes available numerous free resources. She's lovely, and I always feel better just seeing her photo, reading her blog, or watching her video updates. Adding her suggestions to your toolbox is a great way to continue to work on yourself by managing and reducing your pain between medical appointments.

10. Create your team. By now, you're probably starting to identify who can or may be able to help and support you. It takes a village! It's important to identify your team—the group of people who constitute your go-to resources.

Make sure that you like your team and that they are supportive and actually help. Make sure this is a team that works for *you*. I encourage you to write a list of who is on your team, so that if you are in a crisis, you can grab it and quickly identify who will be able to help.

And remember the most important person on your team... is you! You're the one who chooses your team, you're the one who decides when to connect with which team member. You're the one who makes the decisions, because you know what is best for you. And if you're unsure, your body will be more than happy to let you know what you need.

11. Write it down. Now that you've got your foundation figured out, *write it down*—all your practitioners, your friends, your support team, and your nutritional, sleep, and exercise basics. This will make a good reference sheet, and we'll be referring to it again and again in this book, so keep it handy.

———————

WOW, CREATING A foundation is a lot of work, no? Let's be real, it *is* a lot of work. And it's worth it. You need to be putting yourself first, right now. If that feels selfish, this means that you haven't been making yourself a priority. Now is the time. Your body is giving you the message: look after me! The great thing about this kind of work is that it pays off, it really does. Imagine how good you are going to feel going out on your first date: knowing your boundaries, being willing to enforce them, knowing you have a great team behind you, that you have a solid foundation, and that you can't be rocked by a date gone awry.

PART II
DATING

CHAPTER 4

Getting Ready to Date

CONGRATULATIONS ON MAKING it to Part II. You're working on your foundation, and now it's time for the fun stuff: preparing to date!

MY STORY

I'VE DATED A lot, and I think I'm now a pretty good dater. I like dating—it's fun, and I get to meet interesting new people. Plus, I always have plenty of stories to tell my friends. I think I've mastered dating.

I've discovered that deciding I want to date is one thing; being truly ready to date is something else altogether. This is a lesson I learned (the hard way) throughout my 20s and early 30s, a time fraught with insecurity and the lack of a strong personal foundation. I had no plan, no vision for the future. My focus bounced from one thing to another, one man to another, and my timing was often terrible, as evidenced by the following dating blunders:

- I decided to start dating a few days after I separated from my husband. Ummm… yeah. Can you say rebound?
- I got back into dating while in immense pelvic pain, pain I was ignoring and pushing through. That lasted about two dates. Barely.
- I tried online dating for the first time when I was desperately lonely. I don't recommend that either.

But I was impatient. I didn't want to wait until I was in a healthy, stable place in my life and mentally, emotionally, and physically ready to meet someone. I wanted a relationship *stat*. I wanted, *needed*, love *now*.

Early in my quest to find my soul mate, I experienced varying degrees of desperation, loneliness, self-doubt, and insecurity:

- I cried myself to sleep at night.
- I threw myself into any party, gathering of friends, or other social event I could find, so I'd never be alone at home in the evenings, especially on weekends.
- I wished, hoped, and prayed that the eye contact I managed to make with some cute guy was going to turn into the love story of my life.
- I tried to appear mysterious and seductive while having stains from a spilled drink on my blouse. (Because the only way I was going to get through that party was drunk, or at least glowing moderately.)

- I smiled at any and all (well, most) men who passed though my line of sight, insecurity escalating exponentially with each unreturned smile.
- I felt the frustration of being out at a bar or party where no one was approaching me.
- I experienced the desperation ramping up as my nights out went on. Was it my hair? Was I too intimidating? Was I not skinny enough? Not artsy enough? Not interesting enough? Could they tell I had pain in my undercarriage and therefore wasn't good girlfriend material?

What I couldn't see in those days was that what I was presenting to the world was not going to attract what I wanted. That my attempts to meet men and find a relationship were ineffective, that there were better strategies, *much* better strategies. Feeling lonely and desperate to meet someone and not having a foundation of support attracted men who were up for a one-night stand, who would use me, who were not willing to commit to anything. And the more I kept searching for rescue from the outside, the further I got from what I was looking for.

I finally figured out that if I'm searching for someone else to fill a hole, provide a distraction, or stop the desperation in my life, I'm not going to find what I *actually* want. The most powerful thing I can do is to shift the focus onto myself and work on my own issues until the time really *is* right to introduce someone new into my life. The time to venture back into dating is when I feel confident, calm, and happy, and I'm not on the rebound. The outcome is so much better, because then I am *truly* ready to meet someone special and will be much more likely to attract someone who respects me and treats me as I would like to be treated. As Hamlet said, "The *readiness* is all" (emphasis mine).

And these days, I'm ready, so now what? Well, I'm an old-school gal. I'd love to meet my next boyfriend in person—at a party or some other event, where our eyes meet and we just click and that's it. But I don't spend nearly as much time going to outings as someone who's living more or less without pain. My life is different. A lot of the ways that I have met men in the past aren't possible anymore because of my limited energy and various symptoms. And thank goodness for that, because I'm no longer willing to go to parties and gatherings every week, stand for hours in heels, make small talk, drink to excess, and scout out who's not wearing a wedding ring.

Thankfully for me, technology has changed so dramatically over the past 10 years that much of meeting prospective dates now takes place online. I don't have to put in the hours in person. Online dating, however, like anything else, has its pros and cons. While it can be a great starting place or backup plan, it can also be a big time-waster—I'm talking *hours and hours* down the drain. I'm not going to get into a big discussion about online dating, but—because there certainly is a lot to say—I will recommend the book *Modern Romance* by Aziz Ansari. He takes an in-depth, scientifically researched, and very funny look into today's dating world.

I'm really not sure where I'll meet my next guy, but I'm more than happy to get creative and find new ways to meet men, ways that don't involve parties, cocktails, or computers. Online dating is my backup plan. It's where I go when I haven't met any new people lately, when I'm in the mood for another round of dating. Before I dive back into dating, though, I *always* check that my foundation is still strong.

LET'S DISCUSS

I'VE WRITTEN A whole chapter on Getting Ready to Date because I'd like to make sure you set yourself up for the best possible dating experience. You have your mental, emotional, physical, and spiritual foundation in place. Now you need to do some administrative work around dating. There are some important questions to be answered:

- Are you ready to date?
- How do you know when you're ready?
- What are your dating goals and expectations?
- Who do you want to meet?
- How do you want to present yourself to others?
- What are your dating limitations?
- How will you meet people?
- Should you be willing to settle for less than what you want?

All right, let's get started then!

Are You Ready to Date? Are You Really?
This is an interesting question and one that everyone will answer differently. Your response shouldn't be based on what your mom or your best friend thinks. It's about how *you* are feeling and what *you* think. If you want to date, great. That's one step in the right direction. If you feel you have a good foundation, even better. If you're nervous or unsure because you have a lot of pain, discomfort, or fatigue,

that's ok, as long as you are functioning at or close to your maximum level and you're looking after yourself as best you can. You can still date if your maximum is a 4 out of 10. Your condition is what it is. It doesn't mean you're not ready to date, it simply means that there will be various limitations on your availability and ability (we'll talk about this more in a short while).

And it's ok not to be ready. Maybe you need some more time to build a stronger foundation, or to adjust to the idea of dating. Perhaps you need a bit more time to do some healing and reach a higher level of functioning. Or maybe you just want a little longer to wrap your head around how it's all going to work. And that is just fine.

If you don't feel ready, however, I would like to challenge you with a question: are you genuinely not ready, or are you making excuses and putting it off because you're feeling scared, insecure, or unsure (maybe all three)?

Perhaps you're having one or more thoughts like these:

"After I lose five more pounds, I'll start dating."

"I need to get in better shape first."

"Once I get a new job, I'll start dating."

"Once I get my own place, then I will be ready."

"No one is going to want to date me."

No. Uh uh. Those are not legitimate reasons to postpone dating. Those are excuses. If you keep waiting for the last five pounds to drop off, you're never going to start. Excuses such as these are a result of distorted beliefs you have about yourself. Time to go back to Chapter 1 and clear out a bit more of your emotional closet. What's holding you back from dating? What are you most afraid of? Investigate until you're ready to kick excuses to the curb!

On the other hand, if you're waiting for your current health flare-up to pass, then yes, wait. If you are waiting for some healing to occur, or for some answers to your medical issues, please wait. Your health is your number one priority.

How Do You Know When You're Ready?

You're ready when you have a strong foundation in place. You're ready when you're no longer coming up with excuses not to date. You're ready when you know what you want. You're ready when you're excited about the idea of dating!

You will be even more ready once you've read the rest of this chapter and have more clarity around how dating is going to look for you. It might be a strictly online relationship if you have difficulty leaving the house. It might be long-distance. It might involve seeing someone once a week. It might mean diving in right away and getting married after a few months. Everyone is different. Be yourself. Listen to your intuition. Do what feels right. Do what increases your sense of well-being. If dating is going to *decrease* your sense of well-being at this point, then it's probably a good idea to postpone it while you direct a little more attention to yourself and your healing and/or well-being. If dating is going to boost your enjoyment of life, then you're ready! Go get 'em!

What Are Your Dating Goals and Expectations?

Dating is a different experience for everyone. We all have various opinions on what a good date is, what a bad date is, and what a fulfilling relationship looks like. Ask yourself a few questions:

- What does dating mean to you?
- Are you looking for someone to date short-term or long-term?
- Do you want to get married eventually?
- If you're in a lot of pain, would you like to look for an online romance with someone you don't meet in person?
- Would you rather date someone in person for a short while—maybe dip your toes into the dating pool and see how it goes?
- Or are you looking for a no-strings-attached, casual hook-up booty call?

Whatever your dating goals, be clear on them *before* you put it out there that you are ready to date.

This clarity will help you avoid situations where you end up in a casual sex encounter when what you really wanted was a long-term relationship, or vice versa. Be clear. Be clear with yourself so you can be clear with the people you meet and date. Make your intentions specific and unambiguous.

Part of this process involves looking at your expectations about what kind of relationship you *can* have. Are your expectations reasonable, given your condition? Also, look at the expectations you have of a potential partner. Are your expectations of *him* reasonable? It's not reasonable to expect your partner to be your caretaker, because you want a relationship, not a caretaker, right? If you want just a caretaker, then this is not the book for you. Having no expectations that your partner will take care of you is the best way to go. Take responsibility for yourself and for your condition. Take initiative, find caregivers (who are not your partner), and seek treatments and support on your own. This is your job and will not become your future partner's job. The key is in the word—"partner." That means an equal, not a caregiver. Once someone becomes your caregiver, an imbalance develops in the relationship, and you are no longer partners.

Who Do You Want to Meet?

You're ready to date. You want to meet someone. Who is this "someone"? Have you thought about what you would like in a partner?

Just as it's important to get clear about what your dating goals are, it's important to know what you are looking for in a partner. That way, you'll recognize whether you are on track or off when you start dating. This is something I didn't do for a long time and I suffered the consequences (unsuitable mates)!

When it comes to your ideal relationship, what things are musts and what are you willing to compromise on? Do you even know what you want in a partner, or are you thinking that anyone who likes you is great? If that's the case, it's time to revisit Chapter 1 for some self-confidence building. No one, including you, needs to settle for a subpar partner. I'd like to see you pick someone as marvellous as you are. And you *are* marvellous. You're a survivor. You deal with things on a daily basis that most people can't even wrap their heads around. You deserve someone special because you are very special.

If I had it my way, dating would be romantic, smooth, and magical. There would be no real life interfering with your love life—no speed bumps, hiccups, or reality checks. But alas, we don't live in a fantasy, which is why it pays to be well prepared when you start dating. In the Take Action! section of this chapter, I provide you with four excellent tools to get you focused on your ideal mate and relationship.

How Do You Want to Present Yourself?

I'm guessing you probably don't want to present yourself as desperate and insecure, like I did in that oh-so-frantic phase in my life.

Picture the ideal you. You sweep into the room to meet your date. How would you like your date to describe you? I would like to be described as happy, creative, elegant, smooth, successful, connected, loved, excited, affluent, and a little kooky. Envision the pain-free, completely healthy, ideal you. Close your eyes and imagine. And then imagine the now you stepping into the ideal you, and know that you *are* the ideal you, *right now.*

You may not be able to physically present yourself the way you would like if you are in a wheelchair, confined to your bed, walk with a cane or, like me, walk at turtle speed, but you can feel that way on the inside. And when you feel that way on the inside it will radiate on the outside. I promise.

I know it's not easy to radiate happiness, elegance, and sophistication when you're in pain or don't feel well, when you're dizzy and anxious, or when you can't leave the house. I get it. But it's about being your ideal self in the *present moment.* Right this second. How do you want to feel in this very moment? Don't worry about an hour from now, 10 minutes from now, or how you're going to sustain the feeling for more than a short time. It's all about the right now.

In this moment, as your ideal self, what is your attitude?

What is your personal style? What sort of first impression would you like to make? Have some fun with it. I encourage you to be "you" as much as you can. Don't try to be someone else, and don't let your condition limit your imagination or creativity.

And now for the trickiest part about presenting yourself: How much of your condition do you want to reveal, and when?

I've spent a lot of time thinking about this and trying different approaches. I've been completely up front about my condition from date one, I've hid it until after having sex with a partner, and I've done the slow reveal—a little more on each date. I've gone so far as to reveal in my online profile that I have a disability, but I found that put guys off, perhaps even ones who would have been ok with it had they met me first and gotten to know me. I've also waited until the time felt right intuitively.

The reactions I've experienced have run the gamut from never hearing from someone again to a shrug and him saying, "That's all? No big deal. I thought you were going to tell me something really horrible." Everyone is going to have a different perception of what your condition means and how they think it will affect them, all based on the life lenses they are looking through.

And here's what I've learned: while you don't have any obligation to reveal or explain anything about your health to anyone, it's a good idea not to go out of your way to hide it. If someone feels misled or lied to at the beginning of a relationship, chances are the relationship isn't going to go much further.

When and how much you say about your condition is

really up to you and your comfort level. I found what worked best—surprise, surprise—was when I followed my intuition. I found I didn't need to reveal anything on the first date, because what if I didn't want a second date? I didn't need to disclose a lot of personal information to someone I wasn't going to see again. I now tend to discuss my condition once I've gotten to know someone well, know that I like them, and have decided I want to continue dating them. I do my best to present myself as Kira: friend, pop-culture aficionado, dog lover, romantic, meditator, fresh air addict, funny person (at least, I hope so), writer, life coach, and counsellor. I do not want to present myself as Kira: sick person. So I don't. I am all the things I listed, and I happen to have a condition, but it's not *who I am*, so I don't like to disclose it right away.

If you have a visible impairment, your date may ask you a question about it right away, or you may wish to let people know ahead of time that you are in a wheelchair or walk with a cane. And again, it's your choice how much you want to reveal about what got you into that wheelchair or requires that you use a cane. If you are mostly confined to your bed and are looking for an online relationship (emailing, messaging, Skyping, phone calls), you also have the choice about whether or not to reveal your condition right away. You always have a choice.

So, in a nutshell, present your true self, your glowing self. Go with your gut. Listen to your intuition. Don't lie or hold things back if it feels wrong to do so. Share with integrity and honesty. Reveal what feels right, when the time feels right.

What Are Your Limitations and Boundaries?

Ok: you're ready to date, you know how you'd like to present yourself, and you know what you're looking for in a partner. Great!

Now is the time to look at setting some boundaries— with yourself and your prospective dates. You're likely reading this book because you have chronic pain and illness, and you likely have some (or many) physical limitations.

Let's look at those limitations and consider how they will affect you when it comes to dating. Think about what is realistic, and stick with it. Maybe it's one date a week, maybe two. And what are your time and distance limits? How much can you reasonably do physically? If you need to be in bed by 9pm every night, then what is the latest your dates can end? 8pm? 7:30pm? Figure it out, and consider doing a test run with a friend.

Again, it's really important to be honest and clear with yourself when establishing your boundaries. For example, when I first got back into dating a few years ago, I was able to sit in a chair (especially one with no padding) for an hour at the most. Anything more meant intense pain and at least a day or two of recovery. So one of my limitations was no sitting for more than one hour. Did I push that boundary? Sure. Did I suffer for it? Yes. Was it worth the suffering? Not usually.

It can be difficult to explain why you can't sit for more than an hour. You don't have to. Instead, you can start by going for coffee dates and saying that you only have an hour, or that your parking meter runs out after an hour. Again, no need to explain your condition at this point; you don't even know whether you like the guy! Or, if you just need to move, have your hour-long coffee date and then suggest a short walk afterwards. That way you can extend the date with no extra discomfort for yourself.

Can't go far from your house? Meet at a nearby park. Can't walk more than half a block? No problem. Have someone drop you off where you're meeting, take a cab, or find parking out front. Are you in a wheelchair and your date wants to meet on the art gallery steps? Absolutely! Say you'll meet him at the bottom step.

The key is to use your creativity and come up with all kinds of solutions. If you're having difficulty generating ideas, ask a friend for help. It's important to keep your limitations clearly in mind and be realistic. You may be tempted to push your boundaries if you're having a particularly good date or if you really like the person you're out with, but this is about more than just one date. If you push too hard and need a lot of recovery time, what about the second date? If you push at each date, you're going to spend all your time between dates recovering from them, and that's not ok. You need to have a date–life balance.

Also, if you push yourself too much at first, the person you are dating may develop unrealistic expectations around how much you can do. Set the bar low. That way, both of you can be pleasantly surprised when and if your stamina increases.

Along with establishing your physical and temporal boundaries, get clear on what you are able to contribute in a relationship. What do you bring to the table? Do you bring love, humour, and comfort? Do you bring intelligence, wit, and patience? How much do you have to give emotionally? Your emotional stores may be limited due to your condition, so be aware of how your physical limitations affect your mental and emotional capacities, and vice versa. Maybe you get brain fog after talking for more than 45 minutes. Good to know! Adjust your dates accordingly. Do you feel like you need to follow your date's lead? Well guess what: you don't. You have the power to decide how much time you want to spend with someone and what you will do during that time.

If you set your boundaries at the beginning, and you respect them yourself, others will respect them too and be less likely to push them. If you show from date one that you *sort of kind of* have boundaries but you're willing to bend them for your date, then your date will bend them. And the longer you wait to set a strong boundary, the harder it will be to successfully implement that later on, both with yourself and with your date.

How Will You Meet People?

This is the million-dollar question, and it has a million possible answers. What I do know is that the more effort you put into meeting people, the more likely it is that you will get dates. If you stay at home and don't change your routine other than a grocery store shop once a week, not much will happen. If you put it out there that you want to date, and take some steps in that direction, things will start to happen.

What can you do? Here is a pile of suggestions to get you started:

- Do the exercises in the Take Action! section of this chapter.

- Tell all your friends (and family) that you are ready to date and want to meet someone.
- Accept blind dates.
- Read *Soul Mates and Twin Flames: The Spiritual Dimension of Love and Relationships* by Elizabeth Clare Prophet, and do the meditations in the book.
- Allow your friends to set you up.
- Talk to people everywhere you go—in the elevator, grocery store line-up, on the bus. Everywhere. You never know where things may lead.
- Be open-minded.
- Go to parties and social events.
- Try speed dating.
- Pursue what you love—spend time on your passions and interests.
- Join a club centred around an activity you love.
- Smile at people as you go down the street.
- Join an online dating service.
- Investigate other dating services in your area, and join if they're appealing and manageable.
- Change up your walking route or grocery store once in a while.
- Show an interest in other people.
- If you have a dog, take your dog to the dog park and chat with other dog owners you meet.
- If there is someone you know and like, ask them on a date.
- Give up on dating because, as everyone knows, that's when you meet "the one." (Just kidding, although some people swear by this method.)
- Be yourself!

For those of us with pain or illness, internet dating is a good option because we can meet hundreds of people without leaving the couch, or bed, or standing computer station, or floor, or hard-backed chair. We can be in our comfort clothes, ruling people out without moving more than our fingers.

There are all kinds of online dating sites. There are ones for people with disabilities, Christians, Jewish people, married people, women looking for sugar daddies, people with STIs, geeks, Trekkies, farmers, travelers, pet owners, parents, and women behind bars. And then there are ones for "normal" people—and no matter how much pain we're in and how tired we are, we're still "normal" people. I've tried the disability dating sites, without much success. There are not many people on them compared to, say, OkCupid. But hey, you never know, right?

Should You Be Willing to Settle for Less Than What You Want?
I've spoken with a number of people dealing with chronic pain and illness who feel that if they meet anyone—anyone at all—who is interested in them, they need to take the opportunity, even if it means settling for less than what they want.

No! You are no less worthy than anyone else, regardless of your health status. You are whole and complete just as you are, and you deserve a wonderful partner and companion just as much as the next person. It may be more difficult to find the right person, but it is possible. Who knows, maybe it will even be easy, and you'll meet someone great right away. You never know. But please, don't settle.

Settling often means ending up in an unhappy relationship, which means more stress for you, which may well worsen your condition. If you find yourself feeling tempted to settle, come back and read this chapter again!

TAKE ACTION!

THIS CHAPTER HAS been about setting yourself up for a good dating experience. Do as much as you can beforehand to get clear on what you want, what you are able to do, and how you are going to do it. You may wish to get a "dating notebook" so you can make lists of intentions, limitations, boundaries, and goals. If you write things down, you are more likely to achieve them than if you simply keep them in your mind. So grab a pen and paper (or your laptop or tablet) and answer the following questions:

1. Are you ready to date?
Be honest with yourself. If you need to go back and work on anything from the first three chapters of this book, then do so. Rest some more first. Heal from your previous marriage a little longer. Whatever you need to do. There is no rush. And if you're ready, then you're ready!

2. What are your dating goals?
Get clear on what you want: a relationship, a casual encounter, something in between, or whatever else it is you desire.

3. Who do you want to meet?
The following are four effective tools for envisioning and attracting your ideal partner. Try all or just one or two, and be ready for the results.

a. **Visualize.** Find a comfortable spot, somewhere you can relax. Close your eyes, and envision yourself out on a date with your ideal partner. Notice the details, where you are, what you are doing. Look at your partner. Notice his clothing, eye colour, hair colour. What is his voice like? How does he smell? Picture as many little details as you can. Where are you going, and what are you doing? And now for the most important piece: How do you feel? What emotions are you experiencing? Connect to the feeling you have when you are with your ideal partner. Feel the sensations in your chest, your stomach, up and down your spine, or wherever you experience them. Bask in the wonderful feeling of being in that dream relationship.

Feels good, right? Now connect with this feeling as often as possible throughout the day and as often as you remember during the week. When you have time, go through this visualization again, picturing all the details and connecting with the feelings.

By conjuring up the sensations you have around your ideal mate, you will attract more of those sensations, and when you are dating, and you meet the right person, you will recognize the wonderful feeling you have been looking for when it happens. It's the law of attraction, baby!

b. **Write it out.** Take a pen and a piece of paper and jot down a list of the qualities you are looking for in a partner. Grab a sheet and just go for it. Mine is four pages long—but don't tell any of my dates, they might get scared! List anything and everything that is important to you. Your list might look something like this:

- Intelligent
- Funny
- Good conversationalist
- Empathetic
- Happy
- Emotionally stable
- Financially stable
- Enthusiastic
- Patient
- Generous
- Kind
- Likes to travel (but is not too adventurous)
- Reads
- Is punctual
- Smells good
- Likes to play board games

Put anything on your list, even if it seems silly. Be clear. The clearer you are with yourself, the more likely you are to get what you want. Keep the wording positive. Rather than writing "doesn't spend too much money," write "saves money," or "is financially stable." If you're struggling with this one, you can write a list of things you don't want and then, on a separate piece of paper, write down the opposites of all the things you don't want. You will end up with a positive list of your ideal mate's qualities. Then throw out or burn your list of "don't wants."

Once you've finished your list, keep it. Put it somewhere special, or keep it under your pillow. Hold on to it. Keep it around and review it once in a while, adding and taking off items as required.

c. **Ask for him**. Here's what I mean: I recall a time when I was lonely and just wanted someone in my life. I sat down and meditated. I asked my higher self to bring me someone, someone to date, even if just for a little while. Shortly thereafter, I met someone and we became a couple. While I was in the relationship, I realized that what I really wanted was something long-term. Alas, this relationship ended after a year, and I was pretty broken-hearted. But I had gotten what I had asked for: someone to date for a little while. After that, I changed my tune. When I meditate now, I ask for exactly what I want.

Go for broke. Take some time to sit quietly and ask for who or what you want. Ask for the sun and the stars and be willing to accept less. The more you ask for, the more you are likely to get.

And who are you asking? I ask the universe and my higher self. You may wish to pray, or to ask your ancestors who are watching over you. It doesn't matter where you direct your requests, just ask. You don't have to have a specific target. Just put it out there. And I don't mean go and ask your friends to find you this man (although that might not be a bad idea either): I mean ask the universe, karma, fate, whatever you call it. Make your intentions clear.

d. Make a Man Chart. I went on a couple of dates
with a guy who told me about a dating chart he had
made, to track his dating experiences and rate his
dates. At first, I was thinking, "Whaaaaat?! How
dare you rate me!" Then I realized that he was on
to something, especially for a person like me, who
tends to plunge into the excitement of a new relationship and lose my vision around things that are
no-nos for me. I now use the chart frequently. He
gave me permission to use it in my book, so here
is a sample:

Man Chart

	JEREMY	TIM	STEVEN	KEVIN
Respectful	Y	Y	Y	Y
Honest	N	*	Y	N
Intelligent	Y	Y	Y	N
Punctual	Y	N	Y	Meh
Good kisser	Y	N	N	N
Attractive	Y	Meh**	Y	N
Sexually adaptable	N		Y	N
Good manners	Y	Y	Y	N
Funny	N	N	Y	Y
Financially stable	N		Y	N
Does not live with his mother	Y	Y	Y	N
Does he really do it for me?	Y	N	N	Y

* A blank cell means "I don't know the answer yet."
** "Meh" means "It's not a no, but it's not a yes either."

List your top 10 or so must-haves for your next partner on the left-hand side of the chart. After listing your must-haves, add a row for "Does he *really* do it for me?" As you date, write your date's name at the top of the first available column, and rate away! At the end, ask yourself whether he *really* does it for you, otherwise known as "Do you have chemistry?" Does he turn your crank? Do you smile when he's not around and you're thinking of him? Do you feel connected while you are physically apart? Does he just *rowrrrrr* do it for you? Because, at the end of the day, his column could be full of Ys but he still may just not do it for you. On the other hand, his column might be full of Ns but he may *totally* do it for you. And that's called a bad boy. They're best to avoid unless you're looking for a quick, hot fling.

By using these four tools, you will have a much better chance of meeting the right person for *you* than if you dive in with no vision or plan. Proper preparation prevents poor performance!

4. How do you want to present yourself to others?

Visualize your ideal, best self; see yourself stepping into that self; and then list the adjectives that describe you. Write them down. Write about what makes you *you*. What do you love to do? What are your interests and passions? What makes you unique?

Read over your notes and familiarize yourself with the characteristics and traits you've listed. Embody them on a daily basis. Be your ideal self despite your pain and discomfort. Show *who* you are, not what your condition or illness is. Don't lead with your disability or pain. Lead with your authentic self. Easy to say, harder to do, I know. But try, be this person, if only for a few seconds or minutes at a time. With practice, it will get easier.

5. What are your dating limitations?

Please don't skip this very important step! It's so crucial to get clear on how much you can reasonably do on a date—physically, mentally, and emotionally—before you start going on dates, before you get swept up in romance and kissing and love. *Sigh*. It's important to decide where your boundaries are. Write them down, and make an agreement with yourself to stick to them. Whether it's limiting dates to one hour, not leaving your neighbourhood, avoiding coffee and other stimulants, or only having daytime dates; jot down all of your rules, big and small. Taking care of you is the most important thing. No matter who you meet, keeping your level of well-being and quality of life as high as possible is your number one priority!

6. How will you meet people?

Consider the many options I've suggested earlier in this chapter, then list all the ways you feel you could meet people. If some of my suggestions aren't feasible for you, then no problem. My list is by no means exhaustive. Be creative and have fun with brainstorming.

Once you've written your list, it's time to start working your way through it. Get the wheels in motion! What is the first thing you are going to do towards getting that first date? What is the next thing you are going to do? Great. Now do them!

———————

THIS HAS BEEN a work-intensive chapter. I've suggested quite a bit of visualizing, reflecting, and writing, and this will be worth your time and effort as you continue through the next chapters. The work you've done around preparing to date will also considerably strengthen your foundation. Once you reach this point, you will be clear on what you want from a relationship, who you want to have it with, and how you will go about finding it. You're ready for success. Now, on to the first date!

CHAPTER 5

The First Date

MY STORY

FIRST DATES CAN be terrifying. They can be fun. They can be both terrifying and fun. And they get easier. These days, I'm a first date expert. I have a great foundation in place, which gives me a lot of confidence. I love meeting other people and am curious about each guy I meet. I know how I would like to present myself, and I know how I do present myself. Even though I feel open and comfortable, I still come across as reserved. And I know some of that is because of the pain, because part of my mind is on the pain. My body often appears a bit rigid because I'm in discomfort, and I'm ok with that. There are worse things than seeming reserved. When people get to know me, that assessment usually evaporates.

I've had some amazing first dates and some run-for-your-life-in-the-opposite-direction first dates.

The first date I had with my now ex-husband, over 20 years ago, remains one of the best. We started by going for dinner at a fancy Italian restaurant, one of my favourites. Then we went to a play. And he fell asleep during the play. Oops. But the play was a minor bump in the road. Afterwards, we went to a nightclub called Celebrities, had drinks, and danced to some of the best dance music of the '90s. One of the songs that pumped through the speakers still sticks with me today—"Mr. Vain" by Culture Beat. After the club, we walked down to the beach, sat on a log and kissed for hours. I got home around 4am. It was a magical night, one I would not be able to replicate now, but what a wonderful memory.

I've also had first dates that haven't gone as well. Some were just awkward, and some were downright awful. Truth be told, I don't like to label dates as "bad." I will say I've had some difficult first dates. Some dull first dates. Some batshit crazy first dates.

I met a guy one morning as I was walking down my back alley. Red flag already, right?! But I was in my 20s and had a really open mind. Gary. Oh Gary. Gary told me I was beautiful and asked for my number, and I gave it to him right there in the alley. He was not a big guy, fairly lean, a little taller than I. Dark hair and eyes. Seemed safe enough. He called me, and we set up a breakfast date for the next weekend.

Saturday rolls around, and he's prompt. We meet at my building and walk to the Elbow Room, then sit down and start chatting. So far, so good. He seems to have a lot to say. I ask where he lives, and he says Kitsilano.

"Oh, do you have roommates?"

"Well no, yes, sort of."

"What do you mean?"

"I'm still living with my ex-girlfriend, but I'm moving out at the end of the month."

"You're still living with your ex? When did you break up?"

"Oh, a few weeks ago. But it's totally over. It's been over for a long time."

Riiiiiight.

So Gary was still living with his girlfriend, possibly ex-girlfriend, while looking for his next conquest.

We order our food. He then tells me that he was really sick when he was younger and has a pacemaker. Apparently, you can feel it through his skin. He has me feel it. It's in his chest, above his heart, and feels like a small box under his skin. I'd never met anyone with a pacemaker, let alone someone so young. And that was fine. Maybe he would understand my pelvic pain better since he had gone through some serious medical issues.

We're finishing up our meal when another couple is seated next to us. If you've ever been to the Elbow Room in Vancouver, you'll know that the tables are squished together like sardines. Gary is very chatty. He starts chatting with the couple next to us. It all seems pretty normal. And then he says, "This is the first time my girlfriend and I have eaten here." What?! Me? Your girlfriend? After an hour of dating?

At this point, I'm starting to suspect that he wants to get a new relationship going quickly so that he can move from one girlfriend to the next—literally—otherwise he'll have to find a place to live on his own. I'm also starting to notice the neediness seeping out of his pores.

Finally, we leave. He wants to take the little aquabus

over to Granville Island so we can walk around. I would rather end the date immediately, but I agree to go with him for reasons I can't for the life of me remember.

As we walk down to the water he holds my hand, then puts his arm around me and tries to get as close as he possibly can. I subtly move away. Clearly he doesn't understand because he's wrapping himself around me once again. And then he leans in for a kiss. Uggh!! I've never felt so smothered in all my life. I finally push him away and tell him to stop. He comes in closer to touch me, and I back away.

"Stop, just stop. You're smothering me. I can't deal with this."

"I thought we were having a good time. I really like you."

"You're a nice guy, Gary, but this is just too much. I can't handle the smothering. And I'm not your girlfriend. We barely know each other! Please stop trying to touch me. This is just too much. *And* you're still living with your girlfriend."

"She's my ex-girlfriend, I swear."

"I don't care—you're not done with that relationship."

"It's been over for a long time. We were just going through the motions. We're more like brother and sister." He goes for my hand again.

"Gary, please! I have to go home, I can't deal with this, it's too much."

"You're ending our date?"

"Yes!"

It takes a lot for me to abandon a guy mid-date, but it had to be done. I refused to hug him goodbye and dashed off home as quickly as possible.

I rarely smoke. I love nothing more than a good cigarette,

but I don't want smoking to kill me, so only on very rare occasions do I indulge. As soon as I got home from my date with Gary, I lit up, hanging out my window. Aahh, sweet relief, escape. It felt surreal; people actually act like this?! I finished my cigarette just as the phone rang.

Gary.

I answered.

"Can you come down for a minute? Please?"

"What for?"

"Please, just come downstairs. I'll only take a minute of your time."

"Ok."

So I head down on the elevator, conscious of my cigarette breath, but whatever—all the more repelling to him. The elevator doors open on the ground level and there he is. I hadn't buzzed him in, so he must have followed someone else. There is a mail room just to the side of the elevators, not visible from the street or the lobby. He says nothing but grabs my hand, pulls me into that room, pushes me against a wall of mailboxes and kisses me passionately. Or what I assume he meant to be passionately. It felt more like a messy, sloppy, confused meeting of willing and unwilling lips.

I push him away. He looks at me intensely. I think he's trying to be sexy. He says, "I'll leave you with that," or something to that effect, and walks out of my building.

But that wasn't the end of Gary. He called me frequently, pleading for another chance. I stopped answering, but he kept calling, leaving long messages that would get cut off by my voicemail. He would call and hang up. Call and hang up. Call and hang up. He would ring the apartment buzzer. He continued to call and buzz long after I stopped answering. I had my very own stalker.

Not too long before I met Gary, I met Christine, who has become one of my closest friends. We were out one day and I happened to be talking about Gary without using his name. I told her I had a stalker, that he was really needy and had a pacemaker, and she said, "Is his name Gary?" Apparently he was stalking her, too. Gary really got around.

I lost track of him a couple of years later (it took me that long to shake him off). Now, I think of Gary as a sweet soul—scared, needy, and trying to navigate a world that possibly hadn't treated him well. Christine would still talk to him on the phone once in a while, but last time I asked her, she hadn't heard from him in several years. Gary, wherever you are, I hope you found what you were looking for.

LET'S DISCUSS

THE FIRST DATE deserves a chapter in itself because it's a big deal, especially if you haven't dated in a while. There's a lot involved in meeting someone new, even when not facing chronic pain and illness. Luckily you've got your foundation in place and you're prepared to start meeting potential mates. As you begin to date, it's crucial to make sure that the foundation stays in place and that you continue to build upon it.

You never know what you're going to get on a first date, and that uncertainty can be a challenge when it's structure and pre-planning that keep your symptoms at bay. You can do your best to plan a date that feels safe and comfortable, but you can't plan for surprises, so it's important to be ready for whatever happens.

Planning Your First Date

When you have chronic pain and illness, planning and preparation are a big part of dating. Let's say you've met someone you would like to get to know better and you've both agreed to go on a date. It's now time to figure out when and where to meet and what you're going to do on the date.

Location

The most important thing is that you meet in a place where you are comfortable physically, both in terms of your condition and your physical safety. Meet somewhere public where there are other people around, that you can get to easily (and from which you can make a quick getaway if needed) and where you can sit (or stand) comfortably. I like to scope out my neighbourhood ahead of time (via the Internet) to find a few suggestions that I can present to my date. It's also a good idea to let a friend or family member know that you are going on a date with someone new, where you are going, and that you'll call when you get home. And keep your cell phone on you at all times. You can't be too safe.

If your date suggests a location, look it up online and check in with yourself to make sure you feel good about it. If not, don't be shy. You know you need to look after yourself, so suggest an alternative. You don't need to give a long explanation—you can simply say you're more in the mood for X rather than Y. Don't be afraid to be the one to choose where to meet.

If you aren't mobile, or your date lives in another city, planning where to meet may be simple, as you will likely have a virtual date online, through a video chat service such as Skype or FaceTime.

Date and Time

If you've had chronic pain and other symptoms for a while, you probably know by now what your best times of the day are, when you have the most energy and the least pain. If in doubt, you can consult your symptom journal and see what it tells you about when you are at your best. Consider both the day of the week and the time of day. If you have something planned for Wednesday morning, Tuesday night might not be the best time to go on a date. If you work and are usually exhausted by the end of your work week, then that night is a no-go. If you don't work, perhaps most nights are good nights. And if nights are tricky, then suggest a daytime date—brunch, a matinee, a coffee, or a visit to the park. This is a good opportunity to exercise your creativity.

Don't feel you need to accommodate your date. If he only has time on Friday and Saturday nights after 8pm, and you like to be in bed by 8:30pm, then sorry, that's not going to work for you. Maybe the stars aren't aligned and it's not meant to be. Please don't sacrifice your well-being to fit into someone else's schedule because when you've done that once, you'll probably be expected to continue to do that. Remember: boundaries!

After you've established the day and time you're going to get together, determine how long you are willing to spend with your date and commit to sticking to it. One hour for a coffee date or an initial meeting is just fine. And if you can only manage half an hour, that's fine, too. Two hours works as well, as long as your body agrees. If you're having a wonderful time and don't want to end your date, just remember that there can be more dates; you don't have to pack it all in to one day.

Activity

The activity you plan for your date deserves just as much thought and attention as the day and location. Ensure the activity is reasonable for you. If your date suggests something you *think* you can do but know is probably going to be too much, don't be afraid to suggest an alternative. You are just as important as he is, and you don't have to go along with what he suggests because you think it will make him happy or like you more.

For example, when I first stopped drinking alcohol some of my friends gave me a hard time, encouraging me not to give it up or to have just one drink. One girlfriend even told me that not drinking would make dating so much harder because I would have to meet a guy who didn't drink either.

I'll admit, I did at first feel a bit insecure about telling guys I was dating that I didn't drink alcohol. I knew that most people like to have a few drinks and don't like to drink alone. I stuck to my guns, though. As I became more confident about the fact that I didn't drink, I found that people were more willing to accept my choice. I also started meeting guys who didn't drink either. The more I owned it, the more it became acceptable to others.

If there is an activity in which you do not wish to participate, don't. Don't try to please others by compromising your health or values. Use your creativity and choose an activity that you find fun and easy, that will add to the date rather than have you struggling through it.

First Dates and Monkey Brains

If it's been a while since you've been out on a date, a lot of thoughts and feelings are likely to come up—especially if you are dealing with chronic pain and illness as well.

What will he think of me?
What if I'm not good enough?
What if I'm not smart enough?
What if he's not attracted to me?
What if he's not willing to date me because of the pain and illness?

These are normal thoughts to have. Are they useful? No. So scratch "what if" right out of your vocabulary. You *are* good enough. You *are* smart enough. You are strong and you are remarkable. You are a survivor. "What ifs" are useless.

When I first started dating after a serious worsening in my condition, all my monkey brain could think about was my condition and how my date might judge me for it. I was convinced he would only see my illness, not the rest of me. The what ifs in my head were out of control. When I met someone on a date, I felt like a fraud if I didn't tell him about my illness—like I was tricking him into something. I felt duplicitous.

After a while, though, I saw the flaws in that line of thinking. I realized that I was giving my power to the guy I was dating. I was allowing *him* to be in control of whether or not I was adequate, of whether this was going to turn into a relationship. My illness had created such great insecurity in me that I was unable to see that I could take the reins. I felt unworthy of a relationship, of love. I believed that my illness made me inferior and therefore unlovable. This may or may not be your experience. Perhaps you are much more confident than I was. If so, you're a step ahead!

You may realize after a while that you actually have a lot more choice and control than you expected. You may begin by going into dates worried that the guy won't like you, yet after a while realize that *you're* actually not interested in *him*. And that's a good sign, because it means you're not settling or compromising yourself.

We are all worthy of love, regardless of the condition of our bodies. We deserve to have a loving relationship just as much as the next person. We are not our illnesses; we are whole and complete just as we are. There is no reason why we wouldn't be worthy of loving relationships. Sure, they might be more challenging to find for those of us with physical conditions and disabilities, but it's still possible. Don't let your monkey brain convince you otherwise. Our relationships may be different than the traditional "married with two kids, living in a house with a white picket fence," but it doesn't matter what the eventual relationship looks like, as long as it works for us and we're happy.

First Dates and Feelings

When heading out for a first date, it's normal to feel a variety of emotions, both enjoyable and uncomfortable. Once you quiet your monkey brain's "what ifs," criticisms, and doubts, take some time to notice your feelings. Are you scared? Nervous? Excited? Feeling inadequate? Dreading the event? Or are you stoked and ready to dive in? Allow yourself to experience your feelings and notice them. Be aware of where in your body you feel them and what they feel like. Do you have fireworks in your chest or a brick in your stomach? Don't judge the feelings, just take note. These emotions are 100% ok, and I encourage you to have them, feel them, and then let them pass. Enjoy the happy ones; let go of the rest.

Expectations

Your date has been planned, your monkey brain tamed, and your emotions experienced and identified. Now all that's left to do is wait for the main event.

You probably have some kind of expectations of your upcoming date. If you've been talking to, texting, or emailing the guy you're going to meet, you've likely developed an idea of what he is going to be like in person. You may even feel that, based on your conversation so far, he's definitely going to be your next boyfriend. He's funny and intelligent, and he texts you back right away. It's true love!

On the flipside, you might be unsure of the guy you're going to meet. Maybe he is a bad speller and takes a long time to text you back. You're wondering why you're even meeting him at all. You picture him as unreliable and distracted. You don't really like him, and you haven't even met him yet. You're thinking that maybe you should cancel the date and not ever meet him in person.

Either way, you've created some expectations in your mind about what your first date with this guy is going to be like. High expectations can lead to big disappointments. And low expectations can lead to pleasant surprises. If you'd like to avoid disappointment—and be willing to give a guy a chance even though he may not present himself in the best light by text or phone—dropping any expectations is a great strategy. Go in curious: "I'm about to meet someone new; I wonder what he's like?"

Avoid making any assumptions as to what he'll be like

or what will happen on your date. If you walk in with assumptions, they will come across in your attitude, body language, and communication. If you drop the assumptions beforehand, then you open up a new realm of possibilities. Dropping them will also make it easier for you to be yourself, be present, and enjoy meeting someone new.

The First Date

It's finally time for your date. This is the easy part, believe it or not. You've prepared yourself well, you know your limitations, and you've promised yourself that you are going to stick with them. You're solid. Now is the time to have fun!

Fun? you say. What's that? How can I enjoy myself or the company of someone else when I'm hyperaware of my condition and symptoms?

Do your best—that's all you can ever do. Take it minute by minute, one second at a time. Know that in this moment, you are ok. Remember that you are not your condition. Allow your true (glorious, funny, intelligent, eccentric, creative) self to emerge while you focus on getting to know your date. Breathe, relax, and have fun with it!

But what if things don't go as smoothly as you had planned?

No problem! Here are a few common scenarios, with tips on what you can do should these situations arise:

The conversation is awkward. This is pretty normal for a first date, especially if one or both of you is nervous and you're meeting in person for the first time. Ask questions, share interesting tidbits about your life; once you find some common ground, you may notice that the conversation becomes less awkward. If it's easier, talk about things unrelated to either of you, such as the activity you're engaging in, the people around you (people-watching is a great conversation starter), a movie you recently saw, or goings-on around town.

You have nothing to say. Ask your date about himself. People generally love to talk about themselves. Ask him lots of questions—about his family, where he grew up and went to school, what his interests, hobbies, and passions are, what three things he would want to have with him if he were stuck on a desert island. Keep it light and avoid a police interrogation-type conversation.

He's on his phone. If it bothers you, speak up. If you let it go, you're letting him know that it's ok to check his phone while he's on a date with you, and he will continue to do so. You can ask him to put his phone away: "Would you be willing to put your phone away for the rest of our date, so that we can get to know each other without so many distractions?" Or, you can make light of it and see how he reacts: "Are you on a date with me or with your phone?"

You're on your phone. Stop it! Switch off your phone, put it away, and pay attention to your date!

Your pain and symptoms flare up or become overwhelming. If this happens, you need to take care of yourself ASAP, and that probably means cutting the date short. You may wish to explain why you need to leave, but if you're not yet ready to discuss your condition, you can simply say, "I'm sorry, I don't have much time to meet today, but I would love to see you again and get to know you better" (that is, if you *do* want to see him again).

He talks about his ex-wife or ex-girlfriend a lot. What a turn-off! And more importantly, red flag! Red flag! It doesn't matter whether he's dissing her or simply reminiscing, you probably don't want to hear about his ex. Try changing the subject whenever he brings her up. If that doesn't work, you can use a more direct approach, such as: "How about we not talk about our exes today? I'd like to learn more about *you.*"

He's rude and crass, and you just want to get away. This guy sounds miserable. If this is him putting his best foot forward on a first date, there's no need to stick around and find out how things turn out. Do what you can to exit grace-fully. Say something like: "I'm sorry, I don't have much time to meet today, and I have to go now. Thank you for the date." Don't suggest or agree to another date. If he suggests another date, you can say, "No thank you," or, if that feels too awkward, "Text me."

You can't get a word in edgewise. This does happen from time to time. You meet a guy who's a motormouth, doesn't ask you anything about yourself, talks over you if you start to say something, and barely pauses for a breath. These guys loooove to talk, and they will think a date went really well if they got a chance to go on and on the entire time. Ha! Sometimes all you can do is sit and listen, and then go for the graceful exit as soon as you find an opportunity.

(Just a note about the talkers—some people babble when

they get nervous. If you're not sure whether he's a natural motormouth or a nervous babbler, it might be worth giving him a second chance so you can see what he's like when he's feeling a little less nervous.)

These have been just a few possible dating glitches. I can't cover them all, but you get the idea, right? If something isn't working for you, ask for what you want, and if that doesn't happen, go for the graceful exit. Remember to have compassion for yourself and for your date. Be kind and take the high road, even if he doesn't.

A Reminder About Revealing Your Condition

We talked about timing the reveal of your condition in the last chapter, but it's worth mentioning again briefly here, because it's likely to come up, at least in your mind, while you're on your first date with someone.

Remember, your health issues may become someone's business if you are to have an extended relationship with him, but you don't owe anyone anything on the first date. The person next to you is on a date with you, not your illness. If you don't want to bring it up, don't. Think about what you want to lead with. What does your intuition say? As long as you feel clear in your heart and you're listening to your intuition, you won't go wrong.

After the First Date

Hurrah! You've navigated your way through your first date with a new guy and hopefully enjoyed it, too. Now what? Right after the date is a good time to reflect on it.

- Did you enjoy yourself?

- What did you enjoy about it?
- If you didn't have a good time, why not? What got in your way?
- Was there a connection between the two of you?
- Were you able to stick to your boundaries?
- How is your body feeling?
- If you're not feeling well, what would you do differently next time to feel better after the date?
- Do you want to see him again?

This is also a great time to fill in your Man Chart that lists your "must haves" and where you ask "Does he really do it for me?" So, does he?

Give it some thought, and be honest with yourself. You can take as much time as you need to think about the date. Sleeping on it often brings more clarity in the morning. Whatever results from the date is just fine, whether it's a relationship, friendship, or nothing further. It can be disappointing when things don't turn out as you had hoped, but more important than any guy is your well-being. As long as *you* remain your top priority, you are on the right path.

TAKE ACTION!

1. Butterflies in your stomach, shaky hands. It's normal to feel a range of emotions before going on a first date. Close your eyes, take a few deep breaths, and notice your emotions. How do they feel in your body? Allow yourself to really feel the emotions, know that they are just fine and completely normal, and allow them to pass. Do this as often as you need to.

2. If you're having doomsday thoughts, rein them in.

Here's one of my favourite negative thought-wrangling tools, which I learned from Dr. Arseneau. First, write down on a sheet of paper all the self-doubting and negative thoughts you have around your date. Then, choose one and write it at the top of a fresh sheet of paper or a cue card. (Cue cards are best because you can wrap an elastic around your stack and keep them in your purse, car, or somewhere else convenient for easy reference.)

Example: He's not going to like me because I'm too shy.

Below that, write down the following headings:

Negative thought: He's not going to like me because I'm too shy.

Emotions:
Behaviour:
Physical sensations:

Valid:
Useful:

New thought:

Then go ahead and fill out each heading. For example:

Negative thought: He's not going to like me because I'm too shy.

Emotions: sad, lonely, angry, frustrated (These are the feelings you experience when you have the thought.)

Physical sensations: tightness in chest, sick to stomach (These are your physical sensations when you have the thought.)

Behaviour: cancel the date (This is your behaviour that results from the thought.)

Valid: no (Is the thought valid? No. I have no idea of knowing what he will think of me. He might be really shy, too.) Note: sometimes you might find that your thoughts are valid, and that is ok.

Useful: no (Is this thought useful to me? It creates negative emotions and unpleasant body sensations and takes me away from my goal of meeting someone, therefore it is not useful.)

New thought: I may be shy, but I'm a pretty interesting person. I'm looking forward to meeting someone who gets a chance to know the real me.

Whenever you have the negative thought, immediately and deliberately think the new thought you've chosen. Pick up the cue cards and refer to them as negative thoughts arise. Read over all of them at least once a day to start retraining your brain to think more positively about yourself.

If you like this technique and would like to explore it more deeply, I highly recommend a book called *Self-Coaching 101* by Brooke Castillo. She breaks it down even more and shows how to use a similar technique on all your negative thoughts, not just the ones around dating. This is a great book that provides a lot of useful information very succinctly.

3. Get in touch with who you are and how you want to present yourself. Bring yourself to the forefront and shrink the importance of your illness. Let your spirit and soul shine through. Ask yourself, "Who am I?" or have a trusted friend or family member ask, "Who are you?" over and over for at least 10 minutes. Answer with whatever comes into your mind, no matter how silly it might sound. If you have to reply, "I don't know" a few times, that is allowed. Just go with it.

If you are doing this exercise on your own, you may wish to write your replies into a journal (or your laptop or tablet) rather than speak them out loud. Go with whichever you prefer.

Notice how you feel after the exercise. Bask in your authenticity, in your soul, in who you are at your core. *That* is who is going on this date.

4. Make sure your plan for the date fits your physical abilities. Have some suggestions on hand if your date asks for ideas of what to do and where to go. If your date plans the meeting, don't commit to anything that doesn't feel right. Set yourself up for a good, comfortable date. Speak up if your date's plans will not work for you, and arrange something that will.

5. Leave your expectations and assumptions at home, and approach your date with a sense of curiosity.

6. Prepare in advance for common difficult or awkward scenarios, such as the ones we looked at earlier in this chapter (or other ones that occur to you), so that if they arise, you aren't thrown off.

7. *Have fun*! Even if it's not the best date, it might end up making for a good story later on.

8. Finally, after the date, take some time to reflect on the experience and fill in your Man Chart.

CONGRATULATIONS ON TAKING the leap and going on a first date! This is a big deal, so please acknowledge yourself for the hard work you've done to get to this point. You deserve recognition for your courage and willingness to take a risk given all the challenges you already face. Depending on how your first date went, you will be moving on to the next phase, either a second date or meeting someone else and going on another first date. Both of these situations often involve that dreaded word "rejection," so that's what we're going to discuss in the next chapter: how to deal with and overcome rejection.

CHAPTER 6

Rejection

SO YOU'VE GOT a first date under your belt. Well done! What now? A couple of things are likely: (1) you or he may suggest another date, and he or you will then agree or decline, or (2) there may be no communication after the first date. If you go out with him again, wonderful! If not, you may be facing some form of rejection.

Rejection. Ugh. It's awful. It straight up sucks. Many of us are petrified of rejection—so afraid, in fact, that it stops us from doing things for fear of being rejected. Is rejection any different when you're dealing with chronic pain and illness? The reality is that experiencing rejection is never easy, regardless of your situation. It is, however, what you make of it. If you feel you've been rejected because of your condition, you might sink into self-pity, thinking that life is unfair, that your health is preventing you from having a boyfriend or getting married. But if you were completely healthy, you might still feel like life is unfair and indulge in a bit of wallowing.

In this chapter we'll talk about dealing with rejection in the early stages of a relationship. Some of this will also apply to break-ups of long-term relationships, but we'll talk specifically about those in Chapter 13.

MY STORY

I'VE FACED MY share of rejection. Sometimes I've handled it gracefully, other times not at all. It often involved copious amounts of crying, agonizing, theorizing, candy, and ice cream, depending on the severity of the rejection. On occasion, I have used my condition as an excuse: "He rejected me because I'm faulty." That was almost a relief, because then I had a reason for not being wanted, something I could blame for the rejection. It wasn't me, it was my condition. The condition became a shield from deeper pain.

There are small rejections, like a guy not calling me when he says he will or not asking me out on a second date—especially when he had previously mentioned getting together again. Or I might ask for a date and be turned down.

Then there are medium rejections. Perhaps I've been dating a guy for a few months and he decides to end things. Ow. But it's only been a few months, so I'm not as invested as with longer relationships.

And then there are the biggies: long-term relationship break-ups, the worst. Our lives are intertwined. We own pets together. Some people may have children and be married. It's complicated, messy, and upsetting.

I've faced rejection from more than simply the guys I've dated. Since my condition worsened, I've been rejected by friends who can't seem to accept having a friend with a serious medical condition, and by family to some extent. It hurts. It burns. It makes me extremely sad.

I've been through all types, more than once—sometimes being rejected, sometimes doing the rejecting. It's never easy, no matter what side you are on.

A few years ago, I was in a long-term relationship. My health was decent when I met Jack, but it declined considerably throughout our relationship. (That was a sign I didn't notice at the time but now know is a big ol' red flag. If your health is declining due to your relationship, it's time to look at your relationship!) I thought this man was my soul mate. He was so handsome (dark eyes, dark hair, strong jaw, cleft in his chin), intelligent, strong, charismatic, and funny. I loved him fiercely and would have done almost anything to be with him, even though the relationship was far from perfect. There was some verbal and emotional abuse. Jack had different plans for his life than I had for mine. And yet there was something between us, something unique and special. The good times were some of the best of my life (and the bad some of the worst).

I started feeling rejected in increments in that relationship. Jack's harsh words and dark moods left me feeling rejected. After three years of being together, he decided to move to another town, didn't involve me in the decision, and didn't suggest that I move with him. As I write about this years later I can clearly see that the move was when our break-up should have happened. At the time I didn't have this clarity of thought. Yet I stuck in there. I loved this man and, since I have a fear of abandonment, I just held on tighter. After a year of long-distance, I announced my decision to move to be closer to him, and when I did, Jack suggested I not do that and just give it a one-month trial. Ouch. More rejection. Why didn't he want me with him? Why didn't he want to be with me as much as I wanted to be with him?

I wasn't ok with the one-month trial, so I flew out to visit him and attend a few job interviews. He would barely hug me, kiss me, or tell me he missed me—my heart ached. When I got home, he called and suggested, over the phone, that we split up. Jack was sure. I was stunned. I had put so much work into this relationship, I had held on so tightly and done everything I possibly could to make it work, and it was over with a few words.

I hung up the phone. It was over. I was shocked, and yet I wasn't. My intuition had known things were leading here— all those smaller rejections over the past couple of years had started to add up. No, I really wasn't that surprised. And you know what else I felt? Relieved. I no longer had to try so hard. I didn't have to hold on to someone who was trying to shake me off. I didn't have to be in a one-sided relationship anymore. I was free. And it was a great feeling. I mean, yes, there were still some tears and bowls of chocolate chip mint ice cream, but it was a positive thing for me. Being rejected, in this case, was ultimately good.

Some time later I went through a different type of rejec- tion. This time I had a good foundation in place, one that I had created since my relationship with Jack. I had a great support team, I had done a pile of work on myself, and my health, while delicate, was on the upswing. I knew my lim- itations: dates had to end by 10pm so I was in bed no later than 11pm; no intercourse, because my body wasn't ready for that; no more than three blocks of walking.

This was when I met Juan. He was Dominican and a simply beautiful man, inside and out. Dark eyes and hair, of course. Long dreadlocks, dimples, adorable laugh, incredible body. He was intelligent, and so kind and gentle. And he smelled so good, my god, I couldn't get enough of him. Our chemistry was electric, but that was also a problem. I wasn't able to have sex at this point because I was experiencing too much pelvic, back, and stomach pain. Yet he was very sexual. Excuse me while I fan myself for a moment.

I told Juan pretty early on about my condition because things were moving quickly. I don't like feeling pressured to have sex. I don't want to spend one more minute gritting my teeth and counting the minutes and recovering from the pain of sex. No thanks. There are lots of other things I can do sex-wise, and I would rather do those things, at least for now. I do believe one day I'll be back in the saddle again, so to speak, just not quite yet.

I was prepared for the possibility that he would not be on board with the no-sex rule. I know that most men love sex, and that is normal, human, and healthy. If sex is really important for a man, then I don't want to deprive him; if a guy needs a relationship where sex happens frequently, then I'm not the right girl—end of story. I also know that there are men whose libidos aren't as strong, who can love just as deeply but aren't as interested in sex, for whatever reason. And I know that I would be better off with a man like that.

When I told Juan about my condition, I was direct. I felt comfortable and emotionally safe with him, and my intuition told me it would be ok to talk to him about this. He was lovely, a real gentleman. He expressed his concerns and doubts but said he really wanted to try to see whether things could work between us. So we dated for about a month. We fooled around, had some fun, and then he confessed that it wasn't going to work for him. He needed to have sex. He wanted it, with me. And he couldn't go celibate; it just wasn't his nature.

I felt upset. I felt rejected and angry at my condition. How unfair! And at the same time, I understood. I had known from the beginning that sex is really important in relationships, and that I didn't want to force someone to be in a relationship where they were unhappy because they were sexually unfulfilled. I had known this was a risk I was taking by dating Juan. He was very kind in the way he told me, and I was able to retain a certain amount of objectivity, which helped a lot. I didn't take the rejection personally, because it wasn't personal. He really liked me, and I liked him, but it wasn't going to work out because of an insurmountable physical hurdle. He wasn't rejecting me—my soul or my spirit—he was simply declining to be involved in a situation that he thought wouldn't work for him.

I was sad, I cried a little, but there was no ice cream involved, just some hugs from good friends and some long talks. I was feeling like my old self in no time. Juan and I are now good friends and spend time together on a regular basis—platonic time. He's lovely and I appreciate him as a friend plus I still get to smell him—although I try not to be too creepy about that.

Rejection never feels good, and I'm not sure it ever gets much easier. At any rate, the big ones don't get easier; I think the little ones do. I'm not as fussed anymore when a guy doesn't call after he says he will. In my 20s, I used to spend hours agonizing, wondering, making assumptions, checking my phone obsessively, and debating whether to call him myself. Now I'm of the mind that if he really liked me, he would call me, and if he's not calling me, then it's not meant to be and there will be someone else. Maybe it's age, maybe it's experience. I'm not sure.

So being rejected sucks. But what if you're the one doing the rejecting? I find that this is often just as hard. I feel awful letting guys down. I've tried all sorts of different techniques: not answering the phone, not replying to messages and voice mails, avoidance, avoidance, avoidance, lying, awkward letters. I used to be so afraid of conflict that I wasn't able to be honest with someone when I wanted to end a relationship, however short it had been. Over the years, I've realized that if I want to be treated with respect, I need to treat others with respect, and that means breaking up with them in the same way that I wish to be treated in the reverse situation. It took some work to build up my courage and learn how to communicate in a clear and caring way. Now it's easier. I still feel bad for letting a guy down, but I tell him how I'm feeling from my heart. I let him know that I don't sense that we have a connection, that I rely on my intuition to guide me, and that I don't feel we are a good match. Clear, honest, and respectful communication. No blaming, no finger pointing, and no attacking his character; just kindness and respect, because that's what I would want for myself.

LET'S DISCUSS

CHRONIC PAIN AND illness or not, rejection hurts; but it's part of the human condition. So what can we do to better cope with rejection? I have a few ideas.

Strategies for Overcoming Rejection

Feel the Feelings, Then Act

We all have similar, and at the same time different, experiences of feeling emotions. For example, some of us feel sadness in our chests, some in our stomachs or even in our throats. Is yours a weight, or a clenching? A pressure, or a butterfly feeling? Do you know what your emotions feel like?

I've worked with a lot of people, and I've noticed that many (most?) of us aren't in touch with our emotions. We can't tell right away where we experience an emotion and what it feels like. Often, we aren't even sure what emotion we're feeling. We stuff our emotions down, cover them up, distract ourselves, or run away from them. But for those of us with chronic pain and illness, it's so important that we don't suppress our emotions. Emotions trapped in our bodies can increase stress, which in turn increases pain and other symptoms. Our bodies are by no means separate from our minds or emotions; our whole organism works as one.

Allowing ourselves to fully feel emotions can be scary. What if it hurts too much? What if we lose control? What will other people think if we just let our emotions go? I've heard so many doubts, rationalizations, and excuses, but the truth is, the only way out is through—through your emotions. You can't avoid them. If you try, they will still be there, trying to come up, popping out in strange ways at inconvenient times. Ain't nobody got time for that!

When you feel rejection, notice what is happening in your body. Where do you feel it? What does it feel like? What other emotions are coming up at the same time? Rejection may be a cocktail of emotions including, for example, hurt, sadness, anger, frustration, and fear. What are the ingredients in your rejection cocktail? Allow yourself to feel the feelings. Once you feel them fully, they will start to pass. Push them down and they're going to be there, just waiting for you.

Don't Take It Personally

You know that common phrase, "It's not you, it's me"? There's a lot of truth to that. It's never about you. It's always about the other person. This is the most important thing to remember if you're feeling rejected.

We all see our lives through certain lenses, and these lenses are tinted with our past experiences, starting from when we were born, or—some would argue—since we were conceived in the womb. We perceive our present through our past experiences and usually allow the past to dictate our perceptions and reactions to current events. So if your date turns you down, whether due to your condition or for any other reason, know that it is actually his past experiences that are turning you down. Unless he's done a lot of work on himself and is very conscious, his past is dictating his reaction to you. The quality of his parents' relationship as he was growing up is a deciding factor in how he responds to you. He doesn't necessarily know this consciously; his subconscious is looking after all of this for him. He is looking at you through his own tinted lenses and allowing his subconscious to react based on his distorted interpretation of the present. And you are receiving this information through your own tinted lenses and allowing it to be interpreted, in part, by your subconscious and your own cognitive distortions.

Whew! That's complicated. Essentially, my point is this: How can we take others' actions personally when they're not even reacting to us? They are reacting to the idea they have of us, to what we are triggering in them, to what we stir up in their memories and subconscious.

Here's what Don Miguel Ruiz has to say about it in *The Four Agreements*:

> Personal importance, or taking things personally, is the maximum expression of selfishness because we make the assumption that everything is about "me." . . .We think we are responsible for everything. Me, me, me, always me!
>
> Nothing other people do is because of you. It is because of themselves. All people live in their own dream, in their own mind; they are in a completely different world from the one we live in. When we take something personally, we make the assumption that they know what is in our world, and we try to impose our world on their world.

If you don't believe me, believe Mr. Ruiz. Or believe Dr. Guy Winch, who, in his blog, *The Squeaky Wheel*, notes:

> Most romantic rejections are a matter of poor fit and a lack of chemistry, incompatible lifestyles, wanting different things at different times, or other such issues of mutual dynamics.

It may absolutely feel like it's about you. And it may be about your shared circumstances, but it's not about *you*. As

Dr. Winch says, romantic rejections are mostly about a lack of compatibility, spark, or connection. They're about the energy that occurred (or didn't occur) between you and someone else. If one of you isn't feeling the connection or the spark, then it just isn't there. It's simply a matter of two people sharing an energetic exchange and not clicking, and that's ok. Not everyone is going to click. I mean, if we all clicked with everyone, how would we possibly choose who to have a relationship with? It would be chaos.

You may be asking, "But he's dating *me*, so how can it not be about me?" Believe it or not, no matter how personal it seems or feels, it's never about you. Whether you feel that he is rejecting you or your condition, you need to change your perspective on the situation: be objective, know that we all go into relationships with our tinted lenses on, and realize that you can't change someone's past. That past, along with your chemistry (or lack thereof), is usually going to dictate how a guy responds to you.

Don't take anything personally. He's just not that into you. Let it go. Find someone who is. And as one of my favourite teachers, Dr. Keith Condliffe, used to say, "So what? Who cares? Doesn't matter."

Accept It Early

Have you had any experiences of rejection where you spent hours, days, weeks, or longer analyzing, breaking things down, repeating conversations in your head? Trying to figure out what went wrong? Feeling sad every time you rehashed the relationship, however short or long? Contacting your ex and attempting to convince him to try again? And what have you got to show for all that time you spent agonizing? If you're anything like me, you have nothing to show for it.

The best thing you can do is accept the rejection early. Feel your feelings, don't take it personally, and accept it. He's not that into you, and you won't be able to *make* him be into you. Time to move on and find someone who *will* be into you, who *will* be happy to accommodate your special needs, firm boundaries, and physical limitations. Dwelling on the past isn't going to change anything.

I'm not trying to be a hard-ass here. It's really important to allow your feelings to come up and have compassion for yourself. But this is about how long you stay there. Mulling over the rejection endlessly is stressful. And stressful = increased pain and symptoms. No guy is worth worsening your health, especially if it was just for a few dates.

What is going to help you get past rejection is the solid foundation you have built based on the first three chapters of this book. A big part of that includes connecting with friends and your support team. Let's talk about that next.

Talk to a Friend

In *The Squeaky Wheel*, Dr. Guy Winch says:

> Rejection destabilizes our "Need to Belong." We all have a fundamental need to belong to a group. When we get rejected, this need becomes destabilized and the disconnection we feel adds to our emotional pain. Reconnecting with those who love us, or reaching out to members of groups to which we feel strong affinity and who value and accept us, has been found to soothe emotional pain after a rejection.

Pull out that sheet you created in Chapter 3, where you listed all the elements in your foundation. Who are the friends in your support circle? Call, text, or email them, then connect with them in person as soon as possible. Re-establish the feeling of connectedness, and feel the love you share with your friends.

You may also wish to talk to your counsellor. Having an objective third party can really make a difference. It's a great opportunity to check in with your self-esteem and get a boost if you need one. Your counsellor may also have some great ideas on overcoming rejection.

Be with your people, your tribe. This is key to overcoming rejection.

Stop Dwelling on It

Still trying to figure out the rejection? Stop! Dwelling on it isn't going to help. Dwelling on the rejection and negative feelings may, in fact, increase your pain. According to Dr. Winch,

> [r]ejection piggybacks on physical pain pathways in the brain. fMRI studies show that the same areas of the brain become activated when we experience rejection as when we experience physical pain. This is why rejection hurts so much (neurologically speaking). In fact our brains respond similarly to rejection and physical pain.

I don't know about you, but I have enough pain. I don't want to go lighting up the pain pathways in my brain if it's not absolutely necessary. I want to calm those pathways, not turn them on. It's pretty amazing when you think about it: our thoughts can create more pain and symptoms in our bodies. That means we also have the power to reduce the amount of pain in our bodies. Let's reduce it!

Do Something Else

If you have time on your hands, you have a lot of time to dwell on what happened. Even if you're busy, you'll probably be making time to think about being rejected. Ooof! It doesn't make you feel any better, does it? How about doing something that does make you feel better?

A question I like to ask is: What do you need, *in this moment*, to feel better? Is it a bath, a good book, or a talk with a friend? Do you need to scrub your bathtub or clean the kitchen sinks? Or create art or music?

What do you need to *do* to feel better *right now*?

If you're looking for something to read, other than this book, I highly recommend the book, *He's Just Not That Into You*, by Greg Behrendt and Liz Tuccillo. It cuts through the BS and basically tells us that if a guy isn't calling us, asking us for another date, or giving us the attention we need, he just isn't into us. And if he isn't into us, nothing we can do is going to change that—and he isn't going to change, so move on.

On the other hand, if you need to escape from reality for a bit, go for some fiction, something that really holds your attention, whether that's Nora Roberts or Marcel Proust.

Don't Allow It to Control Your Future

Remember those lenses we look through when we view our lives? If we're not careful, every rejection we face will add a new layer to them and, before we know it, we'll be looking at life as a "rejectee." No thanks! Dr. Winch has some wise words for this situation:

> Rejections send us on a mission to seek and destroy our self-esteem. We often respond to romantic rejections by finding fault in ourselves, bemoaning all our inadequacies, kicking ourselves when we're already down, and smacking our self-esteem into a pulp. . . . Blaming ourselves and attacking our self-worth only deepens the emotional pain we feel and makes it harder for us to recover emotionally.

Woe is me. I'm not good enough, pretty enough, smart enough, thin enough, fit enough, funny enough, healthy enough. Do you find yourself coming up with all sorts of reasons for being rejected?

The more you have these negative thoughts about yourself, the more likely they will turn into beliefs. If you start believing that you are inadequate, that's going to shape your future in a way that doesn't sound too attractive. Your life is going to be very different if you go through it believing you are inadequate versus knowing you are unique, interesting, fun, and lovable just the way you are. Remember Mark number one and Mark number two, who didn't get to go to the Elton John concert? Just like the Marks, you have the power to determine how a rejection is going to affect your future. Are you going to let some guy(s) determine how you feel about yourself and thus shape your future?

Please don't allow one or several rejections to control the rest of your life. Don't let them affect your self-esteem, because they're not about you. Pull out your cue cards from Chapter 5 when the negative thoughts creep in.

Get Your Spiritual Fix

Spirituality can really help you get through the crunchy times. If you're feeling rejected, this is a good time to connect with your spiritual world and fill up your love tank. Do things that nourish your spirit, get you in touch with the bigger picture and your purpose in life. Feeling part of something bigger can make it easier to let go of the smaller things, like being turned down for a second date. What makes you feel like you are a part of something meaningful, something bigger than just you or your immediate surroundings?

Your Date's Reaction to Your Condition

Let's be totally honest. There are some people out there who don't want to be with someone who has a serious health condition, and you may run into a few of them on your adventures in dating. Some will tell you outright, some may give you a different excuse, and some you might just never hear from again.

You can't control how your date is going to react to your condition. There is absolutely nothing you can do about that. And that's what makes telling someone about your pain scary. What you *can* do is keep in mind your foundation. Remember that there are people who know you and love you for who you are, just the way you are. Leave your expectations at home, and approach his reaction (positive or negative) with curiosity. *Hmmm, I wonder what in his past is causing him to respond in this way? Interesting....*

Whatever you do, don't take him turning you down due

to your condition personally. (Are you tired of hearing me say this yet?) If you've been dealing with your health issues for a while, I'm sure you've already experienced a wide range of reactions from various people. This is no different. It's not about you, it's about the person's beliefs and lenses— and it's not your job to change those.

Many people twist themselves up in knots worrying that they are going to get rejected because of their health conditions. And then, what do you know, *they* end up being the ones turning down second or third dates. Why? Often it's because they have a solid foundation in place, and therefore have the confidence and awareness to realize that their suitor is not a good fit. They are not willing to accept just anyone, because they know they are worthy of finding that special someone. And you are worthy of finding your special someone too.

Turning Down a Second Date

We've talked a lot about being rejected, but what happens when you're the one doing the rejecting? The shoe is on the other foot! Maybe the next paragraph will seem familiar, or you'll soon experience something similar.

I remember feeling, at first, so grateful that someone wanted to date me. And then he wanted a second date; I was thrilled! My condition was not stopping me from dating, and I had found a guy who wanted to see me again, even though my physical limitations were so rigid. I felt like I needed to be thankful just to be wanted. But then, as the second date approached, I started dreading it. He had been a bit boring, talked a lot about himself, was a smoker, and lived in a suburb about an hour away. He had been 45 minutes late for our first date because of traffic, which really cut into our time because I had budgeted two hours maximum to be sitting in the restaurant where we were meeting. Honestly, I really didn't want to see him again. I knew I was not going to be able to drive out to visit him because I wouldn't be able to drive for that long. But I felt I *should* go; I *should* be willing to settle, since I have this cumbersome condition, and here was someone willing to accept it, at least so far.

Stop! Halt! Cease! Desist! When you notice your inner voice telling you that you "should" do something, it's time to stop and re-evaluate.

You are allowed to say no to a request for a date! In fact, I encourage you to say no when it doesn't feel right. Saying no can be difficult, especially when you feel like you've found someone who is willing to accept you—pain, illness, and all. But it's still important that *you* be interested in him, that you feel the spark, and that he is really doing it for you (remember the Man Chart you've been filling out?). You are under no obligation to say yes to anyone. Cut the "shoulds" right out of your vocabulary.

Once you've decided to say no, how do you go about it? Turning someone down is not easy. If you're anything like me, you probably really dislike hurting other people's feelings. Here's my advice: try to treat others the way you want to be treated. Let them know as soon as you realize you're not interested. You're not here to waste their time. Be direct, and be kind. Let them know that you enjoyed your time together (if you did) but that you don't feel the connection you're looking for.

Some guys have a hard time accepting excuses or understanding why you don't want to see them again. Even if your reasons are legit, they may sound like excuses, especially lines like these:

- I'm super-busy and don't have time to date.
- I need to focus on my career right now.
- I'm not over my ex.
- I need more space.
- I'm trying to find myself, and I need to be alone to do that.
- I'm going through a lot right now.
- I'm not ready for a relationship.
- I just want to be friends.
- Things are moving too fast.

Many guys will argue and try to convince you otherwise. I like to explain that I rely heavily on my intuition, and it's telling me that we would not be a good match. It's really hard for someone to argue against your intuition and your feelings. Attraction and love are not things you have control over—they either happen or they don't, and guys seem to get that. Also, while you don't owe anyone an explanation for why you don't want to see him again, it can help him move on if you are somewhat specific (yet kind, considerate, and diplomatic) about why you're not interested. This will help *him* move on more quickly so *he* won't end up dwelling endlessly on the rejection.

Overcoming Discouragement

Adding dating into your life can feel overwhelming when most of your time is dedicated to resting and caring for yourself. It can be easy to get discouraged if you've been on dates with several different guys and nothing has worked out, especially if you find yourself feeling rejected. Between the pain of your condition and the pain of unsuccessful dates, life can get discouraging.

I used to work in a restaurant as a hostess. It was a fancy place and often not that busy. At times, I spent hours standing at the hostess station, doodling and staring at the menu, waiting for people to come in. I would always tell myself: "The longer no one comes in, the sooner someone will come in." I apply the same concept to dating: "The longer I go not meeting my life partner, the sooner I will be meeting him." By simply going through the dating process (sometimes over and over), you are one step closer to meeting the right partner. Some people get lucky and meet someone quickly. Others have different karma and may be late bloomers when it comes to finding the right relationship. As long as you are taking care of yourself, working on yourself, and doing what makes you happy, it will come.

If you are feeling discouraged about dating, it doesn't necessarily mean you are doing the wrong thing, or that there is anything wrong with you, or that you're not meant to have a relationship. We are all worthy of relationships, and we are all worthy of love. It may just be that you are doing the right thing in the wrong way. Try a new approach. Shake things up a little. Change your perspective.

How do you go about changing your perspective? One step at a time. One belief at a time. Shift your focus from the grey cloud to its silver lining. For example, if you ask a guy on a date and he says no, instead of telling yourself, "He rejected me," say, "He said no." This way, you aren't framing the rejection as something bad about you. He isn't rejecting you, after all—he's simply saying no to a proposition you made. "It didn't work out" is another great way of putting it. That way, no one is being rejected.

Find a way to shift your idea of dating from stressful, awkward, and potentially embarrassing to enjoyable. Go in with curiosity and no expectations. Revel in the infinite ways we are all so different. Be entertained by and grateful for your experiences. Be happy when a date with a great guy goes really well and a second one comes of it. Be ready to move on when a date doesn't go that well, or if the guy doesn't want a second date. If he's not interested, so be it. Don't be attached to the outcome of your first, second, or even third date. Simply explore the possibilities. Be grateful for your ability to date, however that may be. Be present and enjoy the small moments.

All you can do is do your best not to become discouraged about dating. You are living your life to the fullest within your capabilities, and if a relationship happens, it's a bonus.

Discouragement is a choice. If you feel discouraged, it's because you've chosen to feel that way. No one is forcing you to feel bad. I know this idea will rub some of you the wrong way, but it's true. If you are feeling discouraged, it's due to your perspective and due to the lenses through which you are viewing the world. How about switching up those lenses and viewing a bad date not as an awful or failed experience, but as a learning experience and a good story to tell your friends later on?

TAKE ACTION!

REJECTION FEELS AWFUL, no matter how you cut it. The good news is that you can soften the blow, both for yourself and for others. There are things within your control and abilities that will help you heal and move on, without dwelling on the painful emotions around rejection.

Here is a little rejection checklist for you to follow when you're feeling like you need a boost:

1. **Feel the feelings.** Sit quietly for a few minutes, notice the feelings in your body, and allow yourself to experience where they are and what they feel like. What are the ingredients in your emotional rejection cocktail? Do they move around? Do they dissipate once you've given them some attention?

Cry, punch pillows or your mattress, scream (into a pillow if your walls aren't soundproof), ask for lots of big hugs (big means they last at least 20 seconds, because it takes that long for the feel-good hormone oxytocin to be released), sing, create, clean, or do whatever will help most at that moment.

Once you've experienced the emotions, doing something with your body to help the energy move can transform the uncomfortable feelings into something positive, like a song, a piece of art, a clean bathtub, or a weed-free garden.

What feels best to you?

2. **Do not take it personally!** I am going to sound like a broken record by the end of this book, but if there is only one thing you take from it, please let it be that you stop taking rejection so personally. It's never about you. It's about the other person's lenses.

3. **Think about your own lenses.** Are there flaws in your beliefs about yourself, especially in the ones that aren't supportive of you? Might your perspective seem true to you but not to others? Think about how you would like to adjust your lenses—take out the grey, and add a little more rose.

4. Let go of expectations and attachment to outcomes in the early stages of dating. That will help reduce disappointment and feelings of rejection. Instead, go in with an attitude of curiosity.

5. Accept it early. He said no. Ok, he's just not that into you. Cry, hug for at least 20 seconds, have ice cream, move on.

6. Talk to a friend. Friends are wonderful. They can hug and listen at the same time. Pull out your support foundation sheet and call, text, or email a friend on your list. If you can connect in person, that's ideal. The more human contact you can have, the more your feelings of rejection will be lessened.

7. Stop dwelling on it. Still thinking about him? It's time to stop, right now. He's not going to change, he doesn't need a little more time, he doesn't need space, he doesn't just need to see how great you are. Time to move on.

8. Do something else. If you've already been through the cry–hug-a-friend–ice cream process and you're still replaying your last conversation with him over and over, it's time to distract yourself, because now you're dwelling on it. Do something that engages your brain and transports you elsewhere. It might be reading, painting, getting outside, doing a little exercise, whatever appeals most to you.

9. Don't allow rejection to control your future. Are you really going to let one, or ten, bad dates dictate the rest of your life? I know I might be exaggerating a bit, but really— that's just ten people out of *billions*. You are special. You are worthy. You just haven't connected with the right person yet. Take a look at your Man Chart; how many guys actually had all your "must haves" and "does he really do it for me" checked off?

10. Treat others the way you want to be treated. This is especially true when you are letting someone else down. How would you like someone to treat you? Would you want him to just stop replying to your texts, or would you want an explanation—or maybe just a simple but kind, "I'm not interested." Show the universe how you want to be treated by treating others that way.

11. Connect spiritually. Fill up your unconditional love tank. Reconnect with the big picture and with the things that are really important to you. Take a walk in nature. See friends. Go to church. Meditate. Whatever it is that floats your boat.

REJECTION'S A BITCH, and there's no avoiding it. Luckily, *you* determine how you handle it. You now have the skills to guide you through feelings of rejection and come out on the other side feeling confident and resilient. The more you use the tools provided in this chapter, the easier it will become for you to enjoy dating and not be bogged down by insecurity and doubt.

Next, we're going to put rejection aside and talk about what happens when things are going well and a new relationship is blossoming.

CHAPTER 7

Pacing

PACING? WHAT'S PACING? Making sure I don't overdo it? Oh yeah, I can do that, once I've finished my work, done my exercise, visited a friend, helped out my dad, run errands, gone to the grocery store, and made dinner.

Does this sound familiar?

MY STORY

WHEN I WAS younger, I was more than happy to take care of myself—as long as it was the last thing on my list. And pacing? No, that's ok. I'll just keep going until I'm exhausted. And then I'll do it all again tomorrow because I'm young, and other people are doing it, so why shouldn't I be able to? Why, indeed.

I recall when I first developed my bladder condition. That was the first time I felt crazy, 11-out-of-10 pain.

Keep-me-awake-at-night pain. Constant pain. At that point, I was very athletic, and the only thing I cared about when the pain started was that it was stopping me from working out. There was no way I could go without a workout for more than three days. As soon as the pain would ease just a little bit, I'd head to the gym and run on the treadmill for at least half an hour. Running and pounding, jiggling my insides—really great for my bladder. Guaranteed, I'd be writhing on the couch, clutching my pelvis, within 24 hours. But I could not give up on the running. Over and over. Pain, less pain, run. Pain, less pain, run. I was determined to fight through it, when in fact I was wearing my body down even more. Soon, not just my bladder was inflamed, but my whole pelvis. You want to talk pain? This was an ER-worthy pain. Unfortunately, the ER doctor told me I had pulled a muscle and to take ibuprofen.

I knew my body, and I knew ibuprofen wasn't going to help (it certainly hadn't in the past). Part of me knew that I had to stop exercising and start resting before my body would be able to heal. But I buried that part, didn't want to listen. I wanted to maintain my size-six figure and toned body. I was at the height of my perfectionism at this point, and my priorities were all screwed up. I wanted to be cool; I had a hot boyfriend and cool friends. I kept having sex, even with the pelvic inflammation—less frequently, but I was determined not to lose that part of my life. Sound painful? You have no idea. But I was so afraid of losing my boyfriend, and I believed that sex through gritted teeth (off the charts on the pain scale) was the way to avoid that. I went to social and cultural events and had a great job. I liked to drink and party. I didn't want to give up this lifestyle. "This is the life everyone else has, so I deserve it too!" I tried to force my body to co-operate. I reduced the pain with analgesics, but that was only slightly to moderately successful. I ignored the pain. And I cried a lot. I didn't even consider going on disability, because that was for other people, not "normal and healthy" people like me. I still believed there was nothing wrong with me, because my doctors couldn't find anything wrong—certainly nothing that would explain the pain.

It took me *seven years* to finally give it up, and only because my body quit, said, "No more!" I was hitting 50 on the pain scale. I was in agony 24/7. I had zero energy. I wasn't sleeping at all. It took all I had to climb the stairs to the kitchen. I was horribly depressed and wanted to die. That was my rock bottom.

Please don't hit rock bottom before you slow down and put yourself first. Get medical help now. Rest now. Rest frequently. Don't overdo it. You don't need to be a martyr. This is not the sword to die on. Listen to your body *now*, not seven years from now.

You might be thinking, "Well, at least she had seven years when she could still do what she wanted." Let me clarify: they weren't good years. They were excruciating, sad, frustrating, and fearful years. Also, I believe that had I stopped during year one, and rested deeply and taken care of myself, I could have prevented, or at least significantly delayed, the onset of the other syndromes I have since acquired.

Fortunately, after a year of deep resting (i.e. lying in bed or on the couch 23.5 hours a day), proper medications, and rehabilitation, I was in a good place and happier than I had been in years. Why? Because I had created a solid foundation: I had a support team, I listened to my body, and I did what it asked. I may still have pain and various other symptoms, but I am happy. I find it kind of hard to believe, but it's true. When I finally put myself first, I became happier. Duh, right? But it was so hard to actually do. And, after putting myself first for a year, I had the energy to do volunteer work on top of a part-time job, and to care for my ailing father. Had I not looked after myself first, I wouldn't have been able to help anyone else.

When I started dating again, I set a limit for myself: two dates a week, max. After a month or two, I decided I was feeling a little better and snuck in an extra date, and then another, and before I knew it, I was at four dates a week. I was having so much fun. Remember Juan? I was really taken with him around this time, and, when we were together, the clock stood still. I hardly noticed the pain, and I wasn't as tired. And when we weren't together? I was feeling overwhelmed. I needed the entire following day to recover from the date and from staying up later than usual. At four dates a week, I needed four days a week for recovery. I was getting nothing else done and things were piling up.

Clearly, I was not pacing myself.

Time for an adjustment! I recommitted to my two-date-per-week rule. I negotiated a slightly later bedtime for myself on date nights (11pm instead of 10pm, but not midnight or 1am, as I had been allowing to happen) and stuck to it. I made sure our date activities did not involve me physically overdoing things. (Haha! I know what you're thinking, but we weren't having sex.) We stuck to hanging out at his place most of the time, with the occasional short walk. And after a week or so, I felt much better—stronger, more rested, and less chaotic.

Pacing isn't glamorous, fun, or exciting, but it works. And if you pace yourself *now*, you will be able to experience more glamour, fun, and excitement in your life in the long term.

LET'S DISCUSS

WHETHER YOU'RE THINKING about preparing to date, dating, or being in a relationship, it's time to take a breath and check in with *you*. In the previous few chapters we've put in quite a bit of time and effort thinking about others (our dates or partners), but now we're going to step back and take a little time to evaluate what's going on with ourselves.

If you've started dating, I have some questions for you. Please be honest! The more candid you can be with yourself, the better:

- How are your boundaries working for you?
- Are you getting enough sleep?
- Is dating or your relationship wearing you down?
- Do you need to adjust your limitations and boundaries?
- Have you realized you can comfortably do more than you thought you could do?

It's always possible that adding something positive into your life has actually meant that you feel better and can do a little more than you previously thought possible. If this is the case, high fives! If it's not the case, that is ok. We are going to look at ways for you to build up some energy stores.

Let's talk about pacing in relation to dating. You might meet someone amazing. He may feel like your soul mate.

You want to be with him 24/7. You're stretching yourself and going for more dates than you had planned, or maybe you're talking on the phone for hours every day, or Skyping or emailing. Stop, take a breath. What impact is this new-found exuberance having on you? Be honest.

According to Dr. Arseneau and Mara Shnay's *Living with ME/CFS, FM and Related Disorders Program Manual*, pacing is about "living according to a plan rather than in reaction to symptoms." (Shout-out to Dr. Arseneau for sharing the information that provided the basis for this chapter.) The plan is how you set up your day. It includes the boundaries you establish around time and place, your set mealtimes, bedtime, wake-up time, and how much activity you do in a day. Pacing ensures that you don't just keep going until you feel symptoms or until symptoms worsen. It means you go for an allotted amount of time that you know won't trigger or exacerbate symptoms. It's about being consistent in both activity and rest.

One rule I like to follow is to think about how much I can do in a day, and then do half, because I know I tend to push myself too much. Now that I'm feeling better, I often do three-quarters of what I think I can reasonably do in a day, but never more than that. Ultimately, only you know how much you can comfortably do.

Pacing requires you to do some *realistic* planning. To quote Dr. Arseneau, "Failing to plan is planning to fail."

In what areas of your life are you failing to plan?

What can you do to set up a plan in those areas?

Make Your Life Easier

Pacing makes your life easier. You end up with less stress and more energy. Making a plan ensures predictability, and predictability reduces relapses and stress. Let's talk about how to do this.

Listen to Your Body

We've talked about this before, and I'll say it again: pay attention to the messages your body is sending you. If you're not familiar with your body's signals, start to pay attention to how you feel in your body. Mentally scan yourself from head to toe, and notice the different sensations. What is your body telling you? Ouch? Slow down? Stop? Eat? Sleep? Bust a move?

Once you identify what your body is telling you, respect what it's saying! Don't try to override your body's signals. If you're tired and you keep going, you're going to get more tired—and probably more sore. If you're hungry, your body needs sustenance. Ignoring hunger signs isn't helpful, especially if you're like me and many others who get hangry—angry when hungry.

You need to nurture yourself and love your body even if it's not behaving as you want it to. You'll get a whole lot more co-operation from your body with love than you will with punishment; and you're punishing yourself when you're tired and force yourself to keep going, or when you're hungry and you don't eat.

Reconnect with your body, get familiar with its language, then reply by providing what it needs.

Take Rest Breaks

Depending on the type of condition you have, you may benefit from rest breaks. If you're suffering from chronic pain, rest breaks are definitely for you. Pain is exhausting and wears you down. You need and deserve breaks—lying down eyes closed. Lying down and watching TV doesn't count, nor does reading, or standing up with your eyes closed. You don't have to nap, but if you drift off, that's great. If you don't fall asleep, a rest break is a great opportunity to meditate or do some deep breathing. The key is to keep your breaks to 15–20 minutes. Anything longer may interrupt your sleep at night. You will be amazed at how rejuvenating it can be to have a 20-minute lie down.

Two things to remember. First, schedule rest breaks into your day, make them part of your routine. Use them to help pace yourself. Second, don't skip them if you're feeling good. You might think, "Oh, I don't feel tired today. I'm going to skip my lie down." No! Stay consistent, and take your breaks whether you are tired or not. Not only can they rejuvenate, but they can also help you *stay* feeling good and prevent you from getting as tired as you would without the rest.

Determine Limits for Your Activities

We've talked before about boundaries and determining ahead of time what you can do. Have you been sticking to your rules? Setting limits on your activities before you even start helps ensure you will stick to the limits. When it comes to dating, set a time limit on in-person dates, phone calls, Skype/FaceTime calls, and/or on how many emails or texts you send in a day. Set these limits with yourself *before* you become overwhelmed. By setting limits right away, you will manage the expectations of the person you are dating so they won't expect more than you can do.

You may wish to share some of your limits with your date or partner. For example, it can be useful to make clear what time you go to bed and what time you wish to be home. Other limits you may prefer to keep private.

Are you worried your date might think you're weird or rigid because you have all these rules or limits? That he might not be interested in you because you have these restrictions? Here's what you will notice. The more you respect yourself and your limits, the more others will respect you and your limits. If you present your limits confidently, people will act within them. If you present them in an unsure and insecure way, you will gain less respect, and people will cross your boundaries more often.

Boldly be yourself, and enjoy the results.

Switch Up Your Activities on Dates

If you're anything like me, you probably have trouble doing one activity for very long—sitting, standing, reclining or lying down in one position for any length of time. In your normal day, do you shift your body regularly, making sure you don't stay in the same position for too long? If you do, high fives! If not, it might be something to try. Either way, being on a date is no different than the rest of your day, so it's vital that you remain as physically comfortable as possible. If that means sitting, sit. If it means reclining, go ahead and make yourself comfortable. If it means rearranging yourself every 15 minutes into a more comfortable position, then so be it.

A couple of years back, when I was going though a bad flare-up, I wasn't able to sit up straight, so if I was going to a restaurant, I would suss it out ahead of time to make sure it had booths, and I'd request one. That way, I could arrange myself on the bench in a semi-reclining pose and reposition myself frequently to avoid getting too achy. No one really seemed to notice or care. Sometimes I'd even bring a pillow with me. I encourage you to use devices if that helps—pillows, small blankets, anything that makes you more comfortable.

Being comfortable starts with a plan for a date that is do-able for you. And while on the date, if you need to shift or stand for a bit, go ahead and do that. If your date questions what you are doing, and intuitively you are not ready to tell him about your condition, all you need to say is that you're feeling uncomfortable and need to stand for a bit. You don't owe anyone an explanation of your health, especially not on the first few dates.

You can take this further. If you had allotted two hours for the date, and you're having fun, but it's only been an hour and you can't sit another minute because if feels like your back is going to snap in half, then suggest a walk or a different activity that doesn't require you to continue sitting where you are. Switch your activities rather than force your body to keep doing the same one for too long.

The other night I went on a date to a comedy show and had to sit in bleacher-type seating for two hours. I have long legs, and there wasn't any room to stretch out. After two hours my body ached, my knees throbbed, and when I reached home I got a migraine. I realized later that I could have switched my activity. If I were to do it all over again, I would have gotten up and stood at the entrance to the section we were sitting in because I would still have been able to see and hear the comedian. I would also have had the opportunity to get up and stretch and move around, which would have prevented the aching and possibly the migraine. In addition, I could have gone into the outer area of the stadium and walked around a little bit because the show was being broadcast in the corridors as well, so I wouldn't have missed anything. After 20 minutes or so of walking and standing, I could have returned to my seat, then repeated again if necessary. Sometimes I forget about these options in the moment, but they are always there.

We can get carried away by a good date and forget about taking care of ourselves. We may try to fight our body's signals because we're having a good time and don't want it to stop. Stay aware of your body no matter how much fun you're having. The fun doesn't have to end; it may just need to continue at a different venue.

If you are developing an online or phone relationship with someone, this task becomes easier because you can move around as you like, taking your date with you wherever your go, whether it's the couch, the kitchen, the garden, or the bedroom (ooh la la!).

Keep an Eye on the Time of Day

Is there a time of day when you feel better than at other times? I'm a morning person (9:30am–11:30am), and I also feel pretty good just after dinner (7pm–9pm). So I like to schedule morning coffee dates (make that herbal tea for me) or evening meetings. I pity the man who has to deal with me mid-afternoon. Zzzzzzzzz.

Perhaps you already know what time of day is best for you. If not, start to pay attention to when you feel your best. That's relatively speaking, of course. It's the time of day when you feel a little more alert, the pain lessens a bit, your thoughts become more positive, and you are able to do a few things. That's the sweet spot. I highly recommend scheduling your dates during your sweet spot, whether they are in person, over Skype/FaceTime, or by online messaging. That way you can be at your best, and you're not forcing yourself to do something during a time when it would be more natural for you to rest.

Avoid Sensory Overstimulation

Crowds, lots of traffic, loud music, strobe lights. Aagh! Where are my ear plugs and eye shades? Get me out of here! Certain things, like the ones l listed above, can be incredibly overstimulating, especially when combined. You may find it helpful to avoid big crowds and loud anything because they increase stress levels, and when stress increases, fatigue and other symptoms are likely to come on more quickly. And if you avoid these things on a day-to-day basis, why would you want to expose yourself to them on a date? Is a guy really worth a crash or a relapse? (I'm really hoping you answered no!) I'll wrap up this section by asking you two questions:

What do you find overstimulating?

What are the best ways for you to avoid those things, especially on a date?

Accept Your Limits

I don't know about you, but sometimes I want to be able to go out with friends, have a bunch of drinks, dance the night away, stay up until sunrise, have a quick sleep, and then go for a hike in the mountains or a jog along the seawall. And those days are over. It took me a long time to get over the unfairness of it all, especially since my friends are still doing these things, albeit a little less often because they're not spry chickens anymore either, and some now have children to look after.

I'm lucky not to feel a burning desire to have children; I've been very ambivalent about it, and I'm fine with not having kids, especially because I know I wouldn't be able to physically manage it. But sometimes when I get lost in my fantasy of adopting a child from Africa, I do feel frustration and a sense of unfairness around my inability to care for someone else. Caring for myself is a full-time job; I don't have the energy or ability to add a dependent.

I've accepted most of my limitations, usually after a period of denial, anger, and sadness (aka the grieving process). Sometimes my limitations have changed for the better. Limitations aren't set in stone for the rest of your life. They fluctuate and vary. For example, since I've started to get proper rest, I've been able to do a little more. It's about accepting what your limitations are *right now* and knowing that they probably won't always be your limitations. Nothing ever stays the same.

Once you accept your limitations, you will be able to adjust your expectations—around what a date or a relationship might look like, for instance. You will now be able to reasonably know how much you can do on a date. Acceptance does not mean defeat or giving up. It means acknowledging the situation and then making the most of it. Acceptance allows you to be compassionate with yourself, take the pressure off, and let go of the need to do everything, to be perfect. You now have a wonderful opportunity to be creative with your time and energy.

The other great thing about accepting your limitations is that you can then communicate these to your date. That way, you can start managing his expectations of you early on, and he won't be expecting you to go on a 10km hike or stay up until dawn. He will accept your limits because you set them out for him.

Not accepting your own limitations can get you into hot

water. Let's say you force yourself to go on that 10km hike because you really like this guy and want to go because it's something you used to be able to do. The hike is hell, you want it to be over with every step, the pain stabs and burns, yet you continue because you want to be a trooper or prove something to yourself. And then it takes you two agonizing weeks to recover.

Not only did you suffer unnecessarily, but that guy you went on the hike with now thinks you can hike. He doesn't know the agony you endured (unless, of course, you complained every step of the way—in which case you probably don't need to worry about seeing him again). He will have a harder time understanding why you won't hike with him now, since he's seen you do it once. Better to accept and set your limit at the beginning and not hike at all (or go on a one km hike instead).

Postpone, Simplify, Delegate, Eliminate

If you're reading this book, you probably aren't able to do as much as you used to, or as much as you would like to do. You might still feel like you need to do as much as you possibly can because you don't want others to think you're lazy. Maybe you live alone and feel you don't have a choice but to do everything yourself. Perhaps you're like I was and think that you have to do each and every last thing on your to-do list.

Guess what? You *don't* have to get it all done! *You* know you're not lazy, and that's all that matters. If you've got too much on your plate, it's time to lighten the load.

Postpone it! If something isn't of burning importance, then postpone it. Very few things actually must be done ASAP.

If you're trying to get things done for other people because you've committed to them and feel obliged, quit it! Your body is more important than your people-pleasing. I have a to-do list. I look at it every few days. I make plans to tackle an item on a certain day, and if I'm not up to it that day, that's just fine. It'll still be on the list tomorrow. I've been wanting to buy a lamp for my living room and sell my bike for four months. I know I'll get both things done, but on days when I have the time and feel up to the tasks. And that is ok. Same goes for dates. If you have a date but your body is saying, "I need rest!" then postpone the date. If you have plans with your partner to do something but you need to slow down, postpone the plans. The world won't end, and you'll have a lot more fun if you feel your best on the day of the event.

Simplify it! Do you complicate your life needlessly? I do sometimes. It used to be that when I grocery shopped, I would have to hit three different stores to get everything I wanted because I was really particular about my food. My grocery shops wore me out! So I decided to simplify, and now I'll go to one store—sometimes two on a good day. And that's just fine. I may not be getting all the particular things I used to like, but it's a change I was willing to make to simplify my life. There are endless ways to make things easier for yourself. What can *you* do to simplify your life?

Delegate it! This is one of my favourites. I learned to ask for help a couple of years ago and then couldn't believe I hadn't done it sooner. People love to help; they like feeling that they've done something good for someone else. It can be hard to ask for help, especially in a society such as ours that values independence. But we are social creatures who by nature live in community. We are meant to help each other. So ask for help—whether it's with getting groceries, or a ride to a medical appointment, or cleaning your home. Delegating can also mean hiring someone to help, if you are able. Hire a cleaning person, or someone to cook meals for you once a week, or someone who can lighten your workload by doing the mundane administrative tasks while you take care of the important stuff. Wherever you need help in your life, it is completely ok, *more than ok*, to delegate. If you could do it all yourself, you would, but you have a damn good reason to ask for or hire help.

Eliminate it! What are you doing that you don't need to be doing at all? Time to slash and burn all the energy drainers, whether they are commitments, activities, or friends. Eliminate activities without feeling guilty. Hey, if you're not well, it's the perfect reason to drop things you never liked doing in the first place. You can say no to a lot more undesirable commitments than you used to. Enjoy the freedom of saying no to things that you don't enjoy. Unless it's a necessary relationship or activity or commitment, cut it out. Bow out gracefully. By eliminating energy drainers, you will have more energy to do the things you enjoy and to spend time with people who lift you up.

Making a list of your energy drainers, and then working your way through it, removing one item at a time, is a huge stress reducer. And you may be pleasantly surprised by the results. I'm grateful that my pain and illness have led me to stop doing things I don't enjoy. There are activities I used to do out of a sense of duty or obligation that are no longer necessary because taking care of myself is the priority. And that brings a great sense of freedom. You can have that, too!

Make Changes Gradually

This book contains a lot of information and suggestions, and it can be overwhelming to have so many things to do. The key is to focus on one thing at a time. Mark the pages to come back to, or take notes. Highlight sections that really speak to you, then reread them once in a while. Or reread the whole book. You don't have to do everything all at once—in fact, please don't. Allow yourself the time and space you need to take one step at a time. Follow your gut as to what needs to be addressed first.

The same goes for anything else in your life, whether it has to do with diet, exercise, work, dating, rest, or healing. You don't need to change overnight. You don't need to complete your to-do list or meet all the men who contacted you online in one day, or even one week. Do things slowly and at *your* pace. Make changes gradually. This is the key to pacing. There's no need to get everything done right away. Take your time.

In fact, making changes works better when you do it gradually, because you will be more likely to maintain these changes than if you go whole hog and do them all at once. Multiple changes are very difficult to sustain if done all at the same time. One change every couple of months is much more sustainable.

Love Yourself

This is easier said than done, I know. Yet it's such an essential piece for you and for your future (or current) relationship. Remember: how you treat yourself teaches other people how to treat you. By loving yourself, you teach other people how to love you.

Loving yourself doesn't have to mean looking in the mirror and saying, "I love you," although it can. You are showing yourself love every time you do something to take care of yourself, to nurture yourself and to put your health first. Love isn't always flowers, kisses, hearts, and chocolates; it may be a trip to the grocery store or a load of laundry. Love is setting rules with yourself about your bedtime, or establishing boundaries with your date around how long you will stay out. Love is listening to and respecting your body. It's taking your rest lying down with your eyes closed, every day.

How does it feel to be loved by you?

When I have trouble loving myself or putting my health first, I have an inner "mom" voice that I recruit to help me out. She'll comfort me and tell me what I can't tell myself. She'll say I've done enough for the day, that I need to rest, and that it's ok to watch some TV. When I'm contemplating doing *just one more errand*, she'll remind me that, "just because you can doesn't mean you should" (she got that one from Dr. Arseneau). She'll ask me, "What's something you can do for yourself *right now* to feel better?" My answer usually involves a bath and/or pyjamas. My inner mom loves me, and I can rely on her to be straight with me. She's essentially my intuition personified.

What's your inner mom like? What advice would she give you right now?

If you're doubting this whole self-love thing, know that you deserve to be loved and valued, not only by others, but by yourself as well. This applies to everyone. And yes, that includes you!

Stop Being a People-Pleaser

"But what will they think of me if I start doing more for myself and less for others?" you ask. Think of me, schmink of me, I say. It's time to stop being a people-pleaser and start being a self-pleaser. This can be the hardest step for people to take. It's scary to leave that role; you face possible rejection and abandonment—at least, that's your belief. Once you start taking steps away from people-pleasing, though, you'll probably notice that it's not as scary as you thought it would be. Your friends aren't running away. Life goes on, and now a pressure has been lifted from your shoulders.

You have a responsibility to put your needs ahead of others' needs because your health is numero uno. If you wait until you are completely broken down before your take steps to help yourself, then you may not be able to recover. The time is now. Choose to drop the people-pleasing behaviour.

Does that seem selfish? So what, who cares, doesn't matter. It's not actually selfish, but I'm not sure I can convince you otherwise in the time I have here, so I'll tell you it doesn't matter. If you look after yourself first, you will have more to give to others in the long run—including your dates or your partner—and that is *not* selfish. If you're a people-pleaser, it's time to stop. Be a self-pleaser. You have to put your own oxygen mask on before you put on anyone else's.

But OMG! They might think you are lazy, selfish, and ungrateful. Sure, and they might think that the best discounts for flights to Europe are in the spring. Who cares what they think? People think a lot of things. *You* know what's true for *you*. You know what you need to do to take care of yourself. Others may judge you, sure; but they would do that even if you were healthy, or even if you were pushing yourself beyond your limits just to please them. People judge—that's what they do. Nothing you can do, no matter how much you work at pleasing them, will stop them from judging. You know what that means? You can let go of your need to please! You have the choice. Make the choice that is best for you.

TAKE ACTION!

PACING IS KEY if you are dealing with chronic pain and illness. You can't push yourself like other people do, because the more you push yourself, the worse things can get. Pacing means going at a comfortable speed that won't exhaust you or exacerbate your symptoms. There are many pacing tools, and perhaps you already have some of your own. Here are my favourites to help you with what we've just covered in the Let's Discuss section:

1. **Listen to your body.** Pay attention to what messages your body is sending you. Are you hungry? Hangry? Tired? Hurting? Sad? Cranky? Notice the signals, then respond accordingly (eat, sleep, stretch/rest, cry, punch a pillow, end a date early). A particularly good time to tune into your body and emotions is during your rest breaks, when you are quiet and not distracted by other things.

2. **Take rest breaks.** Rest once or twice per day, lying down with your eyes closed. Breathe. Relax. Scan your body and listen for any messages it is sending you. If your mind is whirring at warp speed, try a simple counting meditation: Count your breaths, starting at one and ending at ten. Whenever your mind wanders, start again at one. Try to reach ten on your rest break.

3. Determine limits for your activities. Whether it's dating, grocery shopping, or visiting relatives, plan how long you will go for and how much you will physically do. Determine how much you can comfortably do, then divide it in half. How many dates can you realistically manage in a week? What kind of dates are they—in person or virtual? Figure out how much you can do and write it down. Make an agreement with yourself to stick to the limit you initially set. I *know* he's really sweet and nice, and you totally click, and he might be your soul mate—*and* he will still be there next week if he really is your soul mate; now go and get some rest!

4. Switch up your activities. This applies to dating as well as everything else in your day. If you have trouble sustaining one activity, or sitting, standing, or lying in a single position for any length of time, switch it up!

5. Keep an eye on the time of day. Notice when you feel your best, and schedule dates for these times. Do your errands and schedule your appointments for these windows as well. If you don't already know what time of day is best for you, start to pay attention to see whether there is a pattern. Jot down notes to keep track of how you're feeling. This, however, doesn't give you carte blanche to go nuts in your best time of day. It's not about using up every ounce of oomph you have; it's about being able to do one or two things when you're feeling up to it.

6. Avoid sensory overstimulation. If you find yourself overstimulated by things such as crowds, loud music, or other noise, pungent smells, or bright lights, avoid those things. It's as simple as that. Overstimulation puts a lot of stress on your body, a body that's already struggling, so give it a break and avoid situations that make you want to cover your eyes, nose, and ears.

7. Accept your limits. Acceptance is a big step. It doesn't mean giving up, it means accepting your situation as it is right now so that you can do what you need to do to look after yourself. Drop the comparisons to how you were before and to other people. You are where you are. Wishing it were different and beating yourself up over what may or may not have got you here isn't helpful. This is the way things are right now, this is the state of your health. What are you going to do from here? What can you do to make yourself more comfortable, ease your stress, and enjoy yourself?

8. Postpone, simplify, delegate, eliminate. If it doesn't need to be done immediately, or if you don't need to do it yourself, put it off, cancel it, or have someone else do it. It's ok to ask for help. Actually, it's great to ask for help! And it's awesome not to be perfect. Perfect is boring, annoying, and filled with pressure and unreasonable expectations. Do you have more fun with the people who strive to be perfect or with the ones who embrace themselves, imperfections and all? Usually, the happily imperfect ones are more fun. Hurrah for imperfections! Hurrah for putting things off, asking for help, and crossing things off your list without having done them!

This is also a good time to make an energy drainers list. You probably know some people whose visits make you feel great. Energy drainers are the opposite; if you spend some time with those, you end up feeling totally drained, exhausted, and down. Take a sheet of paper and write down all the people, activities, and commitments in your life that drain your energy. Put them all on your list, then start removing them from your life. Gradually, of course, and kindly, if they are human.

9. Make changes gradually. Sometimes change must happen. But it doesn't have to happen all at once, in one shot. Gradual changes usually last longer than quick ones. Whether it comes to shifts in romantic relationships, following the recommended actions in this book, or maybe planning a move, change gradually. There is no rush. Take your time. Pace yourself.

10. Love yourself. How do *you* love yourself? Is it by setting limits and boundaries and sticking to them? Is it by having a warm bath every night to loosen your muscles? Or do you look in the mirror and tell yourself, "I love you"? Notice what it feels like to be cared for and valued by *you*. You are lovable, pain or no pain. Your condition doesn't make you any less lovable than anyone else.

11. Stop being a people-pleaser. Choose to stop being a people-pleaser and to start being a self-pleaser. At the end of the day, you always have choice. You have the choice to leave a date early if you are physically (or otherwise) uncomfortable. You have the choice to put yourself first. You have the choice to say, "so what, who cares, doesn't matter," to what others think of you. If you are centered in your heart, caring for yourself, and pacing carefully, that's what matters.

Chances are the people who might judge you have *no* idea what it's like to live in your shoes. So how can they possibly be qualified to make a judgment on your life? They're not.

UNDERSTANDING PACING AND getting these skills under your belt will be a huge help as you move forward into longer-term dating and possibly a serious relationship. No matter how much fun you're having, it always comes back to how you're feeling and what you need in each moment. Checking in with yourself regularly and responding to your body's signals right away will reduce your stress and give you more energy in the long run.

Now, let's venture into the meatier aspects of dating and relationships.

CHAPTER 8

Getting Past the Third Date

THESE DAYS, THE third date is often when sex is expected to happen. I'm not sure how this expectation came about, but I do know that the three-date rule, as it's often called, is bollocks. There is no rule about how long you have to wait to have sex; the timing is not the same for everyone. Regardless, the third date is a good place to pause and reflect on where things might be going.

MY STORY

WHEN I WAS younger, I was a real people-pleaser. I knew about the three-date rule, and I really wanted guys to like me, so I would often accommodate them on the third date, or even earlier. Because *I wanted them to like me*. Mental head slap. I once even slept with a guy *before* the first date, which resulted in a four-year relationship. Go figure. I've also been known to wait up to three months to have sex with a boyfriend—not because I liked or wanted him any less, but because we were moving slowly, and I liked the pace.

When I was having sex according to the three-date rule, I wasn't telling the guys anything about my pain condition, out of fear of rejection. I was gritting my teeth through sex, faking orgasms, and hoping they would climax as soon as possible. The smaller the penis and the faster the ejaculation, the better. If we continued to date, I would eventually be forced to reveal the pain situation because I wasn't able to have sex multiple times a day, often not even multiple times a week, depending on the recovery time I needed. Something else I needed to tell them: I was using Xylocaine, a numbing gel, on my girly bits, which would often numb them as well. (Remember the guy with the frozen mouth?) You'd better believe there were many more frozen mouths and boy bits after that one. Oops. So much for the speedy orgasms.

On top of everything else, whenever I had a quick encounter with someone I didn't know all that well, within a few days I would inevitably panic about sexually transmitted infections. What if he had one and hadn't told me? What if he didn't know he had one? What if the condom wasn't enough? What if I was dying? I would *obsess* over STIs. Why did I put myself through this? Because I was too afraid to speak up before things got physical. I was scared to communicate about issues that weren't sexy and romantic if sex was about to take place. My fears of rejection, abandonment, shame, and ridicule were so intense that they prevented me from listening to and taking care of my physical body properly.

Being a people-pleaser, I would downplay pain (physical and emotional), which was really not to my benefit. But then, my efforts were all directed at keeping the guy. They weren't focused on what was comfortable for me or what I needed. My self-esteem was very low. I recall at one point sharing with a new boyfriend that I had been sexually assaulted as a teenager. He scoffed and said, "All girls say that." And you know what I did? Nothing. Nope. Nada. Because he was cute and cool and I wanted a boyfriend. Red flags all over the place, and I was colour-blind.

What exactly was I doing wrong in my younger years? I was diving into the deep end of the dating pool without any preparation. Trying to sort out my goggles and water wings, assess the chlorine level, find a swimming buddy, and learn how to do the front crawl once I was already flailing around in the water. Allowing my insecurity and fear to guide me ended in a messy, confused, panicked, and disorganized dating strategy. This was not getting me to where I wanted to be—in a loving relationship. Rather, fear and insecurity resulted in me splashing and thrashing around, dog-paddling, and clinging to the side of the pool. I hadn't established a foundation of self-esteem, confidence, or support before jumping in. The result? I found myself drowning. When I imagine how much easier it would have been had I been prepared, I want to kick myself (gently and lovingly, of course). Planning, preparation, and pacing are all *so* important if you're dating and entering relationships with chronic pain and illness.

I finally established a solid foundation and kicked fear and insecurity out of the driver's seat several years ago. This is what it looked like: I met a tall, kind, handsome, and chivalrous man called Gabe, and we started dating. I really liked him, we both loved football, and we had great chemistry. When he invited me back to his place on the third date, I knew he would try to get it on with me, but I also knew that it was not going to happen because I had set a boundary with myself. Instead, I told him about my condition, about the pain I was experiencing, and about my limitations. I also asked about his degree of openness to alternatives to intercourse. We talked sexual history and birth control and made a plan to get tested before becoming intimate. I made it clear that I was in no hurry and that I didn't know when intercourse was going to happen. And Gabe was cool with that. Really! My little abandonment-fearing heart leapt with joy. This led to a lovely several months of great, stress-free, and as close as it gets to pain-free sex and (almost) bliss, but then Gabe turned out to be an alcoholic and a gambling addict. Bye-bye, Gabe.

LET'S DISCUSS

THREE-DATE RULE, schmee-date rule. There are no rules for when to have sex once you start dating someone, even though your date might try to convince you otherwise. However, at or about the three-date mark is a good time to reflect on where things are going, which includes getting clear on how you're feeling about this person and what you're expecting of him. Let's take a close look at what's developing, shall we?

Do You Genuinely Like the Person You're Dating?

Do you even want to go past the third date with him? I find

that, often, a person with low self-esteem will date someone who is not a good match. When we have low self-esteem, we are more likely to date people because they are interested in us, not because we genuinely feel a connection with them. Since chronic pain and illness can take a big bite out of your self-esteem, keep this in mind as you date. If you're questioning your worthiness, head on back to Chapter 1 and do a little more work on increasing your self-confidence and self-worth before you proceed.

So let me ask you again, is this person really doing it for you? Are you contemplating a fourth date for the right reasons? Have you checked off the "He really does it for me" box on your Man Chart? Does he meet all (or at least most) of your must-haves? Or are you thinking you'll just stick with him because there's nothing better going on right now, or because he's willing to date you, condition and all?

Please remember: what you have to offer is special. You have a limited amount of time and energy to expend on someone else, so your time and energy are precious. The person you're dating had better be pretty great for you to be willing to give your time to him. And yes, you may need to find an especially compassionate and understanding partner—and that is completely possible. Don't continue dating someone simply because he is interested in you. How do *you* feel about *him*? Who is worthy of your time, your energy?

Do You Want to Continue Moving Forward with the Person You're Dating?

Let's say you've had three or four dates. Do you want to continue? Take a look at your Man Chart and determine whether you're happy with his check marks. How are you feeling? If you're excited and looking forward to more dates, great. Go for it and enjoy! Remember to maintain your planning and pacing and to stick with your boundaries.

On the other hand, maybe you've dipped your toes into the dating pool and that was enough. Perhaps you've realized now is not the right time to go any further because you're physically or emotionally not in the right place for it. And that's fine. I've chosen to go significant stretches of time solo during flare-ups, and there's nothing wrong with you doing the same; in fact, it may be one of the most caring things you can do for yourself.

What about if you're not sure whether you like this guy or want to see him again? If this is the case, a little more digging is in order. Where is the uncertainty coming from? Are you trying to talk yourself into liking him? Connecting with someone is about the feeling you have when you're together. It's also about feeling connected when you are apart. Do you still feel that person's presence or energy when you're not physically together, or is there just a cold ocean of nothingness? Feeling closely connected with someone else is special, and when it's not there, we can't wish or think it into existence.

There's another possible scenario here. Do you find yourself backing away because you are afraid of where things might lead? Of what your date might think of you when he discovers the full extent of your condition? Perhaps you've predicted a scenario in which the relationship will blossom, progress, but then end—and since it will end, why bother starting it? If this is you, stop and take a deep breath. Many of us get caught up in thinking negatively, predicting outcomes and making assumptions about what others will think and do. But you can't possibly know what is going to happen. You can't know what someone else is thinking, no matter how many hours you spend analyzing his words and actions.

Here's what you can do, though. You can ask the guy you're dating to clarify things in order to dispel your assumptions. You can be patient and proceed with curiosity, open-mindedness, and open-heartedness. You can recognize when you're having negative thoughts, then change them. You can stop predicting and fortune-telling. Taking these steps will make life easier, less stressful, and more enjoyable. If you're holding back from dating someone because of what might go wrong in the future, you might be missing out on a wonderful relationship. Don't let your monkey brain get in the way of your happiness.

You may or may not be able to determine whether you're really into a guy after three or four dates. If you're unsure, take a little more time to decide whether you want to see more of him. Not everyone knows right away; some of us need time to sleep on these decisions.

Don't Settle

We've already talked about not settling back in Chapter 4, and I'm going to say it again now: Don't settle!

I used to ask myself how I could expect someone to deal with my illness and pain if I didn't even want to deal with it myself. I figured I would be lucky if anyone were willing to take me on, and if they were, I would jump at the opportunity to be with them. This is not a healthy attitude.

The way to find the right person includes accepting your illness, having compassion for yourself, and seeing yourself as more than just a walking pain condition. Recognize yourself as a whole human being, one who has skills and abilities and value, who is funny and intelligent, and who has a lot to bring to a relationship. You will then be able to say to yourself: "Of course someone will be willing to accept my condition, since I am so much more than my condition."

What has this got to do with settling? It's about valuing yourself. When you value yourself, you will be less inclined to settle. People may tell you otherwise, but your condition does not in any way mean that you have to settle for a relationship that is less than what you want. I don't care if you are bedridden 24 hours a day—that is not a good reason to settle. If you've found someone who is willing to have an exclusively online relationship, you still don't have to settle if he doesn't interest you or if there is no chemistry. And never settle for someone who is abusive in any way—physically, mentally, emotionally, or verbally. Aside from the fact that abuse is never ok, an abusive relationship can worsen your condition, pain-wise and symptom-wise. If there is even a hint of the possibility of abuse, get that person out of your life.

Wait for the right mate! Relationships are a bigger deal when you have chronic pain and illness than when you don't. They take more out of you and have deeper implications for your short- and long-term health and well-being. And it's ok that they are a bigger deal. It's up to you to honour and respect that about yourself.

So please don't stick with someone because:

- He likes you.
- He's willing to take on your condition.
- It's convenient.

- It's hard to meet people.
- You don't want to be alone.
- You have no idea when or how you might meet some-one else.

Those are not good reasons to stay with anyone. Stick with someone because he is caring, nurturing, loving, intelligent, funny, and all those other must-haves on your Man Chart. You deserve all of that!

Beware the Red Flags

When we're just starting to date someone, we often have a tendency to overlook red flags because we really want to give our date the benefit of the doubt. We may have high hopes for a relationship with this person, and therefore it's in our interest to ignore the warning signs. Unfortunately, this tendency can get us in trouble and keep us in relation-ships way past their expiry date.

Red Flag Example No. 1

I would like to preface this example by saying that I have dated too many men who repressed their emotions and refused to work on or discuss our relationship. I have cried, yelled, and sulked about this, on my own and in therapy. I've put considerable work into my own communication skills as a result, with the intention that by improving my skills, I would attract someone on the same wavelength. I've also asked the universe to bring me a sensitive man who is a good communicator and in touch with his emotions.

A couple of years ago, I met Antonio and we started dat-ing. I assumed (error #1) that he was a good communicator, because that's what I had asked the universe for just before he came into my life. We went on a few dates. He was kind, generous, and intelligent. He also walked really slowly, which was great for me and my turtle-speed shuffle. I was feeling hopeful. On the third or fourth date, Antonio joked that he couldn't "do" emotions and instead just stuffed them all back in. Somewhere deep inside, I got a sinking feeling. And I ignored it (error #2). The subject came up again a couple of weeks later, and I realized that he wasn't joking—he really could not do emotions, was unable to express how he felt about me in any way (not even an "I like you" or a "You're pretty")—and was unwilling to discuss "us." Red flags flappin' in the wind. And yet, I continued to date him, thinking that my communication skills would be enough for the both of us (error #3).

Antonio and I dated for five unemotional months before I finally admitted to myself that I could not go on this way because I needed more from a relationship. It was time to move on. Bye-bye Antonio. The moral? Don't ignore the red flags: they're legit. You can save yourself a lot of time, frustration, energy, and anguish if you heed the red flags.

Red Flag Example No. 2.

Not too long ago, I met Jeff through an online dating site. We had a great phone conversation that lasted a couple of hours, but something niggled at me: when I had mentioned that I wanted to go away somewhere warm for a holiday but was having trouble finding a friend who could go, Jeff replied, "I totally want to go on a holiday, too! I'll go with you, we can share a room, and if you don't want to hang out with me, that's cool." This was after talking to me for two hours and never having met me. Red flag #1!

Something else niggled at me as well: he said he had just broken up with his wife of 10+ years but kept insisting that he was over her, that the marriage had been over long ago. Hmmm.... Who were you trying to convince, Jeff? The nail in that coffin, so to speak, was when he asked me to the Justin Timberlake concert a few days later—*the day before the concert*. He had bought tickets for us to go, then got really upset when I declined. Flag flag flag! Jeff had not asked me ahead of time whether I was available the day of the concert, would be interested in going or even liked Justin Timberlake (meh, I could take him or leave him). He had created a relationship in his head where there wasn't one. Besides, loud music, crowds, and cramped seats for several hours, with a stampede to get out at the end? Not going to happen. See ya, Jeff.

Neither of my red flag example situations carried the possibility of a good relationship, and neither offered the prospect of creating a solid foundation in terms of being with someone who would be understanding, thoughtful, and communicative around my condition. For me, it's extremely important to be with someone with whom I can (1) have an ongoing and open dialogue about how we're both feeling and how my condition might be affecting the relationship, and then (2) work together to generate creative solutions and be supportive of one another.

If something doesn't feel right to you when you start dating someone, that's a red flag. That sinking feeling, the little voice in the back of your head, your gut instinct—listen to those. If he's anything but supportive and understanding about your condition, especially at first, that's a red flag. Spare yourself a potentially energy-draining situation.

When your intuition is talking to you, *please* listen to it. You are a lot wiser than you may realize.

End It Now if It's Not Working for You

Perhaps you've seen a few red flags and you're feeling a bit uneasy, but it's not *that* bad. You *are* having fun, and maybe he's smart or you admire certain qualities of his. So even though there are some red flags, and things don't feel quite right, you think you're just going to keep dating him. It's not so bad. You'll just try a little harder to like him, or find him attractive, or not be put off by certain habits or things he says. No. No. No. No. No! End it now if it's not working for you. Don't drag it on past its due date. Remember, your time and energy are precious. Who do you want to expend them on? Who is worthy of your limited resources? There will be other men to date. There are always other men to date. If you don't feel good about the person you're dating, then stop dating him.

Start Disclosing Your Condition

I'm going to tell you a little story about disclosure. I met Matt online. We arranged an afternoon coffee date and had such a great time that we went for a second date later that night. (Poor pacing, I admit.) I alluded to my condition that evening by indicating that I wasn't able to walk too far or too fast. Immediately after the first two dates we made plans for a third. Before that date, though, Matt called me to chat. He told me about other women he had dated and how some of them revealed their "crazy" after a few dates. He asked me jokingly if there was anything he needed to know about me. I told him there was, because even though

I felt it was too early to tell him all about my condition, I'm an honest person.

"What's wrong with you?" he asks. Nice and subtle there, buddy.

"Nothing's wrong with me. I just have some stuff going on. I'll tell you about it next time I see you." This is not a conversation I am willing to have over the phone. It's personal and private, and, for me to feel comfortable and safe, I need to do it in person.

"Can't you just tell me over the phone?" he asked.

"Nope. I'm going to be seeing you tomorrow anyway. You'll know soon enough," I replied.

"Why don't you text it to me if you're not comfortable telling me?"

"Text it to you? No way. This has to be an in-person conversation for me." I was feeling pretty proud of my boundaries at this point.

"But it would be easier for me not to do it in person. What if things get awkward?" Selfish much, Matt? Our conversation ended pretty quickly after that. Red flags, insensitivity, bye-bye Matt.

Matt had some baggage, including a set of lenses that created fear around situations that were uncomfortable for him. It was all about him. I didn't take it personally. There was nothing I could do about his perspective, but I could add him to the list of stories I would tell in this book.

So, disclosure. If you haven't told the guy anything about your condition by the third or fourth meeting, it's probably time to start divulging a bit. You'll likely find that it's a balance between revealing too much right away and holding back too much for too long.

Having you share everything about your condition at the start may be overwhelming and off-putting for some guys. On the other hand, if you find yourself lying by omission, you may put your date in an awkward position when you finally do reveal more about your health situation, and he might feel like he's been deliberately deceived.

As I've mentioned earlier in this book, it's always up to you what to reveal and when to reveal it. I recommend starting with generalities within a few dates, then getting more specific if and when things become more serious. If you end up having only two dates with someone, he doesn't need to know much, if anything, about your medical condition. You can save that for the guys you're genuinely into. When you really are interested in a man, you may want to tell him about your limitations somewhat early on so that if they are problematic for him, you can part ways sooner rather than later, thus potentially avoiding unnecessary heartache. Again, that's completely your call. And if someone chooses to stop dating you because of your limitations, that's ok. Remember, don't take it personally; that's his issue, not yours.

While disclosing your condition is one thing, getting your prospective mate to really understand it is another. The truth is that, when it comes to developing a relationship with someone, you don't need him to fully understand what you're going through (realistically, how can he?), but you do need him to respect your situation. If you're going to share your lives, have a home together, and travel together, doing so will be much easier if he has as much information about your situation as possible. As such, it becomes about educating your partner so that he comprehends—just don't expect him to be able to *feel* what you're experiencing.

Sex

The next chapter is all about sex, but I'm going to touch on it here because sex is often an expectation on or just after the third date. Perhaps you're excited for sex, the third date can't come soon enough, and you're raring to go. Or maybe you're thinking sex might happen in six months, if things go well. There is a huge range of attitudes towards sex, and they are all just fine. The important thing is to be clear on where you stand on the issue. What you want to avoid is deciding that waiting six months is right for you, but feeling pressured into having sex much earlier and then having to deal with the negative consequences—physical, emotional, mental, and spiritual.

It's important to consider what you are willing to engage in sexually *right now*. Things change, and what you are willing to do now may be different from what you are able and willing to do in the future. We are concerned with the present.

Start by figuring out your feelings around sex. This is not the time to simply follow your date's lead. It's important to make your own decisions. First of all, consider your definition of sex:

- Does sex mean intercourse?
- Skype/FaceTime sex or phone sex?
- Mutual masturbation?
- Oral sex?
- All of the above?

People have different views on what "sex" means, so get specific with yourself.

Once you've established your definition of sex, think

about the impact that sex will have on your life:

- Is it going to energize you, or will it exhaust you for days?
- Will it increase your pelvic, back, joint, or wherever pain?
- How long will it take you to recover?
- If it will increase pain and symptoms, is it worth doing?

After asking yourself these questions, you can decide whether you're ready for sex, then set about managing your partner's expectations.

If your partner is eager to have sex, the third date is a good time to have "the talk." Here are some important points to cover with your partner before having sex:

1. What is and what isn't physically possible right now, given your condition.
2. Birth control.
3. Getting tested for sexually transmitted infections. Get yourself tested and ask your partner to get tested before engaging in intimacy. You have enough health issues to deal with—you don't need another one, especially one that is preventable.

If your partner isn't pushing for intimacy, you don't need to have the sex talk on the third or fourth date. Allow it to happen at a time that feels right. It is, however, good to be prepared for the talk in case the subject comes up early on.

Don't Get Discouraged

We've already talked about discouragement, but it's worth having a quick reminder. I know what it's like to go on a bunch of first and second dates and never get to the third or fourth because the dates weren't worth my extra-special time and energy. Sometimes it feels like the right person is never going to come along. But the more you continue to set and maintain your boundaries, keep tabs on your Man Chart, and heed the red flags, the stronger the message you put out to the universe about who you are and who you would like to attract. By working on yourself and changing patterns that didn't serve you in the past, you will be moving forward to the right kind of partner. All the work you're doing in this book is setting you up to have better relationships. You might have to kiss a lot of frogs before you find your prince, but I know it's possible for all of us with chronic pain and illnesses to find loving relationships. It may take persistence, perseverance, and a sense of humour—and hey, those are good qualities simply for getting through life.

TAKE ACTION!

GETTING PAST THE third date can be challenging due to the expectations that are often attached to it. Here are a few tips to help you handle third-date issues with ease:

1. Do you like who you're dating, and do you want to continue dating him? The Man Chart is a great tool to help you answer these questions. Continue to fill out your Man Chart as you get to know your date, and evaluate it frequently, especially at first. Don't forget to answer the all-important "Does he really do it for me?" question! That is often the deciding factor in continuing to date or ending the relationship.

2. Don't settle. To remind yourself of your value, take out a sheet of paper and at the top write: "I am valuable because...." Below that write a list of your positive traits and what you bring to a relationship. I challenge you to fill up both sides of the page. Take out another sheet if you have more to say! You might wish to start with something like: "I am valuable because I am smart, intelligent, and have a lot of love to give...." Don't stop until you have both sides of the page filled, no matter how big or small the points. Keep it around and look at it once in a while to remind yourself that someone as awesome as you are deserves to have a relationship with someone who is worthy of you.

3. Heed the red flags. If you see one of those red flags pop up, be honest with yourself. Don't ignore it. This is your intuition trying to get your attention. See the flag, then act on it so you're not eventually in a relationship with a man who's leading a parade of flags.

4. End it now if it's not working for you. That can be easier said than done. There are so many ways to justify staying in relationships that aren't great: "Maybe he'll change. He's really stressed right now at work. He just needs a little more time. He's scared. I just need to be a little more energetic." No! If it's not working, it's time to move on. It's not worth stressing yourself needlessly in an unhappy situation. Your health is number one, and your health is most supported when you are happy, so aim for the relationships that make you happy, and end the ones that make you unhappy.

5. Disclose your condition. We've talked quite a bit about when and why to disclose your condition to the guy you're dating, but what about *how*? Here are a few tips:

a. Allude to it casually in conversation: "Sure, I'd love to go for a walk, but I can only manage about 20 minutes. I have some aches and pains that stop me from doing more."

b. Bring it up during a lull in the conversation, or if the time seems right: "There's something I need to tell you. I have a health condition that limits how much I can do, and I just wanted to let you know about it." Then decide how much more detail to provide.

c. Sometimes I like to reassure the dates that start looking really worried: "Don't worry, it's not contagious!"

d. Don't apologize for your condition. Ever. You haven't done anything wrong.

6. Sex. Being prepared is key when it comes to sex. Start by addressing the following questions:

a. What is your definition of sex?
b. What is your partner's definition of sex?
c. What impact will sex have on your life—physically, mentally, emotionally, and spiritually?

d. Other than physical limitations, birth control, and safe sex, what issues do you want to cover when you have "the talk"?

Knowing and addressing all of this information before you have sex will make things much easier as you forge ahead in the dating process.

PHEW! MADE IT! You're past date number three. If you've been keeping up with the Take Action! sections, you're a pro by now—you're taking care of yourself, pacing yourself, setting boundaries, weeding out the guys with too many red flags, not taking anything personally, and keeping on top of your Man Chart—plus, your foundation is rock solid. It sounds to me like it's time to talk about sex....

CHAPTER 9

Sex! I Said It!

SEX IS AN *extremely important part of a relationship.* I hear this message frequently, and it makes me nervous and unhappy because it triggers a lot of insecurities. My monkey brain used to tell me that if I couldn't have sex, then I couldn't have a relationship—and a lasting, loving relationship is the one thing I really want in life. Having pelvic pain used to make me feel inadequate, damaged, less than, and certainly not good enough for the sort of man I wanted.

When it comes to relationships, sex is one of my biggest challenges. I'm a sex enthusiast, but my pelvic pain dramatically reduces my enjoyment of sex and ability to have it; consequently, my partner's level of enjoyment often plummets. Your chronic pain and illness may or may not interfere with sex. If you have pain-free sex, I salute you. If you *do* have pain during sex, whether it's in your pelvic region, back, joints, abdomen, or elsewhere, I feel your pain.

MY STORY

APART FROM THE first time, I don't actually remember a time when sex didn't hurt. It's more about degrees of pain: sometimes far too high to enjoy myself and other times barely noticeable. I've had many different experiences with sex, ranging from loving, funny, exciting, and mind-blowing to boring, painful, tedious, uninspired, and disappointing. I've spent my fair share of time avoiding sex, as well as gritting my teeth through excruciating intercourse, mostly because I didn't want my relationship to fail.

I've gone through spells when I would think, *Sex? Forget it.* And then a year or two later, I would be in a relationship where the sex was great and the pain minimal, and I was truly enjoying myself. And then there would inevitably be another setback, another year of recovery before I would be ready to be intimate with someone again. The ups and downs required a lot of patience, hope, and faith.

I've invested a fair amount of time and effort into trying to improve the situation in my nether regions. I've gone for pelvic floor physio, which helped a great deal, although it didn't solve everything. I've gone for counselling, meditated, visualized, and tried all sorts of ointments and freezing gels. I've taken various medications—antidepressants, anti-epileptics, anti-what-have-yous. All helped to some degree. Notably, though, I had the least pain during the times in my life when I was experiencing the least stress. If I was worried, reluctant, anxious, thinking about other things, or feeling meh about the guy, then the pain was usually more intense. I also had less pain when I was with someone I liked a lot who was gentle and understanding and who *really did it for me.* The more I was able to relax during sex, the less pain I experienced. It also helped if he was not very well endowed. Yup, you heard it right. *Not* well endowed.

I've read several books on reducing sexual pain. These were not always that helpful, as the messages were often negative. I remember reading one book on female pelvic pain that had a section meant to be "hopeful." Well, it wasn't. It shared stories about various couples, their failures in the bedroom, and how stressful that was for their relationships. The book brought me right back to being 19 years old in the specialist's office and being told that the vulvodynia would pretty much ruin any relationship I might have. Hope schmope.

When I went online to blogs and forums to look for hopeful stories, I usually found only more problems, more failures, and unhappy anecdotes. People are much more likely to post on blogs and forums when they are unhappy and want to complain. They are less likely to post when things are going well. Hence, what's posted online is not an accurate reflection of reality. And it's not helpful to read about all the difficulties and complications that come with my condition. I'm already living them. My solution is to stay away from reading about my condition on the Internet unless I'm reading success stories.

So where did that leave me? I knew that feeling relaxed while having sex with someone who was not overly large was my best bet. I wanted more information, though. I wanted to know what other people in my position were doing, but the resources just didn't exist. So I went to the sexperts. I read books on how to have great sex, written for "normal" people, to see if I could adapt that advice to fit my circumstances, and that worked to some degree—especially when it came to manual and oral sex. But it also got me fixated on needing to please my partner, which too often led to me enduring more intercourse through clenched teeth.

Perhaps you've noticed that, up until this point, I've been talking about what *I* did to figure out sex, while sex, as I'm talking about it, is something that involves *two* people. For the longest time, it never really occurred to me to involve my partner in my quest for a fulfilling, pain-free sex life for the both of us. Face palm.

Why had I cut my partner out of the process?

1. I was completely embarrassed to talk about sex, let alone about pain during sex.
2. I wanted sex to be romantic, sensual, and effortless, the way it is in the movies, and that didn't involve talking about sex-related issues that weren't sexy.
3. My old friend, fear of abandonment, was always there to suggest that if I was anything less than a willing sexpot, my partner would leave me.
4. I believed that ultimately, the only thing men wanted from me was sex.
5. I thought that men needed to have intercourse at least three times a week, every week, otherwise they would find someone else to get it on with. (I have no idea where this notion came from—probably some old-timey women's magazine).
6. I didn't think men experienced feelings the way women did and didn't believe they actually, truly cared. Wow, right?

I was in my late thirties when I figured all of this out and realized that nothing I did physically was going to improve my conundrum. What I needed was to learn how to communicate without fear and to challenge some of my old, misguided beliefs about men (especially that men were robotic sex-seeking machines). A little self-worth work thrown in for good measure didn't hurt either.

Through the process of becoming a counsellor and life coach, I finally learned how to communicate in a healthy way. And through a tantra workshop, I learned that communicating about sex can actually be sexy, although if there's something serious to discuss, it doesn't *have* to be sexy. Talking about issues around sex can make us feel very vulnerable, and I think that's why some avoid it, because it exposes us, our deepest fears and innermost selves. Yet this vulnerability leads to the ultimate reward: connection. And the more connected you are, the better you will communicate with your partner, and the hotter your sex life will be. Woohoo!

When I added communication to my sex recipe, I started getting some great results and experienced a lot of relief. I don't have to, and I'm not going to, endure any more pain—be it seconds, minutes, hours, days, or weeks—just to give my partner 30 seconds of bliss. I still want him to have his bliss, but I'm going to find a way to help him get there that doesn't involve me suffering for days or weeks after. There is no need for me to sacrifice myself like that. If my partner expects me to, then he's not the right person for me.

LET'S DISCUSS

Why is Sex Important?

Sex is important in a relationship because it creates vulnerability and emotional intimacy, which in turn build connection and closeness. According to renowned psychologist

Abraham Maslow, sex is a basic human physiological need, on the same level as food, shelter, and water. According to the Mayo Clinic (mayoclinic.org), sexuality helps fulfill the vital need for human connection. In addition, endorphins, our bodies' natural painkillers and feel-good neurotransmitters, are released during touch and sex, so sex can make us feel great mentally, emotionally, and physically. Not to mention it's a stress-reducer. Sex is a natural and healthy part of living, as well as an important aspect of your identity as a person. Humans need physical and emotional intimacy; that's just how we're built.

The less physically intimate you are in your relationship, the less connected you will feel—to your partner, to life. To have a loving and supportive long-term relationship, intimacy, vulnerability, and connection are vital. If one partner or both partners are sexually unfulfilled, resentment may develop, and resentment is a relationship killer.

Sexual dissatisfaction often occurs when there is an imbalance in your and your partner's levels of sex drive. Finding a partner with a similar sex drive as yours can alleviate many potential difficulties. This also goes for the type of sex he's interested in. I know some guys who are just as happy with oral sex as with vaginal intercourse and who don't mind not humping their way to ecstasy. I've witnessed many thriving relationships where both partners have an equally low sex drive, or lack the desire for traditional sex. For some, intimate touch is all they want or need, and touch alone can help create profound intimacy and connection.

So yes, sex is important. But sex doesn't have to mean intercourse, or whatever other sexual activity that causes you pain or discomfort. Sex can mean what you want it to;

you and your partner can create new activities, rituals, and ways of pleasuring each other and connecting without exacerbating your condition.

The Basics

When contemplating sex, aside from your personal comfort, your physical health also needs to be respected. If you respect your body, your partner will, too. Here's a little story to demonstrate my point.

I had a one-night stand with Clay. Actually, it was the second one-night stand I'd had with him, but the first one had been about five years earlier. Our first night together was incredible, some of the best sex I'd ever had—it ranked in the top ten of all time. The second night, he came over after a party we had been to, and I was a little drunk—ok, more than a little drunk. And I was excited. If our last encounter was any indication, I was in for a spectacular night (apart from the pain I would have during sex, but I was ignoring that issue).

We started by taking a dip in my hot tub. Clay was sexy in a thuggish kind of way. He was also very charismatic and charming, and I was feeling flirtatious and bold. After some bantering and a little kissing in the hot, steamy water, I realized that I had cut my knee on the concrete steps in the hot tub. The blood from my cut was making long, red ribbons on the water. Oops. I did my best to muddle the water and disperse the blood, although I had a feeling Clay wasn't fooled—he hadn't been drinking much that night. The hot tub was intensifying my drunkenness, and my judgement was blurred by the sexy beast that was Clay.

So there I was, drunk, trying to hide my bleeding knee,

doing my best come-hither eyes and imagining what the rest of the night would hold, when I suddenly had a reality check: I was dreading the impending sex because it would undoubtedly hurt. Story of my life—wanting sex, pleasure, ecstasy, and dreading it at the same time. Pain really takes the shine off the good stuff.

After the hot tub, we went back upstairs to my apartment and, after I put a Band-Aid on my knee, fooled around some more. It wasn't as good as I remembered from five years earlier, but I went with it. We migrated from the couch to the bed, rolling around and having an ok time. I wasn't sure what was different this time; nevertheless, I grabbed a condom out of the drawer and handed it to him. He looked at me like I'd suddenly turned purple with green polka-dots.

"What's that for?" he asked.

"A condom? For sex?"

"Really? You use condoms?" He tried to look confused. "Who does that anymore?"

"Ummmm...," I wasn't sure what to say. "Me?"

"Oh, wow. Well, condoms don't work for me. I can't orgasm. No one uses them anymore."

"Well, it's a condom or nothing." I wasn't willing to take the risk.

"Well, good night then."

And that was the end of the sexy night. We rolled over, back to back, and went to sleep.

When we woke up in the morning, he was frisky and suddenly willing to use a condom. Whaaat?

I figured, "What the hell, why not?" but the sex wasn't even mediocre, I wasn't turned on, and then the condom came off. We gave up. I was glad I had stuck to my guns the night before. Clay had been trying to manipulate me into going bareback, even though he was obviously able to use a condom.

Chlamydia, gonorrhoea, crabs, syphilis, HIV, Hepatitis B, Hepatitis C, genital herpes, urinary tract infections, yeast infections—you don't want any of these things, so take steps to avoid them. Sex isn't worth it, no matter who the guy is. I've said this before, but it bears repeating: you have enough health issues, and you don't need another one, especially one that you can prevent. Use condoms, use birth control (if you don't want a baby), pee right after sex, abstain completely if necessary—you know how to do these things. Don't let a Clay talk you into unsafe sex. And if you're planning a long-term relationship with the person you are dating, both of you should get tested for sexually transmitted infections so you can relax and properly enjoy yourselves down the line. Your doctor will be able to advise what tests you should get.

These are the basics, the minimum to protect yourself. The last thing you need is another health complication, so be safe during sex. You are valuable; treat yourself accordingly.

What is Sex?

Define What Sex Means to You and to Your Partner

If you've decided you want to have a relationship with someone, sex will undoubtedly come up.

Having sex can mean a variety of things. What does "sex" mean to you? Does it represent intercourse? Or foreplay plus intercourse? Or oral sex? Does it have to result in orgasm? What combinations or variations represent "sex" for you? Clarify your definition so that when you're talking about sex with your partner, you are able to clearly express what you mean when you refer to "sex." Compare your definitions, and decide whether you and your partner want to use more specific words for the act(s). Basically, get clear on what it means to both of you.

Expand Your Definition of Sex

Sex doesn't have to just mean intercourse. It can represent a variety of different activities. If you have pain during or after intercourse, it's time to expand your definition of sex. Even if you don't have pain, it can't hurt to add a few more activities to your collection. Sex can include but is not limited to:

- Intercourse (and all its various possible positions)
- Oral sex
- Manual sex
- Mutual masturbation
- Sensual massage
- Phone sex[*]
- Skype/FaceTime sex[*]
- Sexting[*]
- Cuddling
- Playing with sex toys and vibrators
- Kissing
- Touching
- Gazing at each other

---

[*] Please be sure that you trust your partner if you are going to send pictures or videos of your sexy self to him electronically. Snapchat is a good option for sending photos because the application deletes them after one to 10 seconds, depending on your settings.

Sex doesn't have to result in orgasm. What matters is that it yields some form of pleasure. It's about intimacy, what makes you both happy and brings you closer. It's about the journey, not the destination.

Get Creative

Sex is beautiful. Intimate. Caring. Hot. Sweaty. Messy. Slow. Fast. Quiet. Loud. Gentle. Rough. Sex is what you want it to be. You have the ability to create the sex life you desire with an open-minded, willing partner and have it be pleasurable for both of you. It might be very simple, or it might require extra pillows, props, and other supports.

There are endless options, so you might like to investigate a bit. Be proactive and research what you can do to make sex a more enjoyable and comfortable experience for your body. Here are a few ideas to get you started:

- Read some of the countless books about sex. Most of them don't address having sex when you live with chronic pain or illness; however, you may find that you can take bits and pieces from various sources and put them together into something that works for you.
- Explore a reputable sex shop.
- Take a tantra workshop. Through tantra you can learn how to create deep intimacy and pleasure without intercourse. Intercourse is still an option, but practicing tantra is a great way to connect with your partner on a unique level and take your relationship to a new place.

Brainstorm, use your imagination, and redefine sex. This is an opportunity for you and your partner to be creative, experiment, and most of all have fun!

Please Each Other

Sex is in large measure about pleasing your partner; it's not about me, me, me. By focusing on your partner's pleasure, you take the focus off yourself. It's your partner's job to give you pleasure. You might want him to give you a sensual massage, and that is enough. He may want something else. And that is ok. What's important is that you both enjoy yourselves.

However, if you start to focus too much on keeping your partner satisfied but are not experiencing any pleasure yourself—or perhaps you're even enduring pain to pleasure your partner—resentment will likely start to build. I've experienced this. I had been warned that this could happen, but I told myself, *No, I'm just happy to have a relationship. I am willing to do this for him.* And what do you know, over time, the resentment did build. He expected me to pleasure him and didn't return the affection because he thought I didn't like sex. I became very resentful. So, please, make sure you are enjoying yourself.

I'd like to take a moment here to make specific mention of orgasms. People with chronic pain and illness often have difficulties reaching orgasm, whether because of the medications they are taking or the pain itself. Orgasm doesn't have to be the goal. And not being able to orgasm doesn't mean you have to sacrifice the intimacy that often comes with it. You have the ability to feel intense pleasure and satisfaction without orgasm. It really is possible to experience physical intimacy and emotional closeness with another individual simply through touch and anticipation.

Communicate

Communication is the cornerstone of any relationship. That means open communication around such things as every-day matters, feelings, future plans, and sex. Communication around sex is vital. I always wanted sex to be as erotic as possible, and in my mind that meant not talking about it—just doing it, perfectly, fluidly, and seamlessly, Hollywood style. The thing is, real sex is not the same as the way it's portrayed in movies. You're bumping into each other. You're accidentally elbowing him in a sensitive spot. Using too much tooth or nail. You're trying to find a condom, then trying to unwrap it and roll it on. And then you have to pee at a most inopportune time. Oh, and don't forget the leg cramps.

Pre-Sex Communication

Sex is not always as sexy as you might like it to be. Some of the less sexy parts will be talking about sex before the act even happens—specifically, about what your abilities and limitations are, about getting tested for STIs, and about birth control. It's not sexy to have to tell someone, "It may hurt me to have intercourse." I mean, who wants to need to have that conversation at all? But you *do* need to, and the best time to have it is *before* you're naked in bed with your partner. Have that conversation when you're fully clothed, when both of you have the time to talk, and in a neutral loca-tion, like during a walk in the park or sitting at the beach—wherever you feel comfortable. Of course, it may take place in bed if you are bedridden, and, in that case, you can simply keep your clothes or pyjamas on, as the case may be.

Once you get the administrative sex issues out of the way (limitations, STI testing, etc), your chat will also give you a chance to share your likes, dislikes, and fantasies. And you get to listen to your partner talk about what turns *him* on. Listen and acknowledge what your partner is asking for (acknowledging doesn't mean you are agreeing to it). You're establishing expectations and boundaries for the sex that's going to happen.

For some of you, talking about sex with your partner might be easy, and for others, terribly awkward and scary. My most awkward life moments have involved discussing impending sex with a new boyfriend. In the end, though, it's worth doing because you will experience less angst and pain than if you didn't discuss it at all. The conversations will become easier over time if you persist, and please do. It's a good idea to have ongoing communication about sex outside the bedroom once you've started having sex, especially when you have chronic pain and illness. You need to be able to inform your partner about fluctuations in your symptoms, mood, and energy levels because those will greatly affect your ability to engage in sex.

Communicating about sex isn't always sexy, but it can set you up to have a very sexy time.

Communication During Sex

Communicating during sex is usually a lot more fun than the pre-sex conversation. Think moans and groans and sighs and yesses. Whispered directions—softer, harder, a little higher, a little lower. Sharing fantasies, a bit of dirty talk, some sensual encouragement. Mmmhmmm.... You know what to do.

Expressing yourself during sex is vital because it will help you avoid unnecessary pain and discomfort, as well as help you communicate to your partner what really does it for you. If your partner hits a sore spot, let him know that's not a good place to focus his attention. And rather than yelling out, "OW!" you can seductively say, "To the left, to the left," in order to better keep the both of you in the moment. But please, if something is uncomfortable, don't let it continue. Don't go with it because you think it's making your partner happy. He is there to pleasure you, so let him know what you like best. Don't endure for the sake of your partner. Guide him gently to a better feeling spot or activity.

Listen to Your Body

Sex can be a wonderful outlet, relaxing and healing. However, if you overdo it, you may end up paying with pain and other symptoms—and not just for the duration of the experience but for hours, days, or weeks afterwards. If you are having pain, stop what you're doing! It is critical that you not sacrifice yourself long-term for your or your partner's short-term pleasure. Allow your body to gauge how much you can do in the sack. Listen to its messages and respond accordingly. Notice which activities are comfortable and which cause you discomfort. For example, if giving oral sex causes pain in your neck or back, then try a different position or a different activity, or try it at a different time of day, when your symptoms are less intense.

It is vital that you pace yourself during sex as well. If you need a break or a rest, take one. You may have some great sex with no symptoms during the experience, but the following day you're unable to sit, stand, walk, or even lie down comfortably. If this is the case, you may need to moderate your sexual activity (shorter encounters, fewer encounters, more rest breaks, etc.), even if it feels good at the time. It might also be helpful to get extra sleep and/or reduce your activity levels on days you are going to have sex. I know, it's not the easiest task, but looking after yourself is paramount.

I've said it before, I'll say it again, and I'll keep saying it: listen to your body. Chronic pain and illness fluctuate; there will be times when you're feeling sick—tired, nauseous, or in pain—and the last thing on your mind is getting sexy. That's ok. And then there will be other times when you think, "Yeah, I could go for a little hanky-panky." Go for it.

Your body will tell you how much you can comfortably do. Don't push yourself beyond that point, otherwise you may end up being able to do less and less—sexually and otherwise. Sex can be fun, exciting, satisfying—and it shouldn't come at the expense of your well-being.

Lack of Libido

You may find that your desire for sex just isn't there. If you'd like to change this, and if pain is the cause, consider speaking to your doctor about either adjusting your present pain medication or looking at different pain-control options. As I've mentioned previously, physiotherapy, massage, acupuncture, and other bodywork may also be helpful.

Some pain medications may reduce or eliminate libido and/or sexual function. If you feel this may be happening to you, speak with your doctor to explore your options.

In the end, there may not be much you can do about your reduced libido if it's caused by pain and/or medications. Know that you're not alone. There are thousands, if not millions, of people in the same boat. If you don't want anything to do with sex, that's cool, you don't have to. If you're not willing to accept losing your libido, see your doctor and consider seeing a sex therapist.

The Right Partner

No matter how right someone may be for you in other respects, if the two of you are not sexually compatible, there are going to be problems and it's best to figure this out right away. I'm reminded here of my beautiful Dominican man, Juan. The one who smelled so good. He had it all. He was intelligent, kind, sensitive, funny, generous, caring, handsome, muscular, and he had a huge penis. *Huge.* For many women, this might sound like a dream. For me, it was a nightmare. He was far too well endowed. It didn't seem fair; he was so right and yet so wrong. He loved sex and couldn't see himself going without intercourse, and I couldn't see myself going with it—with him, anyway. So we decided to end our romantic relationship. I was sad, but I was also realistic. He just wasn't right for me physically, and I wasn't going to force it.

The right partner is right in all the important ways, and that means that the intimate part of the relationship has to work for both of you. You can't force people to be someone they are not. That goes for your partner, and it goes for you, too. If having sex (of whatever kind) is difficult for you, then you need to find a partner who is open-minded, has a low sex drive, and/or is willing to accommodate you. Had Juan had a low libido or erectile dysfunction or been happy with just oral and manual sex, then things would probably have turned out a lot differently.

The right partner is someone with whom you can communicate openly, who is supportive and understanding, who is sexually compatible with you, who meets most if not all of your top 10 "must have" criteria, and who, most importantly "really does it for you." Don't force a square peg into a round hole. Find somebody who complements you so that you have the energy you need to take care of yourself rather than spending it on worrying about keeping a relationship going with somebody who isn't the right fit.

Sex for One

I would be remiss if I didn't mention masturbation here. You don't need a partner in order to experience sexual pleasure, and the endorphins and hormones released when you orgasm can provide short-term symptom relief for some. Orgasms provide a mental and physical release, something that might be quite valuable if you have ongoing pain and stress. If having orgasms feels good and doesn't trigger pain, don't wait for someone else to give them to you, make it happen! Whether you use your hand, shower nozzle, vibrator, or electric toothbrush, enjoy!

Sex for Three (or More)

One last option I'd like to touch on is open relationships, where you are in a committed relationship with your partner but have an agreement that each of you can have sexual experiences with other people. If you have sexual pain and/ or dysfunction, there may be some benefits to having an open relationship if you are unable to fulfill your partner's sexual needs (or if he is unable to fulfill yours). It can be a way to maintain your loving relationship and allow for you and your partner to be sexually satisfied.

On the other hand, if you have chronic pain and illness, adding another person (or people) into the mix can lead to feelings of insecurity, jealousy, anger, and resentment. These emotions have the potential to worsen your symptoms because of the stress they bring. If you do decide to have an open relationship, make sure that both of you want it equally, and that you set clear ground rules for how it's going to work. It's not a decision to take lightly.

In my experience, I have yet to witness a successful long-term open relationship. However, although it's not something I would want to participate in, I think it is important to offer as an option because, for some people, it could be a solution.

TAKE ACTION!

1. The basics. Get yourself tested for STIs. Have your partner get tested as well before you start exchanging bodily fluids. Ensure you have proper birth control, and use it correctly.

2. Define sex. Pull out a sheet of paper (or tablet, laptop, or smartphone) and do some brainstorming about sex. What does the word "sex" represent to you? What does it evoke? Once you've finished brainstorming, come up with your own definition of sex and write it down—it may be a list of activities that, for you, constitute sex, or it may be a descriptive paragraph. Focus on the content rather than the form. Once you're done, you'll be clear about what sex means to you, which will be helpful for when you end up talking sex with your partner.

3. Expand your definition of sex. I challenge you to get creative and expand your definition of sex. If your definition is limited to intercourse, then you have lots of room for additions. If your definition is already very broad, add one or two more things to your list. Don't worry if you feel that an item isn't sexy enough (e.g., having your partner play with your hair)—if you want it on your list, put it there. If it's something that gives you pleasure, makes you feel good, and maybe takes your mind off your pain and discomfort for a little while, then it deserves to be on your list. If you're in a relationship, you may wish to include your partner in your quest to expand your definition of sex.

4. Please each other. Sex is about bringing pleasure to your partner and vice versa. Pleasing does not necessarily have to mean orgasms. It definitely doesn't mean enduring pain so that your partner achieves an orgasm. Please don't do that. Accept your partner's love, and give your own in a way that feels comfortable (physically, mentally, and emotionally) for you. It may be highly sexual or quietly sensual. However it is, what matters is that you *both* enjoy yourselves with as little pain and discomfort as possible.

5. Listen to your body. Hear your body's messages during sex and respond accordingly. If a position or activity is causing you pain, switch it up! Change your position or the location, or postpone until later. Remember to pace yourself in the bedroom (or the kitchen, or the bathroom, or wherever else you're getting it on).

6. Communicate. If you want to have a healthy relationship, communicating with your partner about sex is key. I've divided this topic into two areas:

> **a. Pre-sex communication.** This is the time to talk about sexual history, STI testing, birth control, your abilities and limitations, how your condition affects what you can do during sex, your sexual expectations, and even your desires and fantasies. Discuss the idea of pleasure—what it means to you and how you would like to receive it. This is not always an easy conversation to have, but it is important. You might want to touch on the idea that sex is about pleasing each other and not necessarily about reaching orgasm every time. This might be a new idea to you and/or your partner. Discuss the issues that you need to get out of the way so you can let go of worry and enjoy your sexy time.

> **b. Communication during sex.** Even if you explain to your partner ahead of time what he can expect, and what you can and can't do during sex, you will likely still need to help him navigate your body. Expressing your pleasure can be a lot of fun, so go for it! And remember, if you need him to change things up (don't endure a second more pain than you need to), go for gentle directions rather than aggressive

demands (unless, of course, that's his turn-on!).
And when it comes to post-sex chats and pillow-talk,
I'll leave that to you.

7. Lack of libido. If you are frustrated about lacking libido and you suspect it may be due to pain and/or the medications you're taking, talk to your doctor about your options. If your libido is low and you're fine with that, then carry on.

8. The right partner. It can be really hard to admit when you're with somebody who isn't right for you, especially if it has taken you a while to meet a great guy who you click with and who is understanding of your condition. However, sexual incompatibility is difficult to work with in a long-term relationship. Keep this in mind when first embarking on a new relationship with a new man. It's very important for you to be with someone compatible because the stress of sexual incompatibility and all its consequences can eventually affect your health and well-being. Having chronic pain and illness does not mean that you have to settle for someone who is not compatible with you. You deserve a great relationship just as much as anyone else, and you can have it.

9. Masturbate. As long as it doesn't aggravate your symptoms, get into a comfortable position and orgasm away! It's a healthy way to release tension and stress. If you need some assistance, try a shower head, body massager, or vibrator. If you don't have a vibrator and want one, you can shop for sex toys online without ever leaving your home (and they will arrive in a nondescript package to avoid any embarrassment).

SEX CAN BE complicated enough; add in chronic pain and illness, and you have a whole other beast. In this chapter, however, you've learned how to tame that beast. You now know how to enjoy sexual and sensual pleasure with your partner without aggravating your condition. Take some time to enjoy this new-found knowledge and practice what you've learned before you head on to the next section: Relationships.

PART III
RELATIONSHIPS

CHAPTER 10

Starting a Relationship When You're Already in Pain

SO HERE WE are at the relationship section of this book. Congratulations for getting this far and even contemplating a relationship! It can be scary. Putting yourself out there is a brave step, and it's one that can improve and add a little (or a lot) more joy to your life.

I'm not going to sugarcoat it: pain and intimate relationships are not buddies. I've read some anecdotes in which couples report becoming closer and having more intimacy, because they faced the challenge together.[1] That, however, seems to be the exception rather than the rule. More commonly, people report pain causing problems in intimate relationships, especially trouble with communicating, and difficulty in managing feelings like anger and frustration.

---

[1] See, for example, painaction.com.

Either way, great relationships require work, and great relationships in which one partner (or both) is experiencing chronic pain require a lot of work. So let's get to work!

MY STORY

FOR BETTER OR worse, I have copious experience with starting intimate relationships while in some type of pain, sometimes completely manageable and other times formidable. In the past, during spells of intense pain and flare-ups, the pain ruled my life. I would try to ignore it, but there was no denying it was in charge. Because I allowed it to have so much power over me, the pain had a profound effect on my relationships. I would pretend I was fine but then become crabby, irritable, short-tempered, or withdrawn, and I would take things out on my partner because the pain reduced my ability to cope. Having been in agony all day, I had nothing left in my love tank for anyone. But my cranky tank sure was full!

I had never been a great communicator, and I have a feeling that my partners were often in the dark about most of what was going on inside me. I was afraid to talk about my condition because I thought they would leave me if they found out how broken I thought I was. Besides, much of the time I was trying to tell myself that I didn't have a serious medical condition. I tried various communication styles in these relationships, some more successful than others.

Take Chris. We were together for about a year. I was in my late 20s and at the height of my denial phase. I wanted to be like my friends—going to parties, meeting guys, and having casual sex. And if my body didn't want to co-operate, I was going to force it to, dammit! I would overcome the pain by sheer will and determination! I debated telling Chris about the pain in my undercarriage but decided not to. He was handsome, intelligent, financially successful, and living the life. Chris valued strength and believed that feeling pain was a sign of weakness. I thought he was cool. I wanted to be cool, and pain was not cool.

I aimed to please. I never told Chris when I was uncomfortable, not when we were hiking, snowshoeing, riding bikes, playing squash, or having sex (Chris liked intercourse over everything else, and I wanted to keep him happy, so sex equalled intercourse *every time*). I dreaded sex each time we had it and did my best to get it over with as quickly as possible. If we were spending the day together, I would make sure we got it on in the morning so I could enjoy the rest of my day (apart from the residual burning, throbbing, stabbing pain) without sex looming over my head. I pretended I felt great—even better than great. I held my tongue when I wanted to lash out because I was so exhausted from being in pain all day. I bent over backwards to be the perfect girlfriend.

After about a year, I couldn't take the physical pain or the pressure of perfection any longer and I broke up with him without ever telling him what had been going on in my body or my mind. I left him completely bewildered.

Contrast this with Gabe. I met him when I was in my mid 30s and was completely up front with him about my condition from the get go. I continued to be honest throughout the relationship about when I wasn't feeling well. He was empathetic and didn't want me to push myself for his sake. He checked in with me regularly during sex to see how I was, and was often the one to suggest alternatives to intercourse. Different approach + better fit = happier me.

As I have grown older and wiser, I have learned not only to put my health first and only start a relationship when I have a solid foundation, but also how to communicate clearly and directly. And no more pretending to be ok! Boy, do all those things make life easier and relationships smoother!

Here are some more of the things that I learned *don't* work:

- Enumerating my various aches, pains, moods and medications on a daily basis
- Complaining
- Whining
- Being passive aggressive
- Avoiding
- Blaming and criticizing
- Demanding
- Ignoring
- Denying
- Pretending to be fine
- Being a martyr
- Holding in all my emotions
- Expecting my partner to be my caregiver
- Expecting my partner to fully understand what I am going through

These are some things that I've learned *do* work:

- Being accepting
- Being honest
- Communicating clearly

- Apologizing
- Being patient
- Helping out as much as I can
- Having empathy, compassion, and understanding for myself and my partner
- Journaling my anger, frustration, and crankiness
- Educating myself and my partner about my condition
- Using humour (so important!)
- Using relaxation techniques
- Taking responsibility for myself, my condition, and my emotions
- Loving my partner with my whole heart
- Being willing to compromise

This is by no means an exhaustive list, simply a sample of the types of attitudes, approaches, and behaviours that, from my experience, hinder or help relationships.

LET'S DISCUSS

WHILE THIS CHAPTER is fairly serious, I do want to take a moment to celebrate new connections. Starting a relationship is fun and exciting. It's a time of happiness and love and exploration. Sure, it's not fair that you have to do it with all the extra challenges that chronic pain and illness bring. But this is your life, and you deserve the same happiness as anybody else. If you keep waiting until you feel better, you may wait forever. If you keep putting conditions on what needs to happen before you start a relationship, you may never start one. Yes, you have pain and discomfort, and yet you still want to live fully, so do that! Have fun, enjoy, and allow yourself to be transported by new love and passion. This is a wonderful time!

That said, if you're experiencing a particularly bad flare-up, it's entirely reasonable to wait until it passes or you're able to manage your pain to a reasonable level before starting a relationship. It's not realistic to begin a relationship when you're in the depths of pain, because you need energy to give to your partner. When you're in a flare-up, you don't have anything to give—no time, no energy, and certainly not enough love. This is an example of a time when consciously choosing not to enter into a relationship may be the most loving thing you can do for yourself.

Ok, back to work. If you're starting a relationship while experiencing chronic pain and illness, there are more issues for you to consider than for someone who isn't. All the common concerns are there: financial, cultural, religious, political, geographic, children from previous relationships, custody issues, personality conflicts, old baggage, and more. Those potentially come with all relationships, so I'm not going to spend much time looking at them. What's important are the differences that you face due to your condition. On top of the usual, you also have to deal with:

- Avoiding the rescuer
- Physical limitations
- Social implications
- Expectations that your partner be your caregiver
- Further financial limitations
- Mental and emotional impacts
- Sexual limitations
- Having enough quality time together

- Communicating about the pain and illness
- The need for understanding and validation

I strongly encourage you to talk about these topics with your partner once you decide to become exclusive. The more communication around them, the better.

The Challenges

Usually once you've been dating for a while, there's a point where you have "the talk" about being exclusive. This is when you decide whether you're going to embark on a relationship or jump ship. It's a good time to talk about expectations, as well as how your condition is currently affecting your relationship and how it may challenge your relationship in the future. Both of you need to be very clear on expectations; having a realistic understanding of what each other is capable of and willing to do is invaluable.

This is not the time to minimize symptoms or gloss over the seriousness of your health status. Yes, this is a scary conversation to have, because you're opening yourself up to possible rejection (you may want to review Chapter 6 and any writing you've done in response to that chapter if you know you're about to have "the talk," to make sure you feel ready to handle the possibility of rejection). However, it is an absolutely necessary conversation because it sets the tone for the rest of your relationship. By having this discussion, you will be managing your partner's expectations about your abilities and needs and about what type of relationship he can expect with you. You'll also be showing him that communication is important, that you're willing to delve into these conversations, and that you need him to be willing to have these conversations, too. Save yourself a lot of headaches: figure out, *before* you commit, whether you and your partner are prepared to deal fully with your condition together.

Engaging in such discussions may not seem sexy, glamorous, or cool, but it's important. Yes, it can be uncomfortable and awkward, especially at first. In the long run, though, it will absolutely pay off to regularly talk about your health condition and the challenges it presents to your relationship—and yes, the talks do get easier.

We're now going to look a little more deeply into the special challenges that face couples dealing with chronic pain and illness.

Beware the Rescuer

"The rescuer" is the guy who wants to save you. He wants to take care of you and meet all of your needs himself. He wants to be the hero. Sound too good to be true? That's because it is. What he's actually offering is a co-dependent relationship.

A co-dependent relationship is one in which one partner (the rescuer/caregiver/fixer/co-dependent) has an excessive emotional or psychological reliance on the other partner, typically one with an illness or addiction. Rescuers are people who have learned to "live their lives through others" as a coping mechanism—or, worse, a survival technique. For these people, being needed equals being loved.

Rescuers and co-dependent relationships go together like bread and butter. The central theme of these relationships is: "If you need me, you'll never leave me." As a result, the rescuers go in search of potential partners who are sick, wounded, addicted, and/or needy. This gives them the upper hand and allows them to maintain the pretence of having self-esteem, something they are severely lacking.

The problem with you entering into a relationship with a rescuer is that he will be invested in you remaining ill and needing his help and care. He wants to be who you rely on—completely. If you get better and no longer "need" him, there is a good chance the relationship will fall apart.

In a co-dependent relationship, "taking care" of you will often involve him taking control and denying you power. He wants to look good not only in your eyes, but in everyone else's, too. You needing him allows him to feel important. Sure, rescuers are willing partners, but the price is high: your disempowerment and the stress of a dysfunctional relationship.

Don't get me wrong, though. Rescuers are not evil or the enemy. Co-dependency is fairly common. Rescuers have often suffered severe emotional trauma, usually in the form of an abusive parent who was not capable of providing the affection and emotional connection necessary to show how to love in a healthy way. As a result, they tend to have low self-esteem and high self-loathing. They try to fill the hole they feel inside with something or someone else. They are constantly trying to give others what they did not receive as children. They get their sense of self-worth from people and things outside of themselves, and they do this by seeking others' approval, by attending to others' needs, by ignoring their own needs, and by getting into relationships with people whom they see as in need of being taken care of, rescued, or fixed.

When entering into a relationship, be wary. Ask yourself:

who is this person, and why is he willing to take on my condition? Make sure it's for the right reasons—that he likes you as a person and loves you for who you really are. If someone wants to be with you because you have this chronic condition and you are his next project, then run, wheel, crawl, or call a taxi, and get away as fast as you can!

Physical Limitations

Often it's the physical limitations arising from your condition that can cause some of the biggest relationship challenges. Your physical abilities determine what you and your partner are able to do together, and also the things you're able to do on your own that either indirectly or directly contribute to the relationship. A healthy person can, on her own, work and make a living, run errands, visit friends and family, go to her own medical appointments, and generally get on with the process of everyday living in a very independent way. If you have chronic pain, you may not be able to work and that lack of income can have a deep impact on your relationship. If you are not very mobile, you may need help when you leave the house, and you might be unable to run errands, visit people, and go to appointments on your own. Needing help to do these basic things can put stress on the relationship, but that isn't a foregone conclusion.

In terms of what you can do as a couple, your physical limitations may affect tasks you could normally do together, such as grocery shopping and household chores. And what about activities that you'd like to share—cooking, going to concerts and other events, seeing movies, travelling, hiking, kayaking, even just going for an evening walk? Your ability to participate in these activities may be seriously diminished; maybe you can't participate at all.

And isn't that just the worst? That's what I really struggle with. I want to get out there and have a good time—go to comedy shows and concerts and sporting events. I don't want to have to worry about how long the event is and what the seats are like and where the bathroom is. But I *do* have to know these things and make decisions accordingly. I want to be a regular person who can go to a music concert and spontaneously decide afterwards to eat dinner at a restaurant that's a 20-minute walk away. Realistically, though? I'm only going to a concert if the music is nice and soft (and what are the odds of that?). And eating after the concert, if it's an evening concert...? Nope. I ate my dinner at 6pm, as I do every day, and there's no way that (a) I'd have lasted until after concert to eat dinner, and (b) I'd have enough energy after the concert to go out for a meal. I mean, it's bedtime!

For years I found things like this to be so incredibly unfair, until a switch flicked in my brain. One day, I suddenly understood: "This is my life now, and there is no point in comparing myself with anyone else." Once I stopped comparing myself with "normal" people, I was so much happier, so much more willing to accept my life and be able to find joy in what I *could* do. I stopped constantly thinking of all the things I couldn't do and started listing everything that was still possible. I was surprised by the amount and the diversity, especially given how much I had told myself I couldn't do (pretty much everything). But I was wrong. Question your thoughts, and focus on everything that you *can* do—on your own and with your partner.

The silver lining when it comes to starting a relationship when you already have chronic pain is that you can share your physical abilities and limitations with your prospective partner from the get-go. You can set and manage his expectations more easily, and you don't have to deal with a major adjustment in a pre-existing relationship. Of course, if you have a flare-up during a new relationship, that does change things, but at least you will have had the chance to prepare your partner for what may be to come. By educating him on what your life is like, you also give him the opportunity to decide early on whether this is something he can cope with. Some people may not want this in their lives. And as much as it may hurt if they tell you that, it's considerably better to find out early on in the relationship that someone isn't willing to modify his life to accommodate your physical abilities than to discover this ten years down the line, when there is a lot more riding on the relationship: shared assets, maybe children, and a life that you have settled into and expected to continue for the rest of your days.

Put it out there, be honest about what you can and can't do. Conversely, if your partner is willing to enter into this relationship, be the best you can be. Help when you can. Focus on what you *are* able to do. Show him lots of love. Set your physical boundaries, but don't be a drama queen about them.

Social Implications

Most human beings are pretty social people who want others around us—friends, family, co-workers, acquaintances, and so on. You may have found, though, that after the chronic pain or illness started, your social circle shrank. You weren't able to participate in as many activities; you couldn't be as social as before because you needed to be at home resting or in a comfortable (or at least less painful) position.

During my worst flare-ups, I've often felt extremely alone and wondered where my friends had gone. They hadn't *all* abandoned me; I have a small, very loyal circle of friends who have stuck with me through some pretty dark times, and I love them for it. But outside of that group, people disappeared. This is not uncommon for people in our situation. Chronic pain and illness can be quite isolating.

What happens when your partner doesn't have physical limitations and still wants to experience a fulfilling social life in which you can't participate? This is tricky. It requires communication, understanding and compromise on both sides.

It's important that you and your partner talk about what you both need socially. He likely will want and need to do more than you are able. You have to understand that it's important for your partner to go out, have fun, and blow off steam with his friends. Doing that will help him feel happier and better about himself, and this will have a positive trickle-down effect on your relationship. If you force him to stay at home because you must, he'll become resentful and angry at being cut off from the people and activities he enjoys.

At the same time, he will need to understand that it's hard for you to stay home while he goes out with his friends and has fun. This is where there is some room for compromise. Maybe he will go out a little less frequently than he did before he met you. Maybe you will be willing to encourage him to go and have a good time when (or before) you sense strain in the relationship. And maybe, by working together, the two of you can come up with some creative solutions, such as having friends over, and hosting social occasions that you can attend more easily than if they were not at your home.

Caregiver Expectations

One of my biggest fears is being a burden. I think it probably relates to my mother being ill with cancer for seven years and, later, my father having cancer for five years. Neither of them wanted to be a burden either, but let's be honest: a sick family member is a burden, regardless of how much we love and are willing to care for them. I have read that caregivers to aging spouses have, on average, lower life expectancy due to the stress. And according to WebMD (webmd.com), studies show that partners who are caregivers are six times more likely to be depressed than partners who do not need to be caregivers.

Being a caregiver can be physically exhausting, mentally frustrating, and emotionally draining. It was for me, and I wasn't even the primary caregiver for either of my parents. I don't want anyone to feel around me the way I felt around my parents when it came to caregiving. I want to be independent and self-sustaining, dammit! But the truth is that when I am in a relationship my partner becomes, to some extent, a caregiver.

Your condition may be such that you don't need much help—perhaps love, comfort, and understanding are enough. On the other hand, you may need quite a bit of help with a wide range of tasks. Depending on the severity of your condition, the level of support you have in your life, and your financial circumstances, your new partner may well be faced with some degree of caregiving responsibilities.

It's important to disclose this before getting too deeply

into a relationship because, the fact is, partners of those with chronic pain and illness often face more challenges than if they were in a relationship with someone without pain or illness. They may have to take on extra household, parenting, and financial responsibilities. They may also have to deal with possible difficulties around intimacy and sex. It's no walk in the park. And that's not all. Often partners of those living with chronic pain provide most of the emotional support for their loved one. Doing all of this on a daily basis can introduce a great deal of stress to a relationship.

So what is the answer? **Your partner should not be your primary caregiver.** He should be your *partner*. Once he steps into a caregiving role, the dynamics in the relationship change, and the balance of power shifts in his favour. This can easily create a co-dependent relationship and/or resentment on your partner's end, something you want to avoid. He should also not be your only source of emotional support. That is a huge burden to place on one person.

What works best is separating your romantic relationship from the caregiver and emotional support roles and finding other people to fill those roles, such as a friend, family member, volunteer, care aid, nurse, or community health worker. Some of these options will depend on your financial situation. Either way, no *one* person can do everything for you, especially not your partner. Given this information, you may find that you need to adjust your expectations regarding your partner's caregiving role and the degree of emotional support you request from him. The less he needs to do to take care of you vis-à-vis your condition, the better.

Of course, there may always be small tasks that he does

for you, like cooking dinner or driving, but those are different than him (literally) feeding you, changing your dressings, organizing your prescriptions, or setting up your medical visits.

Establish early on who will be your primary caregiver and who is in your support network (pull out that sheet on which you listed the people that make up your foundation of support, then lean on them). And keep in mind: even if your partner is willing to take on a large role in your caregiving, your relationship will be much healthier and resilient if you do not allow him to do so.

It might seem unnecessary to discuss caregiving expectations and plans at the beginning of a new relationship, because everything is going well and you're both so infatuated with each other that it feels like love will conquer all. (That's been one of my favourite fantasies.) It's important, though, to address the subject of caregiving expectations and support plans and be very clear on what you need and expect from your partner. Your relationship will have a much greater chance of succeeding if you talk about all of these issues ahead of time and when they subsequently come up. If you ignore them, you tend to get a lot more nasty surprises than if you deal with them on a regular basis and know where the issues are at, rather than allowing yourself to let them swing around and smack you on the flipside.

Either way you cut it, your partner will likely end up doing more for you than if you were not living with chronic pain and illness. So what can you do to make things easier on your partner? Aside from forbidding him to be your primary caregiver, love him deeply and completely. Show him your respect and gratitude. Help out when you feel up to it. That might mean washing the dishes once in a while or popping out to the store if you have the energy. It may mean giving him a back rub after a long day. Listen to *his* troubles, be interested in his life and hobbies, and support him. His troubles are no less important than yours, and he also requires bolstering and encouragement from his intimate partner. Listening is a wonderful gift that you can give your partner. Active listening—when you focus completely on what he is saying and give him all your attention—is a powerful tool that helps the speaker feel truly understood.

Further Financial Limitations

I love to spend money. It's exciting. It makes me feel happy and alive, and I often have something awesome to show for it, like new clothes or jewellery or perfume. I used to work in law and was pretty much able to buy whatever I wanted, within reason. After I became ill, I left work and suddenly found myself on a tight budget. Not fun! But even though there was much less money coming in, I still felt that I was entitled to spend as usual, like $50 on my favourite shampoo and conditioner. It took me about two to three years to adjust to the idea that I was financially restricted. It seemed so unfair, and I felt quite angry. This damn pain was taking away my life! I felt inferior to my friends and less desirable as a woman and life partner.

When I finally accepted my condition, I also accepted my financial limitations and realized I had some pretty twisted beliefs about money. I still love to spend, but now I find joy in smaller things, like buying the $5 shampoo instead, especially if it smells like coconut.

If you're suffering from chronic pain or illness, chances are you're not able to work full-time and may not be earning what you did before you became ill. That is a huge adjustment. If you're not working, you may be on disability or some other form of social assistance and likely not receiving as much as you would earn were you working. You may not be able to contribute to household costs as much as you would like, such as food and utility bills—not to mention date nights and other things you and your partner would like to do for fun. There may also be an additional strain due to hospital bills, prescriptions, other medical costs, or alternative therapies. Being sick is not cheap.

So what does this mean for your relationship?

It means being honest and getting clear with yourself about your financial situation, needs, and outlook. It means figuring out what your financial expectations are of your partner. And then it means communicating those matters to him. This is especially important if you are moving in together or getting married and plan on maintaining a household together. Being honest about your debts is crucial. Money is one of the number one stressors in relationships, so if you start out with clear and honest communication on this topic, you're beginning on a good footing. From there, the two of you can develop a plan for how you wish to handle your finances—whether that means keeping things separate, allocating a percentage of expenses based on ability to pay, or pooling your resources. Remember to keep communicating about finances openly as frequently as needed.

Mental and Emotional Impact

The mental and emotional impact of chronic pain and illness on the sufferer can be tremendous. The impact on your partner can also be significant, so the relationship exists in more tenuous conditions than you would otherwise expect.

I go through a huge range of emotions on a daily basis. Distress, sadness, frustration, anger, calm, happiness, insecurity, joy, and so on. Sometimes I find it easier not to be in a relationship because dealing with these emotions can be overwhelming. My ability to cope with emotions and situations is reduced due to the pain I have been experiencing for so long, and I don't always know how to navigate these emotions within a relationship. Plus, adding a relationship can give rise to additional devastating emotions: intense insecurity, fear of abandonment, inadequacy, guilt, the need for control, and dependency. I also find that I start to make more assumptions, and become a little less trusting and more suspicious. "Why is this guy dating *me* when he could have someone without all these physical and emotional issues?" Sometimes I start to wonder whether being in a relationship is actually worthwhile. Then I remember how wonderful it is to be loved and supported, to have a best friend, to feel as though I'm part of something bigger than myself. Nothing replaces that intense feeling of being intimately and closely connected with another human being. For me, it's worth muddling through the emotions to have a loving partner.

Here's what I've discovered: all the assumptions, distrust, suspicions, insecurity, inadequacy, fear of abandonment, and all those other crazy things my brain likes to stir up can often be blown out of the water by an honest and loving conversation with my partner. When I share my anxieties and fears and then hear how he actually feels, I can challenge my distorted beliefs and then change them so that I have a more positive understanding of our relationship. In this way, changing my thoughts leads to emotional relief.

Another emotional trap involves pretending to be fine.

Often people with chronic pain and illness do their best to pretend they're ok. Pretending to be fine when you're not is exhausting, stressful, and increases pain. The toll it takes on your body can make you feel even worse, and then you're more likely to be emotionally reactive. You may become quick to anger or tears; you may lash out. Again, the best thing to do is communicate. Let your partner know when you're having a bad day and that you need a bit of extra space—or a bit more support, an extra hug. Try to communicate how you're feeling *when* you're feeling it so you don't end up having a blow up later on.

I don't think it is possible to go overboard on the numerous things that you can do to build a good relationship. According to Dr. John Gottman, Clinical Psychologist and Professor Emeritus of Psychology at the University of Washington, where he founded the "Love Lab" at which much of his research on couples' interactions was conducted, for every one negative interaction a couple has, they need to have five positive interactions to feel good about their relationship. Five!

If you're not feeling well, and you're grouchy and acting like a temperamental four-year-old (I speak from personal experience) because life is unfair and you're trapped in this body, that doesn't give you the right to take it out on anybody, including your partner. Still, these things do happen, and when they do, once you're in a better state of body and mind, apologize to your partner! Remember: *five* positive interactions for every one negative interaction. And no, apologizing five times doesn't count. Unexpected hugs and kisses count, as do compliments, acknowledgements, and recognition. Small thoughtful gifts and little surprises can also go a long way.

In the "Communicate" and "Take Action" sections below, I'll talk more about effective and open communication, including how to apologize.

Sexual Limitations

We've already taken an in-depth look at sex in the previous chapter, but it bears repeating that it's important to be up front about your sexual limitations before starting a relationship. By telling your partner where you're at sexually, you're establishing trust through your honesty.

If you have sexual limitations due to your condition, be open to being creative. Work together with your partner as a team to come up with alternatives. And if he tells you he needs sexual fulfillment in a way that you can't accommodate, accept and respect this. Better he be honest now before getting too far into the relationship, than have tension build around sex-related issues for months or even years, only to have the relationship fall apart after all the time and work you've both invested.

Keep up the communication around what is happening inside you in terms of your feelings, emotions, and symptoms. Your partner may misread your pain or frustration with your condition as you being angry with him. Pair this with the decreased libido that often comes with pain and/ or medication for pain, and your partner may start to feel rejected, disconnected, shut out, or alienated. It's difficult to get in the mood when you're physically uncomfortable and exhausted, and there is no shame in that. The thing is, your partner needs to know about this so he doesn't have to wonder whether it's his fault that there's no fire in your engine.

Be aware, too, that in the beginning stages of a relationship, both of you may genuinely believe that your sexual limitations are manageable. In the honeymoon stage of a relationship, we are often "blinded by love" and don't think altogether logically. There is a chance that after the honeymoon, your partner may realize that your physical relationship isn't working for him. It's a risk we take when we get into relationships, whether we live with chronic pain and illness or not.

Availability of Quality Time Together

When you're dealing with chronic pain or illness, you may have less quality time to spend with your partner.

So what are some solutions?

Make your quality time together the best it can be. Do things together that bond you but that don't push you to overdo it. Find common interests. The key is to find something that the two of you can do where you are actually interacting with each other. If you're watching a movie or playing video games, you aren't getting that same connection. Perhaps it's as simple as reading and then discussing the books you read. Or maybe both of you like to go for walks or cook together. Something I like to do at the end of each day is lie in bed with my partner and talk. I ask him to tell me about his day and actively listen as he answers. I then ask him to tell me three good things that happened that day; when he's done, he does the same for me. It's such a nice way to come together in the evening, enjoy quality time together, and strengthen our bond.

While time together is important, it's also vital to also have time apart. As I mentioned earlier, it's valuable for your partner to get out and engage in his hobbies and with his friends. It's also crucial for you to have your time to do your own thing—spend time with *your* friends, pursue *your* interests. Spending time apart can enhance the quality time you spend together. If you both engage in your own hobbies and interests and see your own friends, you will be happier over all, and that can only help your relationship. Your quality time with him will be so much better if you are both happy coming into it.

Communicating About the Pain and Illness

I've already talked quite a bit about communication because it is the most important ingredient for any successful, thriving relationship. If you already find it easy to discuss how your condition may impact your relationship, then that's great. If not, now is the time to work on your communication skills. This will take effort, but will be worth it.

What does healthy communication look like? Good question. Here's what it's not: It's not listing your symptoms and medications and detailing your medical appointments to your partner on a daily basis. It's not whining, demanding, criticizing, blaming, complaining, or having a pity party. By all means, if you need a pity party, throw one, but be the only guest and end early.

Healthy communication includes:

1. Listening to your partner—and I mean *really* listening. Stop yourself from thinking of what you are going to say next or how you are going to defend yourself. Listen to hear what your partner is saying, feeling, and wishing you to understand. You will have your chance to talk, but listening is more important. If you both make listening a priority, you'll both feel heard, acknowledged, and understood, which can go a long way.

2. Validating or acknowledging what your partner has said. After he speaks, summarize and repeat back what you understood him to say. Validate his emotions by verbally acknowledging his success, struggles, stress, excitement, or whatever else he is feeling. This is all about him, not you (not yet). Summarizing is an especially useful tool if you find yourself feeling defensive as a result of what he has said. When we feel defensive about what someone is saying, we tend to stop hearing what they're trying to tell us. By repeating back what we think we've heard, we don't immediately jump to the defensive, and we have the opportunity to check our understanding of what was said.

3. Expressing your feelings in a responsible way. This means that you own your feelings and take responsibility for yourself. When you say how you're feeling, it's all about you: "I'm sad. I'm frustrated. I'm feeling angry, and I need some space right now." It does not include blaming your partner for how you're feeling, taking your feelings out on him, projecting your feelings onto him, or criticizing him.

Keep in mind that nobody can "make" you feel a certain way. I know it can really seem that *they're* making you feel angry or frustrated or upset, but you always have a choice about how you react to others. Recall Don Miguel Ruiz telling us to not take things personally because it's never about us. If your partner says something ignorant about your condition, for example, you can choose to be angry and take it personally, or you can choose to have compassion for him because he doesn't understand, and what he said is not about you, it's about him. Which choice do you think will benefit your health and well-being in the long run?

As adults, we need to take responsibility for our emotions and how we express them. Responsible expression of emotions means not directing your emotions *at* anyone— and by emotions I mean here the anger and frustration that chronic pain can bring. Directing love, caring, and kindness at others is a different matter, and in that case, knock yourself out! Also, check out the Take Action! section to learn how to express your love for your partner in his love language.

When you have distressing emotions, contain them until either you're able to express them responsibly around others, you're alone and can kick pillows and scream, or you're with your counsellor and can cry and rant as much as you want. Learning to express your feelings in a responsible way is a loving act that you can do for your intimate relationship.

4. Being honest. I used to lie a lot. I didn't even realize I was doing it—these little lies would just fly out of my mouth. I'd lie about silly stuff, like whether I'd emptied the dishwasher or whether I'd heard what my boyfriend had said to me. It wasn't until one of my partners called me out on it that I even knew I was doing it. Where did I get this habit? I'm not entirely sure, but I think it was the result of watching my father, who seemed to have had the same strange habit, and also an attempt to evade punishment from a very strict mother. At any rate, this was a pretty easy habit to break because I wasn't actually protecting myself from major consequences. Much harder for me was being honest about my feelings and about relationship issues. I wouldn't necessarily lie, but I would be dishonest by omission. I was so worried that if I upset my partner at all, he would leave me. Many of us have abandonment issues, and they can run deep. I needed professional help to overcome this fear, and perhaps you could benefit from that, too.

Communicating honestly about the relationship you're in can be scary, but it will yield positive results. Honesty will bring you closer, deepen your connection, and build trust—exactly the opposite of what you probably fear.

5. Asking for what you need. Asking for help can be really hard. It's also something you need to learn how to do, especially if you have chronic pain and illness. I've noticed that we often expect our partners to know what we need and provide it for us without us even saying a word. The thing is, your partner can't read your mind; he can't anticipate what you need and do what you want him to do *without* you asking out loud. It doesn't mean he loves you any less, it means he's human.

There's so much more chance that you're going to get what you need if you ask for it than if you don't, whether it's a grocery run, a ride to your medical appointment, or a back rub. Ask your partner for what you need; invite him to meet that need, and be respectful if he declines. Just because we ask doesn't mean our partner is required to comply. And if he turns down your request, please don't give up. That's just one request. Keep asking for what you need.

6. Apologizing when appropriate. It can be easy to get grouchy and snappy when you're in a lot of pain. No matter how much we work at expressing our emotions responsibly, there will still be times when we snap, lash out, or say something we regret. This is why apologies are very important. We tend to underestimate the power and importance of a sincere apology. It can be a simple, straightforward expression of the fact that you are sorry for your behaviour. You don't need to include an excuse or a reminder of what the other person may have done before your behaviour—it's actually better if you don't. According to Dr. Gary Chapman, author of *The Five Love Languages*, there are five apology languages—five types of apology—and not everybody responds to every type:

1. Expressing regret—e.g., "I am sorry."
2. Accepting responsibility—e.g., "I was wrong."
3. Making restitution—e.g., "What can I do to make it right?"
4. Genuinely repenting—e.g., "I'll try not to do that again."
5. Requesting forgiveness—e.g., "Will you please forgive me?"

Dr. Chapman says, "The key to good relationships is learning the apology language of the other person and being willing to speak it. When you speak their primary language, you make it easier for them to genuinely forgive you. When you fail to speak their language, it makes forgiveness more difficult because they are not sure if you are genuinely apologizing." In my experience, you may need to hear a combination of two or three of the apology languages to feel the apology is genuine.

The apology languages are a fantastic tool because they really work. You can find out more about them in Dr. Chapman's book with Jennifer Thomas, *The Five Languages of Apology*, and in the Take Action! section below.

Needing Understanding and Validation

When you are in a romantic relationship, you might become tempted to get into the details of your condition on a daily basis with your partner because you want him to really understand what you are going though. It's not unusual for people with chronic pain or illness to look for validation and understanding from loved ones. Having an empathetic partner who understands your condition to some degree makes things a lot easier. However, even the most caring and empathetic person is not going to understand what it's really like to be you, and no amount of explaining and educating is going to make it so. Putting that expectation on your partner is giving him a heavy load to carry.

Instead of spending your precious energy on trying to get your partner to understand your condition, how about giving the understanding, acceptance and validation to yourself? If this seems like an impossible task, ask yourself:

- Why do I need him to understand every little detail?
- What am I actually getting out of it?
- What is he getting out of it?

The more you can let go of searching outside yourself for understanding and validation, the more peaceful you will feel, especially if you work on giving yourself those things. And if you really need more than you can give yourself, consider seeking out friends with similar conditions, or a support group in which people truly will understand what you're going through and be much more able to effectively validate your feelings and experiences.

TAKE ACTION!

1. Beware the rescuer. Check in with why this person is entering a relationship with you, and make sure it's for the right reasons. Avoid men who want to save you, fix you, or be your primary caregiver.

2. Communicate! I know you knew this was coming. If you take only one thing away from this book, I hope it's the importance of communication in relationships. Whether it's about physical limitations, social issues, caregiving, finances, emotions, sex, quality time, pain, expectations, or anything else, when you talk to your partner, be clear, direct, honest, compassionate, and kind. And please do talk about these issues with your partner on an ongoing basis. Address problems as they come up. You aren't the only one who is suffering because of your condition, so listen attentively. Ask for what you need, don't tell or demand. Avoid blaming, shaming, and criticizing. Express how your partner's behaviour affects you, without attacking or commenting on his character. How do you do this? See number three.

3. Use the feedback formula. I talked about this in Chapter 2, but it's worth repeating here. Using this communication tool is an easy way to improve your communication *immediately.* You can use it to communicate about anything, from household chores to sex. Its great strength is that it addresses behaviour, not character. When we start making judgments on or attacking other people's characters, they immediately become defensive or just shut down. In either case, they stop listening. To keep your partner engaged in the conversation, try this approach. Here it is again, so you don't have to flip back to Chapter 2:

When you_____(describe the person's behaviour),
I feel _____(describe the emotion you feel).
The result is _____(describe the effect of that emotion).
Would you be willing to _____(make your request)?

For example, if my partner didn't take out the garbage on his way to work, I would say:

When you leave the garbage in the kitchen before going to work, I feel frustrated and exhausted.
The result is that I'm starting to become more and more resentful of you, and I really don't want to feel that way.
Would you be willing to take the garbage out when you go to work?

The reason this tool works so well is that the person you're addressing learns how his behaviour is impacting you. Most people don't want to be responsible for creating negative emotions in others and are quite willing to adjust their behaviour for the sake of the relationship. Once in a while, you may not get the answer you want, but you have said how you feel, and hopefully you've been heard. You can also use this formula for positive behaviour that your partner does that you want to reinforce. Sticking to the formula when you're first learning it is helpful; once you get the hang of it, you can reword it a bit and make it sound a little more fluid.

4. Express your emotions responsibly. Sometimes when you get overwhelmed with pain and fatigue and you feel grouchy, cranky, and crunchy, the temptation to take it out on someone else can be very strong, especially someone who's super-healthy and ultra-happy. But this momentary desire to lash out ends in regret more often than not. So when you want to whine and complain and bitch and moan, try something else:

   a. Pick up a journal or diary and write about it. I'm not talking about "dear diary" kind of writing, I'm talking about "fuck the world" writing. Bitch, moan, and bellyache. Complain about all of your symptoms. All the stuff you want to take out on someone else, take out on your journal. You might be sceptical about this technique, but you may also be surprised at how much better you feel after a session with your journal. I encourage you to give it a try.

   b. Scream into a pillow.

   c. Punch pillows and kick your bed, if you are physically able.

These techniques are best used when you are alone, without anyone to watch or hear what you're doing. Do whatever it takes to let off some steam and get the anger and frustration out, as long as no one (including you) gets hurt and it's not illegal!

5. Actively love your partner. Given that you need to have five positive interactions for every one negative interaction for both of you to feel good about your relationship, focus on showing your love for your partner and having as many positive interactions as possible. In order to do this effectively, it is helpful to learn your partner's love languages. These languages were developed by Dr. Gary Chapman, who maintains that there are five different ways to express love. Each person has a primary love language (or a couple of top ones) that we need to learn to speak if we want our partner to feel loved. The Five Love Languages are:

1. **Words of affirmation**—e.g., "Thank you for caring about how I feel."; "What a super job, that looks fantastic!"; "You're a great kisser."
2. **Acts of service**—e.g., washing the car, driving you to appointments.
3. **Receiving gifts**—e.g., a chocolate bar, flowers, a card. These don't have to be elaborate or extravagant; it's the thought that counts.
4. **Quality time**—e.g., giving your partner your undivided attention (that means no distractions, including the TV!)
5. **Physical touch**—e.g., holding hands, kissing, sex.

Learn your partner's love language, and share yours with him. Expressing your love to your partner in his language is powerful—and vice versa. He will feel more loved by you when you communicate with him in his language. You can take the Love Languages test together at 5lovelanguages. com. Once you're familiar with your partner's love language, use it!

6. Work on your social lives. I can't prepare you for every eventuality, but I can suggest the following:

a. Openly discuss your challenges around socializing.
b. Understand your partner's needs; they are just as important as your own. Make sure your partner is getting enough social interaction with friends and family. This will benefit your relationship as a whole, even if it might not feel like that while you are at home alone. Recognizing that your partner should be free to do things for himself is one of the best things you can do for him and your relationship.
c. Come up with creative solutions so that you can both socialize together in a way that is manageable for you. Compromise as well, but when you do, make sure both of you are ok with the new plan.

7. Learn your partner's apology language(s) and share yours with him. You can take the Apology Languages Test together at 5lovelanguages.com/profile/apology. Once you're familiar with your partner's apology language, use it!

8. Seek additional professional help if needed. Being in a relationship is hard. Being in a relationship when you have chronic pain and illness adds another layer of difficulty. Sometimes what I have offered you might not feel like enough, and you may need some extra help to get through rough spots. Counselling can be extremely helpful in navigating relationships—overcoming challenges, strengthening your connection with your partner, and creating a solid and lasting partnership. There is absolutely no shame in getting some extra help. In fact it might be the best thing that you do for your relationship.

INCORPORATING THE STRATEGIES presented in this section will get you on the road to a successful relationship. Just as you created a solid foundation for yourself before you started dating, it's best if you begin creating a solid foundation with your partner as soon as you commit to a relationship. The basic tools for creating that foundation are found in this chapter, the most important one being clear, honest communication. And if something comes up in your communication with your partner that sets off a red flag, alerting your intuition that something isn't right, don't ignore it. You haven't come this far just to take a giant leap back. *Trust yourself.*

CHAPTER 11

When Pain Begins During a Relationship

MY STORY

CHRONIC PAIN CAN, and often does, lead to the breakdown of relationships. It's not fair, and it's downright scary at times. I was terrified when my doctor told me this 20 years ago, and as a result I clung to my marriage with all I had. I went for counselling, I went to see a myriad of doctors for second and third opinions, I went to alternative medicine to look for answers, and I tried to include my husband, Rob, in as much of this as possible. He didn't seem particularly interested. He came to counselling appointments reluctantly, and when I asked him whether we could practice the exercises our counsellor had given us, he refused. I reminded him that at our last session, he had agreed to do them, and Rob replied, "I just said I would to shut you both up."

Hmm… not looking too good, right? Rob was often late for other medical appointments I asked him to attend, and I felt that we were really not a team. He wanted me to be "fixed" so we could have sex again, whereas I was going down a completely different road of personal growth. Of course I wanted my pain to go away so that I could have sex again, but I was also embarking on a healing journey that was not only physical but also mental, emotional, and spiritual. The more I progressed, the further apart we drifted, because he wasn't willing to do the work and grow with me. Our relationship ended after six years.

The thing is, we didn't have a strong relationship to start with and I don't think it would have lasted too much longer, anyway.

Years later, I fell in love with Jack. Things were going well—no, more than well. We were thinking this could be it. We were talking marriage. We talked about the future quite a bit, actually. He gave me a promise ring. We were going to get a goat and call him Steve, our cat would be called Doug, and our dog would be called Wayne. We had our whole stable planned out. The sex was pretty good, as I had the pain under control at that point. Things were going along swimmingly, apart from one obstacle: birth control. We didn't want to rely on condoms, I had been on a number of contraceptive pills (talk about crazy side-effects), and I had even tried the NuvaRing. After two months on that, I felt utterly crazy and was convinced men had invented hormonal birth control for women as a conspiracy to keep them subjugated and disempowered. Good-bye NuvaRing.

What was left? Intrauterine devices. My doctor refused to set me up with one because he would only put them in women who had already had at least one baby. But I was determined. What did he know anyway? He was old school and close to retirement. A friend's doctor was willing to do the procedure, so I threw caution to the wind and went to get the IUD.

Prior to the procedure, I had a feeling that this might not be a good choice for me. I already knew that I was extremely sensitive, and had a feeling that inserting a foreign copper object into a delicate area of my body was probably a bad idea. But I felt I had no other choice—there were no other birth control options, or so I thought.

Three weeks after I got the IUD I was in agony. I had a massive pelvic infection and so much pain that the doctors didn't know what to do with me. I ended up in the emergency room a couple of times but experienced no relief. So, after only three weeks, I had the IUD removed.

Unfortunately, that was just the beginning. As I've mentioned earlier in the book, the IUD triggered an excruciating bladder condition, and I was in intense pain for two *years* after just three weeks with that blasted device. At first I thought the infection and pain would go away pretty quickly, especially given the antibiotics I was taking, but after a few weeks of continued agony I started to worry about my relationship. What if the problem *didn't* go away? We hadn't had sex since the IUD was inserted. What if I could *never* have sex again?! My brain was working over-time—pain will do that do you.

I told Jack how scared I was about what impact the pain would have on us, and he assured me that our relationship was so much more than sex. I felt better for about an hour or two. Then the old thoughts came creeping in again: we were now doomed.

To him, I'm sure I appeared perfectly healthy. Some of

his favourite phrases included:

"You need to toughen up."

"Are you fucking kidding me?" (When I would report pain at an inopportune time for him.)

"Quit your belly-aching."

"Deal with it."

"It's all in your head."

Well, yes, Jack, it *is* all in my head, but not in the way you mean. It's in my head because my nervous system has gone haywire and the synapses in my brain are misfiring all over the place, sending pain signals to areas where there technically is no pain stimulus!

I've read that if a person doesn't believe in his partner's diagnosis, he's more prone to respond angrily rather than supportively. I'm pretty sure that's what was happening with Jack—after all, I didn't even *have* a diagnosis. The doctors kept telling me there was nothing wrong! I can understand that it may have been hard to believe the extent of the pain I was in, because on the outside I looked just the same as before the pain started, and I was able to force myself to do things regardless of the pain because I was still fairly strong, physically and emotionally.

Don't get me wrong, Jack could be very sweet. He used to make me hot water bottles every night before bed to help ease the pain in my pelvic area. I really think he tried, I really think he did his best to be supportive. But after four years without considerable improvement in my condition, I think he just ran out of patience and interest. And I really don't blame him, especially given his age. This wasn't something that most 25-year-old guys expected to have to deal with. Your 20s is a time for fun, exploration, and adventure. I *so* wanted things to be good between us, so I pushed myself. I pushed myself constantly, over and over, through the pain. I held it in, not telling him how bad it really was, and that wore me down, emotionally and physically. By the time we broke up, I was so exhausted that I felt as though a light wind would knock me over. Ending the relationship was ultimately a relief.

If I'm going to be completely honest, I don't think my relationship with Jack would have lasted even if I'd been 100% healthy the entire time. There were too many other factors working against us: our age difference (he was 10 years younger); his uncertainty about what he wanted to do with his life; my depression, finite patience, and desire to control the relationship; our dysfunctional communication style, and his consequent inability to understand what was going on in my body.

At the time of my relationship with Jack, I was physically stronger than I am now and hadn't been worn down from years and years of chronic pain and illness, so I decided to stay in the relationship when the IUD flared up my pelvis. Despite being stronger, I was often tempted to end the relationship in order to focus on my healing. I now think that would have been the wise choice, given how the relationship turned out, but I couldn't know the future and I did the best with the information and tools I had. Looking back, I would have set stronger boundaries and focused less on trying to make Jack happy. Jack wasn't happy and, healthy or not, I couldn't make him happy. It was Jack's job to make Jack happy, not mine.

After Jack, I looked at the patterns in my relationships and realized I needed to do additional work on myself if I wanted to attract a more loving and supportive partner. The relationship breakdowns had been due to me *and* my condition *and* my partner.

My most difficult relationships have been the ones in which communication was poor and pain and illness flared up during the relationship. But chances are those relationships probably wouldn't have thrived or survived had I been 100%, either, because there were no solid foundations to build on.

LET'S DISCUSS

HAVING CHRONIC PAIN develop during a relationship is a real bitch. If this has happened to you, and you picked up this book to see whether it would help, please don't read just this chapter. Even though a lot of the book is geared towards dating and starting relationships, much of what the early chapters contain is equally applicable to you—specifically, taking care of yourself physically, mentally, spiritually, and emotionally. This includes doing the work on yourself to get rid of old baggage that's holding you back, as well as creating your personal foundation. These are just a few examples of what will help you succeed in relationships, whether you are currently in one or not. I encourage you to read the book from start to finish to get the most out of it.

It's hard to say exactly what will happen in any given relationship if one partner develops chronic pain and illness. Each relationship is so unique that it's impossible to predict outcomes. However, there are several common situations that occur in many relationships when chronic pain and illness rears its ugly head. Here are a few potential scenarios:

- Your partner is supportive, and you and your partner become closer.
- Communication breaks down and becomes dysfunctional.
- Your partner is unable to provide the support you feel you need.
- Your partner is unable to deal with the situation at all.
- You are unable to deal with your partner and the situation.
- Your partner becomes invested in your illness, would rather not see you recover, and does not support your recovery process.

This is not like starting a relationship when you're already in pain and can set expectations from the beginning. When pain starts during the relationship, you and your partner are being confronted with a massive, unexpected, unwelcome change. This can be extremely trying and drive you apart. However, if you have a solid foundation to start with, and you're both communicating openly on a regular basis, it can actually bring you closer together. It really depends on the relationship that already exists.

For a relationship to survive the onset of chronic pain and illness in one of the partners, a few things are needed:

1. Good, open, honest communication.
2. Both partners being understanding, empathetic, and patient with each other.

3. The partner in chronic pain choosing an attitude of empowerment around their condition.
4. A willingness to work hard on the relationship, including both partners educating themselves on the condition.
5. A great match between two people who have created a solid relationship to start with.

According to painaction.com,[1] research has shown that some people living with chronic pain and illness report improvements in their intimate relationships, such as feeling closer, because they have faced a challenge together. And that makes sense. Facing a difficult obstacle as a team can bring you together. That's actually really good news; it tells us there is hope.

I believe that if you have a strong relationship before the pain starts, it is possible for the relationship to last. If both partners are willing to do their share of the work, as I describe throughout this book, a relationship can survive—and even thrive—despite chronic pain and illness. It *is* possible. The key is to focus on the strengths you both bring to your relationship and use those strengths to help you get through the rough spots. It's crucial that *both* partners do the work. While that sounds simple, not everyone will be up to it, for whatever reasons.

And how do you do the work? Keep reading to find out, and do the suggested homework in the Take Action! section of this chapter.

---

[1] Jonas I. Bromberg, "When Chronic Pain Gets Between You and Your Partner," *painACTION*, December 13, 2010. http://www.painaction.com/members/article.aspx?id=5043.

The Consequences of Pain and Illness Starting During a Relationship

Let's start at the beginning. You develop acute symptoms of varying types. You go through an initial period when the doctors investigate and provide you with a diagnosis—if you're lucky. Many people endure years of chronic pain and illness and see a seemingly infinite number of doctors before finally learning what is causing the problem.

Throughout the process, you and your partner hope and believe that all you need is the right medication or answer and you'll be back to normal. At first, your healthy partner's response is often extreme sympathy and loving support. But when the acute becomes chronic, and it's difficult to get a diagnosis, credibility issues may arise. It's really hard for people to remember how much pain, discomfort, and distress you're experiencing when you look essentially "normal." Your partner may not believe your pain is legit. Chronic pain and illness can have an especially toxic effect on your relationship if your partner is sceptical about your pain or condition. He might think you're faking it or being lazy. If your partner doesn't believe in your pain, you'll probably feel unsupported and misunderstood. This is often why we feel we need so badly for our partners to fully understand what we are experiencing, because if they *really got it*, they would no longer be sceptical about the severity of our conditions.

After several months, it becomes harder for your partner to be sympathetic, because he's tired of what is going on and is being asked/forced to make an unwanted lifestyle adjustment. Time goes on, and nothing changes; maybe your condition even worsens. And there are no answers. No solutions.

Not having an end date for the condition makes it difficult. If you knew you were going to have surgery three months from now that would fix the problem, no worries. But not knowing when—or if—it's going to end? A sympathy-gobbling black hole can develop in you, and your partner may become resentful as a result (been there, done that).

Aside from the physical issues, you likely will not feel the way you did mentally and emotionally before you became ill either. Over time, the pain and illness may lead to problems with your partner around communicating, and around managing feelings like anger, frustration, and depression. And who could blame either of you? It *is* frustrating, anger-provoking, and depressing!

Your partner may not know how to handle the changes in your personality or how to endure watching your suffering on a daily basis. You're not the person he used to know. You've changed. The pain and illness have changed you. Your partner may become overwhelmed by your fluctuating emotions, pain, sadness, and suffering and find it more difficult to be around you and provide support. If you're not feeling enough support, chances are you're not able to fully support your partner either, and so this becomes a vicious cycle. On top of that, if you're not having good, clear, open, and honest communication, you end up in a downward spiral.

Your self-esteem takes a beating, and now you may feel undesirable, so you pull away from your partner. Awareness that your physical and emotional distance is hurting your partner may add to your anxiety, fear, and guilt. Talk about a dog pile of stress! This stress not only can worsen underlying difficulties in your relationship but also intensify your pain and other symptoms.

The strongest relationships can still be challenged by chronic pain or illness. Yes, it's true. Even if your relationship was healthy and solid to start with, things can get difficult. One or both of you may feel trapped, helpless, or out of control. This is not uncommon. Pain causes emotional distress for the person in pain, and that causes emotional distress for the partner—and then distress bounces back and forth like a ping pong ball. That's a lot of distress to deal with.

There are many other possible causes for the distress that arises in a relationship where one partner develops chronic pain and illness. I covered many of these issues in Chapter 10, but they are worth repeating as they apply just as much here:

- Development of a co-dependent relationship
- The healthy partner losing his activity partner
- Decreased socializing outside of the relationship
- Finding someone to look after caregiver duties
- Financial strain
- Mental and emotional stress
- Decrease in sexual activity
- Lack of quality time together
- Dysfunctional communication about the pain and illness
- Lack of understanding and validation (by and for both partners)

I wish I didn't have to say all of this. I wish it weren't

true. I feel sad having to say it, especially as this all seems so unfair—for you, who is experiencing the pain and illness, and also for your partner. At a time when you most need your relationship to be strong, it is most in danger of falling apart. All is not lost, however. Throughout this chapter, you will learn what you can do to nurture your relationship while still taking care of yourself.

Your Healing Journey and Your Relationship

People with chronic pain and illness often find themselves embarking on a quest for healing that takes them to places they never expected to end up. Maybe the following will sound familiar to you. At first, there is a flurry of doctor visits, tests, and medications. Once you have exhausted the options on the traditional route, you may then turn to supporting therapies—physiotherapy, acupuncture, massage, naturopathy, chiropractic, and so on. After that, you might consider counselling or psychotherapy. And then spiritual healing, which may include meditation, consulting a psychic or astrologer, going to church, yoga, qi gong, or whatever else you choose in order to connect with a higher power.

Although healing work doesn't always take place in the order I listed above, in my experience the path to healing does often start at the purely physical level, and if the results are not satisfactory, veers first towards mental/emotional healing, and then to the desire for spiritual connection and guidance. You may look to spirituality to find answers that your doctors cannot give, and to find help with understanding and accepting your situation.

Sometimes this quest results in healing strictly on the

physical level, but, more often than not, people find they also end up healing mentally and emotionally as a result of their journeys back to good health. Others find emotional and spiritual healing, while the physical pain and illness continue to varying degrees. The work you put into healing is never wasted, even if you don't always get the specific results you hoped for. You can't help but get some sort of positive result from focusing your energy on bettering your health.

Getting back to health from chronic pain and illness often requires an enormous amount of soul-searching and change. It's a multidimensional process. The person you are at the end is not the one who developed the condition. Working to overcome chronic pain and illness can change your life. It changed my life, it changed me, it changed my outlook, it changed my values and my beliefs. For me, all these changes were very positive. Although I am not pain- or symptom-free, I'm in much less discomfort than I was before I started out on my quest. In addition, my friends tell me I seem to be a much happier person than I used to be, even before the pain and illness started (and I am!). I credit this to all the emotional and spiritual work I did, and the healing I received on those levels.

You, too, may find that overcoming chronic pain isn't simply swallowing a few pills every day and going for physical therapy, but is in fact much more involved, including self-reflection, personal growth work, and embarking on a complete lifestyle overhaul. Of relevance here is that once you start to change yourself, you also change the dynamics in your relationship. Some partners may be happy that you're helping yourself, and they'll be very supportive of your efforts. Other partners may find it difficult to deal with the changes they see in you because you are not the same person they met. First, the pain changed you; now, the healing journey is changing you. Often that becomes too much change for your partner to cope with.

Some partners will feel threatened or distressed if distance arises from your healing work where previously there was a tight connection. Others will learn, grow, and heal with you, strengthening your bond even more. Unfortunately, you can't control how your partner will respond to your healing. But please don't let that stop you from taking care of yourself and pursuing your healing to the fullest extent possible. Staying sick to hold onto your partner is a bad plan, period.

Priorities: Your Healing or Your Relationship?

Ideally you will find a balance when it comes to the time and energy you devote to your healing and to your relationship. However, in reality, that balance can be quite difficult to achieve. When you are single, you have much more time and energy to invest in yourself. When you have a partner, he requires a significant portion of that time and energy, and that's normal. When you are in an intimate relationship, the relationship is one of your biggest priorities. However, a good relationship, where both of you make it a priority, will nurture you, support you, and give you energy.

In addition, if you make the relationship a priority, your partner will not be as stressed, confused, or depressed about your condition. Your health is a priority, absolutely, and so are the two of you. A good relationship will have more chance of easing your condition than a strained, tension-filled one in which your partner drains your energy. Putting in the effort will pay off when it comes to your health. To have enough energy for that effort, you also need to make your health a priority. So, in summary, your priorities are first, your health, and second, your relationship.

The problem arises when you give the bulk of yourself to your relationship, thus neglecting your health and well-being. Why would you be drawn to sacrifice yourself for your relationship? Usually, it's due to the fear of losing your partner, especially if you have a tendency to be a people-pleaser from the get-go. You believe you must keep him happy in order not to lose him, and in your mind keeping him happy means ignoring your own needs and working extra-hard to keep the relationship afloat. Alarm bells go off in your head at the thought of having to go it alone. You couldn't survive without his help, love, and support (physical, emotional, and/or financial).

If you feel like you're putting more work into the relationship than your partner, that's a red flag right there. You shouldn't be working harder than he is, chronic pain and illness or not.

Maybe you've been with your partner for so long that you can't imagine life without him, especially now that you've developed chronic pain or illness. The fear of the unknown and the fear of change can be so intense that it becomes crippling. This can prevent you from taking steps towards your healing, especially if you think focusing on your healing means neglecting your partner or that it may lead to his unhappiness. Perhaps you've already started to notice that your healing journey and subsequent personal growth is creating feelings of distance between you and your partner, and this scares you because it feels like if you continue down this path, your relationship will probably end.

You may decide that you simply can't lose your partner at this point, and that the relationship is more important to you than healing your condition. That is your decision. But remember what I said in the previous section, that staying sick to hold on to your partner is a bad plan? It is. Why? Because it leaves you not only suffering physically and emotionally, but completely disempowered. Plus, the additional stress of being in a relationship where you're doing your all to please your partner can have devastating effects on your physical health.

So what is the answer? If you are consistently prioritizing your relationship over your health, it's time to swing the pendulum back towards your healing. Refocus on what *you* need. Experiment with ways to continue your healing process while still participating in your relationship. Avoid extremes: it's not you *or* your relationship, it's you *and* your relationship. Open up a dialogue with your partner around this issue, and expose it to the light. Let him know that you need to spend more energy on yourself, and assure him that you will still be there for him. Let go of the need to please and keep your partner happy at all times. After all, he is ultimately responsible for his own happiness.

The uncomfortable truth is that your relationship may not last. Ugh. I wish I didn't have to say that. But you can only do your best—to look after yourself and to do your part in nurturing your relationship. You simply cannot do more than that; the rest is up to your partner. Beyond doing your best, the outcome is out of your control. Your relationship may or may not be able to withstand your condition and the changes that result from your condition and your healing.

And if your relationship doesn't last, and you haven't been focusing on your health, you will be left in a much worse position than had you been taking care of yourself along the way. So start making yourself a priority *now*, and find ways to balance taking care of you with taking care of your relationship.

When Your Partner Is Invested in Your Condition

In some cases, partners of those who develop chronic pain and illness find themselves happier with the new dynamic in the relationship. Perhaps he likes the fact that you are at home more now and he therefore gets more attention from you. Maybe he's a rescuer, so you being ill means he now feels needed and he doesn't want to give up that feeling. Or maybe he likes to be in control in the relationship, and your being ill gives him this control. In his eyes, you are the burden and he is the martyr, and he thrives on the outside attention he gets for this role. In all of these scenarios, it's very possible that your partner will become invested in you remaining in pain because he doesn't want this new dynamic in your relationship to change.

See the whopping red flag? We're in the danger zone now.

If you allow a power imbalance to develop, you are going to end up in a co-dependent relationship. It can be easy to slide into the co-dependent martyr/burden, caregiver/ patient dynamic. If you worry about becoming a burden, or if you consider yourself "less than" because of your condition, and your partner steps into the martyr/caregiver role, then he is agreeing that you are a burden. This results in a power imbalance. In this scenario, you are offering your power to your partner, and your partner is taking it. This is an extremely unhealthy situation. Your partner should *not* be willing to accept your power. Chronic pain does not make you "less than" your partner in any way.

Co-dependent relationships hold you back and prevent you from healing, growing, and changing. It is really hard to move forward and overcome pain and illness when your partner has a different agenda. Your partner will enable you to remain with your chronic pain and illness, similar to the way someone might enable his alcoholic spouse by buying her alcohol. Does this seem like an extreme comparison? It's not. It happens all the time.

Let me be clear here: often, your partner has no conscious awareness of his co-dependent tendencies. It's not that he has some evil scheme to keep you in bed, *Misery*-style. He's simply reacting to the situation based on something in his subconscious that's telling him this situation is safer than the alternative.

But just because you understand what's happening doesn't make it ok. If you are with someone who is invested in martyrdom, who wants to be a caregiver and wants the power, run, don't walk, away! (Or if you're not ready to give up on a long-term relationship, run to counselling, couples *and* individual!) This is not a healthy relationship for you to be in, because your needs are not the priority; the focus is the attention and power your partner is getting because of you.

When Your Partner Simply Cannot Cope with Your Condition

For some partners of those with chronic pain and illness, just dealing with your physical symptoms themselves can prove to be too much. Even before your healing journey begins, or perhaps a short way into it, your partner may decide that he can't handle the situation. Totally not fair. How come you have to deal with this shit and he can just walk away? But it happens.

If he can't handle you because you have bad days when you're in tremendous pain or discomfort, you're upset, can't help around the house, and need extra assistance getting to appointments, then he's not the man for you. Some people cannot cope with others' pain and illness and resulting emotions—they just don't seem to be built for it.

If your partner leaves the relationship, it will take some major readjusting in your life. You will need time and space to grieve. And you will have the solid foundation that you created in the earlier chapters on which to lean during this time. In Chapter 13, we'll talk more about how to deal with relationships ending.

What You Can Do for Your Relationship

You might be feeling a bit overwhelmed right now, having read about some of the many things that can go wrong in a relationship where one partner develops chronic pain and illness. Fear not! I'm now going to share with you some things that can help your relationship survive and thrive. It might seem like you have a big mountain to climb, but I'm giving you the boots, the walking stick, and the map. All you have to do is climb. It *is* possible to make a relationship work if you're in pain. I've seen it happen, so I know it's possible.

Check Your Attitude

What is your attitude towards your condition?

For a long time, I felt like a victim, and I acted like a victim. It simply wasn't fair that I had this pain. My life had been taken away from me. I felt powerless and really sorry for myself. I was keenly aware of all the things I could no longer do. I compared my "new life" to my previous life daily and despaired. I constantly looked to everyone around me for sympathy, validation, and care. I talked about my condition incessantly. I cried a lot. I was depressed. I wanted to die. This was rock bottom.

When I was finally able to accept that I had this condition and it probably wasn't going away anytime soon, I found compassion for myself. The pressure I had been putting on myself to get better and be "normal" again lifted. Sweet relief! I was no longer fighting a losing battle. Instead of wallowing in victimhood, I started *living* my "new life." I began looking for direction and purpose again. Sure, it wasn't the life I had envisioned for myself, but when does life ever follow our plans?

By letting up on the pressure to be "the way I was before," I was able to receive the help I needed from my doctor (rather than being determined to heal myself the "natural" way). I took initiative, becoming proactive rather than reactive. The depression lifted, my mood improved, and I no longer felt like a victim.

Sure, I'm living a completely different life than I was before, and I still have to deal with pain and fatigue on a daily basis, but it's a good life—and I'm not lying. I'm probably happier now than I have ever been because I am focused on the things that bring me joy and make me feel good. I've stopped doing things that I don't enjoy. I am able to be myself, and I'm much more fun to be around. Once you hit rock bottom, you realize how little you have to lose when it comes to living how you *want* to live.

How does this relate to your relationship? How you conduct yourself is what determines the relationship. So, your attitude about your condition is really important. Think about what it would be like to be in a relationship with you. Are you a victim, or do you take responsibility for yourself? Do you lie on the couch and cry a lot, or do you research your condition with your partner and try new possible solutions? Do you dump your daily struggles on him when he comes home from work, or do you ask him how his day was first?

The more responsible you are with your reactions and emotions, the less pressure you put on your partner and your relationship. As someone living with chronic pain and illness, you have more to deal with than someone who is healthy. But it's still up to you to decide *how* you'll handle the life you've been given. What I've noticed in the strongest relationships where someone has chronic pain and illness is that the person with the condition has chosen an attitude of acceptance and empowerment. They take charge (as much as they can). They find purpose and meaning in their lives. They don't complain. That doesn't mean they don't express how they feel or say if they're having a hard day. They allow themselves that, but they don't hang onto it. Their lives are about so much more than the pain and illness.

Sometimes it feels good to hang onto emotional pain, because it's familiar, like slipping into an old sweater. But what's familiar and safe isn't necessarily what's best for you or your relationship. I encourage you to look at what emotional pain you're holding onto and decide whether maybe it's time to let go of it, for the sake of your relationship.

As someone dealing with chronic pain and illness, it

would be realistic for you to expect your partner to make some allowances for you. You can't do all the things that your partner would like you to, and you hope that he will accept that. But making allowances must go both ways. Your partner, while perhaps healthy, will still have ups and downs and go through difficult periods. Relative to yours, his pain may not seem that significant; however, it's not for us to decide whose pain is greater, whether it's mental, emotional, physical, or spiritual. What matters is that your partner is experiencing pain, period. Whether his pain is a result of watching you go through your own suffering or from something unrelated, it's important to remember that you are still half of this relationship and to have empathy and understanding for your partner. Can you imagine how hard it must be to watch the person you love suffer in pain on a daily basis? I can't. It takes a special person to be will-ing to do that, and for that I appreciate my partner, and I support him as much as I can because everyone deserves to be loved and supported equally.

Speaking of which, I have one last comment on attitude: remember to celebrate the good things! Greet your partner with your little victories rather than your top three health concerns for the day. "I actually did XYZ today!" Share and revel in your wins and achievements with him. This is a great way to greet him when you haven't seen him in a while, like after a work day. Show him that you're not your pain. And your partner's wins and achievements? Celebrate those too! Show him that his victories are just as important as yours.

Learn More About Your Condition
Part of choosing to approach your life with an attitude of

empowerment involves educating yourself about your condition. Learning more about your condition and the many different ways you can take action to relieve symptoms and heal will help you and your partner feel more in control. And that's a good thing, because it's the opposite of feeling helpless and hopeless.

The trick is finding a way to educate yourself without bringing on fear and gloom. Here are some tips for non-scary learning:

- Stay off Internet forums where people post about their conditions. More often than not, people on these forums post a lot of negative stories about failed treatments, side effects, and misdiagnoses, which can be rather alarming and depressing. Plus, you have no way to gauge how much of it is actually true or valid.
- If you must trawl the Internet to read about people with similar conditions, read only success stories. This can actually be quite helpful if you avoid the Negative Nellies.
- Be selective about your information sources. Ask your doctor or specialist for further reading.
- Look for books that have received good reviews, and mine their bibliographies for more references.

If your partner is willing, do some or all of this research with him. When you consider your treatment a joint effort, the challenge can bring you together as a team. Both partners should try to learn as much as possible about your condition and, if it's feasible, attend medical appointments together to learn about various diagnoses, prognoses, and options for treatment.

It is very helpful for your partner to hear, in person, what your doctor tells you, including how much you can expect to do in terms of movement, exercise, housework, physical tasks, and work. Learning more about your condition will give you a clearer understanding of what exactly you're dealing with and what your options are. Don't leave it all up to your doctor to tell you—take the initiative. Making it a team effort will help you feel more supported and can enable both of you to feel less out of control; feeling less out of control will lead to a more stable relationship.

Halt the Cycle of Unmet Needs and Unappreciated Effort

Let me explain how this works. If you have pain and you're feeling distressed, chances are you will be thinking more negatively about everything that surrounds you, including your life, your friends, your work prospects, and your intimate relationship. You start to think that you're not getting enough support from your partner, or perhaps you feel your relationship needs are not being met. Your negative thinking may lead you to feel angry or frustrated with your partner, which is something he will feel. On the flipside, perhaps your partner is feeling overwhelmed by the extent of your pain and suffering and as a result finds it hard to give you support, although he's doing the best he can. You don't feel as though your needs are being met, and your partner is doing his best but can feel that you are angry and frustrated with him regardless.

When you feel your needs aren't being met, chances are you aren't going to show your appreciation for your partner. And if your partner isn't feeling appreciated, he's likely going to do less to try to meet your needs, especially if this cycle has been occurring for some time. In this way, you end up in a cycle of mutual unmet needs and unappreciated effort.

So what do you do to break the cycle? Communicate about what's going on in each of your minds and hearts. Negative thinking about your relationship (especially when exacerbated by chronic pain and illness) can have a very harmful impact on it if left unchecked, so talk.

Before having the conversation with your partner, give some thought to the cycle that you're in. Is it similar to what I've described above, or is it different? How is it different? Do you feel like your needs are being met, or are you feeling unsupported? How is your partner feeling? Does he feel unappreciated?

When you do have the talk:

- Honestly express how you are feeling.
- List assumptions you are making about your partner, and give him the opportunity to dispel them.
- Ask for your needs to be met, and not in a roundabout way. Ask directly, and make it clear what you are asking for. For example: "Would you be willing to spend one hour of quality time with me on Monday nights without any interruptions, TV, or cell phones?"
- Allow your partner to do the same—express how he feels, list assumptions, and ask for what he needs. This is your time to *listen* and really hear what he's saying.
- Check in with your partner to see whether he feels unappreciated. If he does, ask him what he needs from you to feel appreciated, and then act on his request.

Chronic pain and illness can worm its way into relationships on the emotional level, creating excessively negative thinking and distorted beliefs. These unhealthy patterns can undermine even the strongest relationships, so it's vital that you take action and halt the cycle before things get out of hand.

Talk, Talk, and Talk Some More

You knew this was coming, right? Yup, I'm still on my communication soapbox, because communicating is the single most important thing that you need to do to keep your relationship alive and well. I realize that relationship issues can be difficult to talk about, but it is imperative that both of you discuss your fears and desires.

And when I say communication, I don't mean you huffing around the house, sighing loudly, or moaning and then becoming angry and resentful when nothing happens. I'm talking direct communication. Tell your partner how you feel. And communication goes both ways: people who are in pain also need to listen to their partners and make an effort to understand how *they're* feeling. Ask your partner for what you need. Listen to your partner when he tells you how he feels and asks for what *he* needs. Remember the feedback formula from the previous chapter? Use it! Both of you!

No matter how long you have been together or how well you know each other, your partner cannot read your mind or anticipate all of your needs. I would love for my partner to do all sorts of things without me having to ask, because for some reason in my mind that means he loves me more. That's my mental BS. Ask for what you need. Your partner will appreciate your clarity and directness a lot more than you sulking around the house, throwing fits, and telling him, "You know what you did wrong!" He really doesn't know what he's done wrong, because you haven't told him.

There are so many opportunities for miscommunication in relationships. For example, you may think that your partner has stopped touching you because he has lost interest or finds you undesirable. Instead, your partner may be fearful of causing you more physical pain or discomfort. Another example: not communicating about pain and symptom severity can lead your partner to underestimate or overestimate your pain, making it difficult for him to provide the right amount of help and support. Not knowing how severe your symptoms really are makes it hard for him to respond in helpful ways.

Each time your partner does something "wrong," you note a mark against him. If you don't speak up right away, you're going to end up holding on to and storing more and more hurt, pain, and anger—often unnecessarily, because the perceived transgression may be a result of miscommunication. The more you hold in and hold on to your anger, the more resentment will grow and the bigger the case you will build against your partner. Soon you'll have enough stored in your memory files to launch an all out class-action lawsuit against him. Wouldn't you rather avoid that? Wouldn't it be easier just to clear up issues in the moment as quickly as possible so you can let go and move on?

Ok, I know talking about communication is one thing, but actually doing it is another. Also, let's face it, hearing about pain can be a drag, and your partner may simply tune you out if you've been talking about it for a long time. So here are a few suggestions to help you effectively talk with your partner about your condition:

1. Be selective when talking about your condition. Your partner doesn't need to hear every detail about your day, all the medications you took and the status of all your aches and pains (do this with your caregiver, not your partner). Unless something really significant has changed (like a doctor's appointment, a new medication, or a new diagnosis), when your partner asks how you're feeling, respond by saying "the usual." Your partner will pretty much know what that means, and if he doesn't, he'll catch on quickly. On a bad day, you can simply tell him that it's been "a bad day." If it was a good day, tell him it was "a good day." Enough said.

2. Be discerning about timing. Plan your talks for a time when you are both able to be present and clear—and by plan I mean discuss with your partner when would be a good time for *both* of you. If you're feeling really angry or upset, take some time to calm down and plan what you would like to say. Deep breaths first, conversation second.

3. Keep in mind that communication is not strictly verbal. Only about 15% of our communication is spoken; the rest is nonverbal, usually body language. It's amazing how much we can communicate without speaking! If you're in pain, you might be signalling anger or distress nonverbally. Be aware of what messages you're sending through your body language, such as facial expressions, sighing, and posture. Think about how you would like to express yourself, verbally and nonverbally, and make any necessary adjustments.

4. Recognize that this situation, your condition, is not what your partner signed up for. Saying it out loud to him is important: "Yes, I get it. This is not what you signed up for. I am grateful for the support. I love you." This will empower your partner, allow him to feel recognition, and encourage him to keep up the things he does that really help you out.

Keep the lines of communication open, and understand that both of you may have a variety of issues with your condition, such as fairness and frustration. Be willing to hear what your partner has to say. Some of it might be difficult to hear, but it's important that it is shared so that it doesn't build up, because when anger, resentment, and frustration are allowed to accumulate, eventually there will be an explosion of some kind. I used to be an expert pyrotechnician but gave that up once I discovered that it wasn't helping me. It's so much easier to maintain a harmonious relationship when you resolve conflicts and problems as soon as possible after they arise.

Relationships can suffer deeply when people don't discuss problems that have no easy or obvious solution. Just because there is no easy answer doesn't mean that you shouldn't talk about it. It means that more than anything, you *do* need to talk. Two people brainstorming a problem can come up with a lot more ideas than one person going at it alone. Finding ways to talk openly about challenges is the first step towards effective problem-solving and generating the feelings of closeness that come from good teamwork. Lack of discussion can lead to feelings of distance and a weakening of intimacy, and that's what we're trying to avoid.

Keep in mind that balance is key. If you never talk about your pain and illness, that's a problem. If you and your partner are consumed with talking about it, that's also a problem. You need to talk about the issues, but over-talking them takes time away from other shared, more positive experiences that lead to bonding, connecting, and increased intimacy. You have to find a middle ground.

Couples who remain aware of the ways that pain and illness can impact their relationship, and who actively work to maintain or improve their bond, are much more likely to have lasting relationships. Many of the issues that pain can cause in an intimate relationship can be overcome with good communication. Making time to talk about how pain affects your relationship is important, as is being open and honest with your partner. I said it before and I'll say it again: don't assume you know everything that's happening in your partner's head. The only way you'll ever really know is by hearing it directly from him, so ask.

Don't Let Your Partner Become Your Primary Caregiver
What? My partner's not supposed to be my caregiver? No! He's not. He's supposed to be your *partner.* If you allow your partner to become your primary caregiver, that will kill the intimacy in your relationship. When your partner is not your caregiver, you feel more independent, self-confident, and self-sufficient. You are able to maintain your dignity in the relationship. These are really important qualities to preserve if you are suffering from chronic pain and illness.

If your healthy partner refuses to act as primary caregiver, you may assume this means that he doesn't love you enough. But no. Loving someone does not always look the way you think it might. One of the most loving things your partner can do is *not* be your caregiver. And that alone may save the relationship. Make sure your primary caregiver is not your partner, especially for the physical stuff. I don't know about you, but I don't want my partner helping me go to the toilet or changing my catheter, for example (if that were needed one day). I would feel humiliated. I would feel inferior. I would want to crawl under a rock. And that's no way to maintain a partnership.

I think a lot of people just fall into the role of caregiver when their partner develops pain or becomes sick, and the unwell partner slides into the role of patient. It isn't usually planned, it just happens. Then, before you know it, you're stuck in those roles.

The sooner you accept that your partner cannot be your primary caregiver, the better. What your partner *can* do is be supportive and advocate on your behalf. Actually, a great task to give your partner is advocating for your health. That way, your best interests are being looked after, your partner is clear on what is expected from him, he feels like he is being helpful, and he's not creating a power imbalance by becoming your primary caregiver.

Admittedly, your partner will most probably end up doing *some* caregiving, but there is a big difference between helping out here and there, and being your primary caregiver. For a more in-depth discussion about caregiving, please refer back to Chapter 10.

Humour

A little humour can go a long way. A lot of humour goes even further. There are so many ways to use humour:

- Find fun ways to address treatments. My ex, Jack, used to get me a hot water bottle every night—it was something he enjoyed doing for me. He would refer to it as "H-dub time" and would sing a song about it.

- If you're in a funk, ask yourself what your favourite character would do. For example, when I'm feeling down or in pain, I ask myself, "What would Bridget Jones do?" and then do my best to follow her example. I like Bridget because she's upbeat, always looks for the silver lining, and doesn't let difficult situations get her down for too long. For example, when she wrongly gets thrown in jail in Thailand for smuggling cocaine, she teaches the inmates how to sing and dance to Madonna's "Like a Virgin."

- Find humorous ways to talk about your moods and emotions. If you're acting and feeling like a victim, perhaps you'll refer to yourself as Vicky the Victim, and your partner can call you out if he sees Vicky coming to dinner.

- Infuse your life with humour generally. Watch funny TV shows, movies, and stand-up comedy.

- Embrace a playful attitude.

- Find a humour role model. I used to work at the British Columbia Cancer Agency in the Oral Medicine Department. There was an older gentleman who was a patient in our clinic, and every time he came in, he was happy and upbeat and joked with all of us. Oral cancer is one of the most painful and distressing conditions I've witnessed; he lost a portion of his jaw and mouth, and he didn't have a great prognosis. Yet he had a fantastic sense of humour and radiated kindness. He was and still is such an inspiration to me. I know I can't force humour and kindness, but I work on growing them every day.

- Brainstorm with your partner and/or look online for more ideas on how to incorporate humour into your relationship.

If you encounter setbacks, try not to become too discouraged or focus on the negative. Keep trying. Keep laughing. You can do this!

Fight Fairly

When you and your partner argue, do you fight fairly? Do you even know what fighting fairly means? Here are some dos and don'ts, which summarize many of the tools and techniques that you've learned in this book so far:

DO...

- ✓ Know your goals before starting the discussion, and consider possible outcomes.
- ✓ Tell the other person you would like to have a discussion *before* addressing the problem.
- ✓ Establish common ground rules.
- ✓ Set a time limit on the discussion (e.g., 30 minutes).
- ✓ State the problem clearly.
- ✓ Use the feedback formula and "I" statements to take responsibility for your own feelings and actions.
- ✓ Be honest and direct about your feelings and what you want.
- ✓ Deal with one issue at a time.
- ✓ Invite the other person to share their point of view.
- ✓ Listen actively and be present.
- ✓ Ask questions to clarify.

✓ Validate the other person's feelings.
✓ Try to put yourself in their shoes to see the opposing viewpoint.
✓ Apologize if you are wrong.
✓ Propose specific solutions and ask for other suggestions.
✓ Discuss the advantages and disadvantages of all possible solutions.
✓ Be ready for some compromise.
✓ If necessary, take a time-out.

DON'T...

✗ Launch a "surprise attack."
✗ Blame, accuse, attack, criticize, use sarcasm, insult, threaten, swear, taunt, or exaggerate.
✗ Store complaints from the distant past.
✗ Apologize unless you really mean it.
✗ Bring up more than one issue at a time, or save up feelings and dump them all at once.
✗ Interrupt the other person, cut them off, or talk over them.
✗ Use generalizations such as "always" or "never."
✗ Make comparisons to other people or situations.
✗ Assume, guess, imagine, take for granted, theorize, surmise, speculate, or pass judgment about what the other person means.
✗ Play games (e.g., poor me; silent treatment; martyr; don't touch me; uproar/tantrum; if it weren't for you...; see what you made me do; if you really loved me...).
✗ Involve other people's opinions of the situation.
✗ Use non-verbal language to antagonize (e.g., rolling eyes, smirking, yawning, making faces, hand gestures).

✗ Expect the other person to read *your* mind.

✗ Argue about details.

✗ Walk away or leave the house without saying, "I'll be back."

This is a good list to post on the fridge and share with your partner. The don'ts are common issues that arise in a lot of arguments or discussions between couples. It's amazing how much more easily we can communicate when we don't blame our partner or allow ourselves to become defensive during an argument. These dos and don'ts will help you out with all of that and more.

I'm also going to share with you some other information that will better help you communicate with your partner. I've included this in the fighting fairly section because these issues often come up during arguments or times of conflict. Dr. John Gottman did some ground-breaking research and work on marital stability, and according to him there are certain behaviours that, if they occur regularly in your relationship, are very good predictors of either a failed or a terminally unhappy relationship. Some of these key behaviours he has termed, "The Four Horsemen of the Apocalypse":

1. Criticism. A complaint addresses only the specific behaviour at which your partner has failed. Complaints are a normal part of relationships. A criticism, on the other hand, attacks your partner's character and personality. Criticism erodes relationships. Here are some examples. *Complaint*: "There is no gas in the car. I'm frustrated that you didn't fill it up like you said you would." *Criticism*: "You never remember to fill up the car! I can never count on you! You're so undependable!"

2. Contempt. Contempt is composed of a set of behaviours that communicate disgust. It includes, but is not limited to: sneering, sarcasm, name-calling, eye-rolling, mockery, hostile humour, and condescension. It's primarily expressed through nonverbal behaviours and body language. Contempt is disrespectful and increases conflict. Dr. Gottman's research shows that couples who display contempt for each other suffer more illnesses and diseases than respectful couples. That alone sounds like a great reason to avoid it!

3. Defensiveness. When you become defensive, the message you send to your partner is, "The problem is not *me*. It's *you*." You avoid taking responsibility for your own behaviour by pointing to something he did *prior* to his complaint about you. You refuse to acknowledge the part that is true in what he is saying about your behaviour. You imply that because your partner threw the first stone, he is responsible for the entire conflict. Also, when you become defensive, you stop hearing what your partner is trying to say and instead rely on the assumptions you're making about what he is saying. Defensiveness is a recipe for miscommunication.

4. Stonewalling. If there is a lot of arguing in a relationship, eventually one partner tunes out, shuts down, and ignores the other partner. This is stonewalling. The stonewaller acts as if he couldn't care less about what his partner is saying or doing. The stonewaller turns away from conflict *and* from the relationship. This is the behaviour that does the most damage to a relationship.

The Four Horsemen destroy the love that is at the core of an intimate relationship. If either you or your partner engages in any of these behaviours on a regular basis or during fights, you have some work to do if you want to ensure the success and happiness of your relationship. Refer to the Take Action! section of this chapter for practical suggestions on how to avoid these behaviours.

Value Each Other

You and your partner got together for a reason. I'm going to assume one of those reasons was love. And now you're both confronted with this challenge in your lives, this unwelcome medical condition that neither of you signed up for. What a bitch. Yet you're dealing with it together. You support each other and love each other, and that's pretty awesome. Please value what you have. Don't take your partner for granted. Keep in mind the big picture, why you love your partner. Don't lose sight of what brought you together in the first place and why you're together now.

I know it's really easy to focus on the things that go wrong in the relationship—the challenges and the struggles, how he never takes out the garbage, how he chews too loudly—but the thing is, he's there. That's something. That's a lot. It's much more than many people have.

When you value each other and work together as a team, your relationship becomes stronger. This is the person you've chosen to spend your life with, so show him how much you value him. This might involve telling him how much he means to you, or doing something kind for him each day. Review his love languages, and show your appreciation in a way that will resonate with him, whether it's an extra-long hug or preparing a meal when you feel up to it. Your thoughtful acts don't need to be grand gestures; they can be small, frequent demonstrations of how much you love and appreciate your partner.

Address Financial Strain

I talked about money issues in the previous chapter, so I'm only going to briefly touch on them here. Money can be a strain for any couple, healthy or otherwise. Chronic pain and illness, depending on the medical care system where you live and on your medical benefits, if any, can be a huge financial burden. You may lose income because your condition makes it impossible to keep working. You may have increased medical expenses and other fees in connection with your condition, such as getting a wheelchair or having ramps installed in your home. As I've said before, being sick is not cheap.

Address financial issues right away as they arise, and deal with them together. This is critical because there is already enough strain on you and on your relationship. Keeping your financial woes from your partner or ignoring them completely is only going to make things worse in the long run. Create a budget and a financial plan together and stick to the financial agreements you make with each other.

If managing money isn't your forte, consider consulting a financial planner who has expertise in helping people with medical conditions. They can be a source of really good advice and often provide information on financial loopholes and tax breaks. Attend your appointments with the financial planner together. It's an issue that affects both of you, and it's essential that you find the best ways to make your money go as far as possible.

Allow Yourselves to Grieve

When I was first diagnosed with myalgic encephalomyelitis and fibromyalgia, I was very upset. I felt like I was losing so much as a result: my job, my freedom, my independence, my social life, my happiness, a large portion of my sex life, my identity, and, for a while, even my home. Who was I now that I wasn't able to be the person I'd been all my life? I felt incredible loss.

I expressed my feelings to a friend, who replied that I shouldn't look at it that way—rather, I should focus on healing and on the positive things in my life. I tried to take her advice, but the sense of loss and sadness kept taking over. When I talked with my counsellor about these feelings, she reminded me that it's completely normal to grieve when you're diagnosed with a condition that affects your life as profoundly as mine has done. She encouraged me to grieve over what I'd lost. Grieving didn't mean I would never get better—it was simply a way to acknowledge my loss, whether or not I eventually would get back some of the things I had lost. And since grief was coming up, it was important for me to let it out. I didn't want to bottle my emotions any longer.

When you are in a relationship, part of the grieving process around your condition will likely involve acknowledging the loss of your relationship as it used to be. And because both partners experience loss as a result of your condition, you can expect that both of you will need to grieve that loss. Allow yourselves to feel and express to each other the emotions that are surfacing. Grieve together. This is normal and healthy. The feelings will eventually pass. And please know that just because your partner is grieving the loss of your past relationship doesn't necessarily mean he is not willing to continue in the relationship in a different direction.

So that you have a better idea of what you can expect, here are the five stages of grieving, according to Swiss psychiatrist Elisabeth Kübler-Ross:

1. Denial
2. Anger
3. Bargaining
4. Depression
5. Acceptance

These stages don't necessarily happen in that order. Sometimes you go back and forth between stages. And although acceptance is considered the final stage, it is still possible to move from acceptance back into the other stages if there is more healing to be done.

So if you notice any of the above feelings coming up around your diagnosis, your condition, and how they affect your relationship, know that this is completely normal. Grieve together with your partner rather than isolating yourself. Isolation can lead to fractures in the relationship and to depression. And while grief does not equal depression, dwelling on or resisting the feelings of sadness and loss for too long can lead to clinical depression.

Watch for Depression

Sadness is a normal response to chronic pain and illness. However, if your symptoms continue at high levels for a long time, you may become clinically depressed. Your partner may also be at risk of developing depression, especially if he has taken on a lot of caregiver duties (and if he has, you both need to go back to Chapter 10 and remind yourselves why your partner should not be your primary caregiver!). If you notice yourself or your partner feeling depressed or exhibiting symptoms of depression, talk to your doctor, because she or he can help. Just because you have chronic pain doesn't mean you have to suffer from depression, too.

Signs and symptoms of depression include:

- Feelings of helplessness and hopelessness
- Loss of interest in daily activities
- Appetite or weight changes
- Sleep changes
- Profound sadness
- Anger or irritability
- Loss of energy
- Self-loathing
- Reckless behaviour
- Concentration problems
- Unexplained aches and pains

This is not a comprehensive list, but it does cover the most common symptoms. If you notice that you or your partner is experiencing some or all of these symptoms, please get help before your depression worsens.

Work with a Counsellor

Sometimes working on your relationship with your partner isn't enough on its own. Getting help from an outside source can make the difference between a relationship surviving or ending. Counselling can help you and your partner work through conflicts and difficult periods and can also provide you with useful coping skills. It can help you learn how to navigate your relationship in light of the major upheaval

your condition has created. You can choose to see a counsellor separately or together, or both (I recommend both!).

I would definitely recommend that anybody experiencing chronic pain and illness talk to a professional. In individual therapy, I have found my counsellor to be hugely
helpful. Talking will allow you to vent your struggles and
suffering to someone who can offer a clear, unbiased perspective. Being able to express all your emotions to your
counsellor on a regular basis will also take a lot of pressure off your partner. Going to couples therapy together
will enable you and your partner to talk openly, in a safe
environment, about how your chronic pain and illness have
changed your lives.

There are many different types of help available, including psychiatrists, psychologists, counsellors, therapists,
social workers, ministers, rabbis, and other trained professionals. Explore your options, and choose the person who
best fits your needs.

TAKE ACTION!

THIS HAS BEEN a hefty chapter, and the discussion section
already contains a lot of recommendations on what you can
do for your relationship if pain starts when you're already
together. I'm going to summarize the main points below
and would encourage you to follow through on them as
much as possible.

1. Choose your attitude. Make it easy for you to be around
yourself, and make it easy for your partner to be in a relationship with you. Don't be a martyr. Don't repress your
emotions. At the same time, though, avoid bellyaching,

whining, criticizing, or blaming. Deal with your own shit so that you're not throwing it at other people. Choose an attitude of empowerment. Take charge, take initiative, find your purpose, and celebrate the good stuff.

2. Learn more about your condition. Learn about your pain and illness together; research, go to information sessions, read books, and do what you can to find out what worsens and what relieves your symptoms. Doing this together can create a sense of teamwork and increase intimacy.

3. Halt the cycle of unmet needs and unappreciated efforts. Are you and your partner working at cross-purposes? Find a way to get on the same track, so you can get your needs met and show your partner you appreciate him for doing so. You guys are a team, so act like one!

4. Communicate. Express your feelings responsibly and ask for your needs to be met in a clear and direct manner. Listen intently to your partner when he shares his emotions and asks for *his* needs to be met. Treat each other with respect and empathy. Talk about problems before things get out of hand.

5. Don't let your partner be your primary caregiver. Look for other solutions. Find people who can help with your care, household tasks, child care, and anything else you need help with or can no longer do. Focus on maintaining a partnership with your partner, rather than creating a relationship with a power imbalance.

6. Humour. I can't say enough about the value of humour. Laugh as often and as much as you can. Period.

7. Post the Fighting Fairly rules on the refrigerator or in another highly visible place and refer to them often and as needed.

8. Ban the Four Horsemen from your relationship. Here are some suggestions for what to do if you and/or your partner are engaging in any of these apocalyptic behaviours:

- When you want to address a complaint you have toward your partner, avoid starting the conversation in a harsh manner. Go for a gentle start. For example, rather than snapping, "Will you stop that?!" say, "Do you have a minute? I'd like to ask you something." This will prevent your partner from jumping to the defensive right away and will make it more likely that he'll really hear what you have to say.
- Keep it simple—address one issue at a time, and don't dredge up the past.
- Use the feedback formula. Address behaviours, not character. Remember to make all requests of your partner clear, realistic, and specific.
- When your partner shares a complaint about you, repeat it back to him in your words to show him that you heard and understood what he said. Not only will he feel heard—it will also bring to light any misunderstanding you may have about what he said and give him the opportunity clarify his words, meaning, and intention.

- Consider what part of your partner's complaint is valid, and address that. No one is perfect, and it's possible that you've done something to hurt him. The most powerful thing you can do is own up to that and take responsibility for what you've done. Apologize if appropriate.
- Speak respectfully, even when angry. Avoid expressing contempt. Refer back to the rules on fighting fairly.
- If you become overwhelmed during a conversation, disagreement, or argument and notice that your heart rate has increased, you're short of breath, your hands are shaking and sweaty, and/or you're having a hard time thinking clearly, take a break. It's impossible to have a calm and rational discussion when your body is in fight or flight mode. Tell your partner you need a few minutes (or half an hour) to remove yourself, breathe and get back to a less agitated place before continuing with the discussion. Then continue the discussion—don't leave it hanging or allow yourself to shut down and stonewall.
- Do your best to meet your partner's needs and requests. A relationship is a two-way street, even if you have chronic pain and illness. Don't ignore your partner's needs. Live up to your agreements—and, if you simply can't, renegotiate.
- Practice sharing compliments, appreciation, love, and praise daily.

These suggestions are simply a starting point to replacing the behaviours of the Four Horsemen with more loving kindness. Depending on the extent to which your relationship has been affected, you may wish to seek extra support through counselling.

9. Value each other. Love your partner; give him compliments and affection, and perform acts of kindness. Express your appreciation and gratitude. This is what being in a relationship is all about. The love, the togetherness, the affection, and the fun. Yes, it's still possible to have fun when you have chronic pain and illness. Your relationship is extremely important and needs to be a priority. If you have a healthy relationship, it can go a long way in supporting you, either in recovering from your pain and illness or reducing the amount of stress and pain that you do experience. Putting the effort into your relationship is definitely worth it.

10. Address financial strain. If you're suddenly no longer able to work due to pain or illness, chances are it's going to affect you financially. Finances are already a hot topic in many relationships, and this additional strain can create a lot of stress and conflict. That's why it's imperative to get on it, sort out a financial plan with your partner, and get help from a financial planner if you need it.

11. Allow yourselves to grieve. It's normal to feel a sense of loss when your life changes so dramatically due to chronic pain and illness. It's important to honour those feelings that come with the loss, especially around what it means for your relationship. Allow yourself to grieve your previous life. Doing this doesn't mean that you are forever fated to live in pain; it's simply a way of accepting where you are now and what you don't have, at least for the time being. Grieving this loss with your partner can be a way of bringing you closer as well.

12. Watch for depression. Keep an eye on each other and notice if you or your partner might be heading towards depression. The sooner you catch it and see a doctor, the better. Depression complicates relationships even more, and avoiding it can make a big difference.

13. See a couples counsellor together. Having chronic pain and illness develop during a relationship is a difficult challenge, and if you don't have to do it without extra help, don't. Consider also seeing counsellors individually for additional support.

––––––––––––

WHEN CHRONIC PAIN and illness develop during a relationship, they can really throw a wrench in your plans. Not only do you have to deal with your condition, but you may also be faced with heightened emotions, strained communication, caregiver issues, sexual difficulties, loss of companionship, extra household tasks, and childcare responsibilities. The only way to deal with these things is to talk about them, so I encourage you to work on your communication skills. The more effective your communication, the easier it will be to resolve the problems that arise. You are stronger if you and your partner act as a team and face your issues together rather than apart. Plan ahead for what you can, be flexible, experiment, and remember to focus on loving, valuing, and caring for each other.

CHAPTER 12

For the Partners and Spouses of Those with Chronic Pain and Illness

ALRIGHT READERS, NOW is the time to hand this book over to your partners or spouses. This chapter is for them.

To the partners and spouses of those with chronic pain and illness:

Until now, this book has been all about your partner. Let's switch it up and talk about *you*. This chapter is here to give you tools and ideas for what you can do to reduce the impact of your partner's chronic pain and illness on you and your relationship.

MY STORY

MOST OF MY story is written from the perspective of someone who is suffering from a chronic health condition. However, I do have some experience on the "other side."

When we first got together, my ex-husband, Rob, suffered from chronic neck pain due to multiple car accidents. I was 20 years old and fairly wrapped up in myself, so I was only vaguely aware of the extent of Rob's discomfort. I knew that he would get a sore neck after long shifts at work and after playing volleyball, which he loved and refused to give up. I was also aware that he went to see his chiropractor and massage therapist on a weekly basis.

Around the time I started seeing Rob, I was first diagnosed with vulvodynia. I was pretty immersed in my own problems, the diagnosis, and all that came with it, specifically, being told by the doctor that I would never be able to have a successful relationship because the pelvic pain would ruin my sex life. Needless to say, my focus wasn't 100% on Rob's neck issues.

When we moved in together, his neck problems became more noticeable. Rob and I didn't have a lot of time to spend together because we both worked shiftwork and usually had conflicting schedules. Since we saw each other so infrequently, I really looked forward to and valued our quality time. But as the months passed I started to notice that he spent a lot of our time together complaining about, stretching, and massaging his damned neck. Always with the stretching and the massaging and the stretching, tilting his head this way and that, back and forth, back and forth. And complaining. Meanwhile, I was heading towards full-blown denial around my recent undercarriage diagnosis and didn't want to speak about it at all. Why couldn't Rob just do the same with his neck?

"Will you come over here and sit with me?" I'd ask.

"I can't, I need to stretch my neck. It's really sore," he'd reply for the umpteenth time. This was the standard script for our "quality time."

I became quite irritated with his neck pain. Even though I logically knew that he wasn't creating it on purpose just to annoy me and didn't have as much control over the pain as I wanted him to, after two or three years I was getting really sick and tired of him complaining about his neck. I started to become angry and resentful because the neck pain was so constant and infringed on our time together. "My neck this, my neck that, my neck, my neck, my neck!" He was always stretching—on the couch, in the kitchen, in bed, at the movies, in the car, you name it, he would be manipulating his neck. It was as if he had developed this problem just to irk me. Obviously he hadn't, just as your partner didn't develop her condition just to piss you off. She probably is much more pissed about it than you are.

I was still fairly young and naïve at the time Rob and I got married, and had yet to develop adult levels of empathy and understanding. I recently read that relationships are less likely to succeed when there is chronic pain or illness if the people in the relationship are young, and that makes a lot of sense to me now, looking back. We tend to be much more self-absorbed when we are in our late teens and early twenties, and we grow into our ability to have compassion for others as we age. Were I to meet someone today with a similar problem, I think my attitude would be very different.

Living with Rob's chronic pain condition was tough, and I didn't even have to take on any extra responsibilities or caregiving duties. What the experience did do for me was give me insight. I learned how you can go from feeling sympathetic towards your partner to feeling very irritated and resentful of their condition. Constantly having to listen to them talk about it is tedious and annoying. My time with Rob also really helped me appreciate the enormity of what my partner experiences now. I had trouble dealing with someone's *neck pain*. My partner has so much more on his plate—my myriad of ever-changing and fluctuating symptoms and conditions.

If your partner has pain and illness and you don't, it can be very hard to understand what they're going through, no matter how well (or how often) they explain it to you. I once attended a presentation given by my internist, Dr. Arseneau, to help the friends and family of his patients better understand what sufferers of chronic pain and illness experience. He took us through an exercise that I think demonstrates really well the difficulty you experience as a partner of somebody with chronic pain or illness.

Dr. Arseneau began by handing out oranges to our friends and family members. He had them hold the oranges in their hands, smell them, feel the skin, and notice all the different colours. He then had everyone peel their orange while paying attention to the texture of the peel, inside and out, and the smell when the peel was removed. I watched as family and friends became engrossed in the experience of peeling their orange and really noticing everything about it. He asked everyone to eat a piece, paying attention to how the inside of the orange was so different from the outside, observing the thin film of skin covering the flesh of the orange, and then tasting the orange as it exploded in their mouths.

After everyone in the group had had a chance to finish up with their orange, Dr. Arseneau asked, "How would you describe this experience to somebody who has never seen or tasted an orange? And how could you be sure that they really understood you?"

This is the dilemma of the patient suffering from chronic pain and illness. How do we describe the experience to somebody who's never had it themselves? How can you possibly understand, even if we provide a detailed description of what it's like? I don't think I could convey in words what it's like to experience the simple act of eating an orange. Sure, I can describe what the colour orange is like, and how the skin feels kind of knobbly, waxy, and smooth, and I can say that the inside has this almost white furry lining, and there is a light skin surrounding the flesh of the orange, which looks like some sort of alien growth. And I can say that the orange was juicy, tangy, and sweet and tasted like summer, but that description really doesn't allow someone to fully grasp the experience of eating an orange. And no matter how carefully or how much I describe my condition to my partner, he will never fully understand it.

LET'S DISCUSS

SO WHERE DOES this leave you, as the partner of someone who has chronic pain and illness?

If your partner has developed a chronic condition, your relationship will inevitably change to some degree. At some point you may find yourself pondering whether to stay in the relationship or to end it. If you decide to stay, stay for the right reasons. Stay because you love your partner, because she is your companion, your partner in life, and you couldn't imagine living without her, and you wouldn't want to. On the other hand, it may be a no-brainer: you love your partner, you're fully committed, and leaving isn't even a consideration for you.

If you do stay, you've got some challenges ahead. Your level of stress will likely be higher, and your emotions may be heightened and/or more difficult to manage. You may, at one point or another, deal with strained communications, sexual difficulties, and caregiver burnout (if you are a caregiver, which I hope you're not!). Your partner is going to go through changes, and your lives are going to be altered. Some of these changes will be difficult, while others may be positive adjustments. Having your partner develop a chronic condition doesn't mean you are going to suddenly be without companionship, intimacy, and love.

However, you're likely going to have to work harder at the relationship than someone whose partner doesn't have chronic pain or illness. And, like your partner, you have a choice about what sort of attitude you want to take in approaching this challenge. Do you want to be a victim, or do you want to feel empowered? Do you want to be angry and resentful, or do you want to accept your circumstances and make the best of them? Do you want to isolate yourself or become closer with your partner? You two are a team, and you can choose to face this problem and chip away at it together, gaining strength, hope, and encouragement from each other.

Don't Become Your Partner's Caregiver

Here's what I know: becoming your partner's caregiver is an intimacy and relationship killer. When you take on the role of caregiver, especially for the physical tasks, you disempower your partner and you allow the illness to take away even more than it needs to. If your partner feels like she is your patient, her self-esteem will decline and her sense of loss will be amplified. It is in both of your interests for your partner to retain as much of her own power as possible. This will allow her to maintain her self-confidence, pride, and sense of independence. It will help you avoid overwhelm, burnout, and resentment. You will be able to remain respectful of her, and she will remain your partner rather than becoming your patient. The balance of power in your relationship will remain equal, which is vital. Yes, you will probably end up taking on *some* extra chores and errands, but do everything you can to avoid stepping into a caregiving role.

You may feel that you have no choice but to become a caregiver. There may be a lot of reasons for not getting outside help. Doing so may create financial strain. You and your partner may not want a stranger helping out. Besides, she might get better soon and then what's the point? The point is, those are all excuses. Where there is a will, there is a way. Find alternatives to you being your partner's caregiver—look to friends, family, care aids, nurses, community support services, your church, or volunteer groups. There are always options; it's a matter of discovering what they are.

Do maintain boundaries and create reasonable expectations of your partner. She is in pain and ill but not completely helpless. Encourage her to find her own way. Be supportive, but other than educating yourself, don't get too pulled into the details of the pain and illness. Getting sucked in often means you're becoming a caregiver and taking on responsibilities that should be hers. Know where your line is, especially around physical care.

Don't try to fix things for your partner. Treat her like a normal person. Don't rush in to rescue her when she's struggling. Allowing her to overcome things on her own will help her keep a sense of independence and confidence. It can be very easy to disempower your partner by doing things for her that she can do herself. If you want your partner to hold onto her self-confidence, dignity, pride and independence (which are extremely healthy attributes for her to have), and if you want to maintain respect for your partner, take a step back and allow her the space to work it out on her own. This is actually a very loving and caring thing to do. If this strikes you as untrue, you may need to re-evaluate what loving and encouraging your partner looks like.[1]

If you don't want to lose your bond, your intimacy, and your loving relationship, take a step back from caregiving duties. If, after reading this section, you still feel you must be the one to take care of your partner, cross the line into caregiving at your own risk.

Teamwork Rules

Here's what else I know: teamwork is key. Yes, this is your partner's illness, and it's important for her to do as much as possible to help herself, but the issue affects both of you as a couple, so it's up to the two of you to work together to make the best of the situation. You're going to come up against a lot of challenges, but that doesn't mean you can't have a rewarding and fulfilling relationship with your partner. You absolutely can.

---

[1] Obviously, if she is in dire need of help and can't help herself, then do absolutely step in, or better yet, get her caregiver to step in.

The more you do together to help your partner reduce symptoms, heal, move forward, and find purpose again, the closer you will become. Leaving your partner to do all the work can create distance as well as anger and resentment, which will start to drive you apart.

There can be a fine line between helping your partner heal and taking on caregiver duties. If you are unsure about an activity, ask yourself: is this something I could delegate (and would be better off delegating) to someone else? If yes, then you know what to do. If no, then consider what your role on the team needs to be, and discuss it with your partner.

What do you need to do for your partner in order to be a strong and valuable teammate? Here are my suggestions:

- Ask her what she needs from you.
- Be open-minded and willing to participate in her healing journey. Consider opportunities for your own personal growth. Be willing to work on your issues, even if you are the physically healthy partner. You're being faced with a very big challenge; how can you take this challenge and transform it into something meaningful?
- One of the most supportive things you can do to help your partner gain and maintain an attitude of empowerment (rather than victimhood) is help her help herself. Call her out on behaviours that aren't helpful, and be honest about what you observe. Support the healing efforts in which she is engaging, encourage her for being proactive, celebrate little improvements and good days, and provide comfort when she needs it.

- Continually work together on strategies for improving intimacy and communication. This is an ongoing process, not just a one-time thing.
- Be kind. Hurting your partner is like hurting yourself. I know the situation can be really frustrating and bring up significant anger. If this is happening, it means that you have a need that's not being met, one that you are assuming your partner will or should meet. It's up to you to figure out what the need is and to find a different way to get it met.
- Don't try to make your partner feel bad for what she is unable to do. She has new limits, so don't ask her to do or think she should do more than she reasonably can. Watch out for passive-aggressive behaviour, like saying, "I thought I would be able to go out today, but now I can't," if she has an unexpected flare-up. And watch your nonverbal body language. You might not be saying something out loud, but your body and your signals may be screaming it.
- Attend your partner's medical appointments. That way you can hear exactly what is going on, what the treatment plan is, and what the prognosis is, without having to guess from what your partner reports. You will be able to pick up more of what the doctor says, for a few reasons. For one thing, your partner may have "brain fog" (an overall lack of mental clarity) and as a result have trouble concentrating and listening. In addition, as the patient she may have triggers and reactions that prevent her from fully understanding and remembering what the doctor has said. You will also be able to ask the doctor questions directly, which can be very helpful.

- Understand that dealing with chronic pain and illness is a full-time job (with a lot of overtime) for your partner. It occupies her mind 24 hours a day.

I encourage you to go back and read Chapters 10 and 11 if you haven't already. They contain many helpful hints and valuable suggestions for creating a relationship that can survive chronic pain and illness, and form a good foundation for the information provided in this chapter.

Regulating Emotions

One of the main difficulties for both of you will be regulating emotions. Pain and illness, whether you are suffering from them or watching your partner endure them, are tiring. When you're tired, it's harder to be empathetic, kind, and thoughtful. You're also more likely to tune your partner out or react with anger or frustration. While understandable, this type of reaction is not helpful for the relationship. So how do you prevent your mood from affecting your relationship, especially when the mood is in large part a result of your partner's health condition?

Here are a few suggestions:

- Be clear about what precisely has frustrated you. Are you angry with your partner or with her condition? Keep in mind that *she* is not her condition. She is someone in whom a condition exists. Express your emotions responsibly and in a timely manner. The previous two chapters explain how to express yourself in a kind and respectful way.
- Don't take things personally. Your partner's condition

is bound to cause challenges and difficulties that you didn't have to deal with before the illness started. But your partner didn't get sick to piss you off, and changes in her behaviour will often be due to her condition. It's not about you, as much as it may sometimes feel like it is. It's also not about either of you not wanting to be with each other, and it's not about what either of you did or didn't do. It's about this condition, which can be like having a third person in the relationship—a very demanding person!

- A partner with a chronic illness may give mixed messages. When feeling good, your partner may want to do things on her own but then become resentful if you don't step up to help when she's not feeling so well. Be aware of this and similar reactions, and don't take them personally. That's not easy to do, but keep in mind: it's about the illness and pain, not about you. Be as patient and understanding as you can, and talk about it with her. Talk, talk, talk!

- Keep in mind your partner may have brain fog or other cognitive difficulties. She may also not have the same level of coping skills as you do and may become easily overwhelmed. This is what happens when someone has chronic pain or illness. So when you are having discussions about your relationship, her condition, or any other serious topic, focus on one thing at a time and be specific. Don't bombard her with a myriad of issues. Make it easy and emotionally safe for her to express her thoughts and feelings on the topic that most urgently needs attention. Choose the right time to talk to your partner; for example, if she is clearer headed in the morning, that's the time to talk.

- Make sure you're taking care of yourself first. It's really important to give yourself what you need in order to keep your tank full before you direct your time and energy to your partner. This may sound selfish to some people, especially those on whom their partners rely heavily. But think about it: if you're unhappy and exhausted, how are you going to be there for your partner, mentally, emotionally, or physically?

- Find a way to listen without trying to fix things. If the doctor hasn't been able to fix the condition, chances are you won't be able to either. It can be a powerful experience for your partner to feel like she's been truly heard. This alone may help reduce her stress levels and emotional distress. You don't need to reply with your thoughts and ideas: simply maintaining eye contact, nodding, listening, and saying, "Mmhmm," can go a long way (and don't you dare pick up your cellphone while you're listening!).

- Please read the section on communication in Chapter 11—it may be the most important section in the whole book. You *must* talk to one another on a regular basis about how you're feeling and about any issues that arise around your partner's condition. You need to work together to develop a solid plan for how to make things work. Keep the lines of communication open, always.

Your Health

While your partner may be the one with the debilitating medical condition, maintaining your own well-being is critical. Let's take a closer look at *your* health and what you can do to ensure you remain as strong, vital, relaxed, and happy as possible.

Maintain Your Health

Taking care of yourself needs to be your number one priority. If you don't have your health, you won't be able to be there for your partner, let alone fully live your own life. Ask yourself the following questions:

- Are you going for annual medical check-ups?
- Are you getting enough exercise?
- Are you eating healthful foods?
- Are you getting enough sleep?
- Are you drinking six to eight glasses of water a day?

If you answered no to any of these questions, it's time to make a few changes and take some proactive steps. These questions cover your body's basic needs for functioning well. I've heard a lot of excuses from clients for why they can't do these things, but that's all they are—excuses. You need to look after yourself, so find a way and get on it!

Accept Help

You're not Superman or Wonder Woman, which means you probably need some help. There is no shame in asking for help or accepting it. You don't have to do it all on your own, and you probably can't do it all on your own without sacrificing your health and well-being. Find out who is willing to lend a hand (friends, family, volunteers, church, community), and take them up on it. You can start with simple requests, like taking your partner to a medical appointment, doing some laundry, or making you a lasagne. People like to help; it makes them feel needed and good about themselves, so it's a win-win.

Take Time for Yourself

Your existence can become pretty focused around your partner and her pain or illness. If you're not careful, your life can start to completely revolve around your partner's health. The thing is, as much as your partner may need you, and as much as you are a committed team and love each other, you are still a separate being with separate needs and interests. To be fully there for your partner, you have to make sure that those needs and interests are fulfilled.

At first you might think this sounds difficult or selfish, but it's really important for you to maintain some semblance of a "normal" life in order to relax and experience happiness. Having a partner with chronic pain and illness can be overwhelmingly stressful, so it's critical that you stay on top of keeping your stress levels down. This might involve seeing friends, playing a weekly squash game (physical activities provide a great outlet for stress), going to the movies, or maybe spending some quiet time alone away from the house—reading, meditating, yoga class, whatever floats your boat. It doesn't matter so much *what* you're doing but that you are taking time for yourself on a regular basis. This is not selfish. This is recharging your batteries so you can come back to your partner without feeling drained by her condition. It will give you more patience and make you less likely to feel resentful—that is a good thing for both of you.

Easier said than done, I know. And you may still be wondering how you can possibly go out when your partner is at home suffering, waiting for you to come back. Actually, though, how can you afford not to?

Educate Yourself

My hope is that you and your partner are working together to find solutions that make your lives easier and reduce your partner's pain and symptoms. It's important that both of you educate yourselves about her condition and what it takes to help improve it. You also both need to become aware of how you can nurture and grow your relationship in the face of the pain and stress that you're confronted with. And on top of those things, it's a good idea for you to educate yourself on what it means to be a partner of someone with a serious medical condition. You're not the only one out there going through this. There are many resources that can help you— online, in books, in support groups, and through counselling. Learn as much as you can about your role. The more you know about your situation, the better you will be able to cope and respond.

- Stay connected. Chronic pain and illness can be an isolating experience for both patient and partner. When pain persists, friends often fade away. Friends and family may not understand what is going on, and when confronted with ongoing rejections to their invitations, they may eventually give up. It's really sad to lose friends over something beyond your control. Yet it's imperative that you maintain social and community ties. If your partner is in a lot of pain or their illness is quite severe, chances are they may not leave the house very often and don't have the energy for socializing. This doesn't mean that you have to stay at home, too. In fact, you need to get out and have some fun. Continue to live your life. Care for, love, and support your partner, but don't give up your career aspirations, friends, or hobbies. This is part of filling up your tank, putting your oxygen mask on first, maintaining your own identity, and safeguarding against depression.

Having friends to confide in and have fun with still needs to be part of your life. Do interesting things and spend time with interesting people. There are things you are not going to get from your partner—maybe you wouldn't get them even if your partner was healthy, and that's normal. It's up to you to get your needs met without negatively affecting your relationship.

Do involve your partner in social activities if she is able to join you. Socializing and being out in the community is extremely beneficial for both of you. And if your partner is unable to leave the house very often, bring friends, family, and community *to* her, as long as she is feeling up to it.

See a Counsellor

You can read this book and a bunch of other books, you can do your best with the situation and communicate as much as possible, and sometimes it's still not enough. You may understand the situation cognitively but still struggle with guilt, anger, and resentment. Perhaps you're really unsure of how to proceed. Talking to a third party who is completely unconnected to your life, such as a counsellor or psychologist, can be extremely helpful. First of all, simply being able to unburden yourself of all your thoughts and emotions, especially if you feel they are "bad," can be a huge relief. Second, the counsellor will be able to offer further coping tools and skills for your situation. Sometimes, a few new tips and tricks can make all the difference. And third, your counsellor may have some ideas that you haven't thought of yet, different perspectives and suggestions for various support systems. There is no shame in going to see a counsellor. If help is available and you can afford it, why not accept it?

Grieve Your Losses

So you met someone you really love, the two of you started a life, and you made plans and goals and shared dreams together. Then she got sick, and suddenly you realize that your goals and dreams are no longer going to be possible, at least not now and maybe not ever. That is a major adjustment, maybe one of the biggest ones you'll ever have to face. You're losing the life you had planned and expected to have. Maybe you also feel like you're losing part of your partner too—it's possible that she's not the same person as before the pain started. No matter how much you try to convince yourself otherwise, your life is drastically altered when your partner develops chronic pain or illness. And it's normal to feel angry, shocked, depressed, resentful, sad, and upset. It's simply human to experience grief over losing something that was very dear to you—your partner as she was, and your shared plans, goals, and dreams.

Allow yourself to grieve your loss. Don't feel that you shouldn't or that it's self-centered. Yes, your partner is in a lot of pain and probably worse off than you are, but your emotions are legitimate, even if just for the simple fact that you're feeling them. Allow them to come out—have a good cry, throw some pillows, or hit a punching bag. The good thing about emotions is that they're not permanent. These feelings will pass as the grief fades. So for now, don't feel guilty about what you're experiencing, just allow yourself to feel. If you're particularly uncomfortable with the emotions, talking to a counsellor or other professional can be extremely helpful.

After your grief subsides, adapt your expectations. Once you have both grieved your losses, it's time to update your plans, dreams, and goals. Her abilities have changed and her desires may have changed, but nothing is stopping the two of you from making new plans, setting new goals, and imagining new dreams.

Create New Shared Activities

Chances are that once your partner developed chronic pain or illness, many activities became infeasible. For me, hiking, biking, kayaking, skiing, running, dancing, and a variety of other physical activities are out of the question. Also difficult is going to see sporting events or shows in venues where the seats are tight and I can't stretch and stand up much. I don't like crowds or loud noises or bright lights. I don't like being too cold or too hot. I'm good for about four to six hours outside of the house, and travelling takes a lot out of me. Sound familiar?

While that list might sound very limiting, there are still many things I *can* do with my partner. I like to play board games, do puzzles, socialize with friends, watch football on Sundays from home while cooking a roast, make craft projects, grow food, discuss current events, go on short road trips (as long as I'm not driving), go for meandering walks, and just be outdoors.

It takes some creativity and imagination, but it is possible to create new shared activities that bring just as much joy and pleasure as others used to. It's vital that the two of you continue to share each other's company while participating in hobbies and activities that you both enjoy. This will help maintain your bond and strengthen your intimacy and friendship. Discuss your interests with your partner, and find some new things that the two of you can do together.

Seek Support from Others in Similar Situations

Although being a partner to someone with chronic pain and illness can feel lonely and isolating, you're not alone. There are so many other people in a similar situation. Consider connecting with other people who have partners with chronic pain and illness. Receiving support from somebody who really understands what you're going through can be priceless. I know that, for myself, having friends with similar conditions to mine has relieved the need for me to feel understood by those who cannot possibly understand what I am going through. These friends really get me, and I don't have to explain much for them to understand what I'm experiencing. The same applies to you; having friends who are in similar situations can be tremendously supportive and rewarding. Where can you find other people in your situation? Ask around, search online, and talk to your doctor.

Know Your Limits and Set Realistic Expectations

We often expect more from ourselves than is realistic. You have more on your plate now that your partner has a serious health condition, and this may take up a fair amount of your time and energy. Have compassion for yourself, and don't set your expectations too high or push yourself beyond your limits physically, mentally, or emotionally. This is important to avoid burning out.

Have reasonable expectations of your partner, too. Really listen to her, and honour her boundaries and limited abilities. At the same time, *do* have expectations of your partner, because that may help motivate her to some extent. Expect that she *will* work to help herself and not just give up, allow depression to take over, and lie like a lump on the couch (although once in a while, lying like a lump on the couch is ok!). Expect that she will keep looking for solutions and ways to relieve her pain and discomfort. Expect that she will do all she can to be as healthy as possible. These are positive expectations that support your partner on her healing journey. You are a team, and you are working together on this. Be aware of both your and your partner's limits, and stick to them.

Things to Watch For

Burnout is a real risk for partners of those with chronic pain and illness. The following are some warning signs that you might be approaching burnout:

- Withdrawal from friends and family
- Loss of interest in activities you previously enjoyed
- Feelings of sadness, irritability, hopelessness, and helplessness
- Changes in appetite, weight, or both
- Changes in sleep patterns
- Increase in illness or sickness

- Desire to hurt yourself or your partner
- Emotional and physical exhaustion

If you are having any of these symptoms, it's time to seek help for yourself and to get support and extra assistance in caring for your partner. Please see your family doctor to start with. Whatever you have been doing up until now is not working well enough, so it's time to make a change. Continuing on this path and hoping things will be different is not going to work.

TAKE ACTION!

IF YOU'VE BEEN feeling that taking time for yourself while your partner is suffering from chronic pain and illness is selfish, I hope that your perspective has changed after reading this chapter. Making your physical health and mental well-being priorities is one of the best things that you can do to help your relationship and your partner. Maintaining a sense of happiness, enjoyment, and fulfillment is key, because you will be much better able to help and support your partner than if you feel run down, worn out, and resentful.

You may insist that you don't have the time to do things for yourself. *Make time!* If you need help from someone else to create an opening in your schedule, then *ask for help.* If you think that having time for yourself isn't important enough to ask for help, please reconsider. You can't afford *not* to take good care of you.

The following is a condensed summary of the discussion section as well as some basic suggestions for what you can do for yourself to live well despite your partner's condition. Use these as a starting point, and build on them as needed:

1. **Maintain your health.** Make sure you're seeing your family doctor for annual check-ups—and in between if you have any concerns about your health. Look after your mental and emotional health by seeing a counsellor or psychologist if you feel you're still struggling despite the support you may already have.

2. **Schedule a time at least once a week to do something for yourself.** Exercise is important, as is spending time with friends (don't isolate yourself!), engaging in hobbies, and possibly just having some quiet time on your own. Once a week is a starting point. Eventually aim for at least three times a week. Start small and work your way up.

3. **Solidify *your* support network.** Take out a sheet of paper, computer, tablet, or smartphone, and list all the people whom you rely on and could potentially rely on for support. Next to their names, write out what sort of support they are able to provide (helping you with household tasks, listening, sporting activities, socializing, etc.). Identify any gaps where you feel you need support but don't have anyone, then find people to fill those gaps. This might even involve going out and meeting new people. Once you have put together a comprehensive list of your support network, refer to it regularly. If you encounter a crisis, pull out the list, and post it somewhere visible. Don't be afraid to rely on others when you need to.

4. Educate yourself. Learn about what it means to be in a relationship with someone who suffers from chronic pain and illness and what you can do to make life as easy as possible for yourself.

5. Read Chapters 10 and 11 of this book. They provide a lot of information on relationships affected by chronic pain and illness, and they offer numerous ideas for increasing communication, connectedness, and intimacy.

6. Last but definitely not least, get together with your partner and make a list of shared activities you can do together. Focus on fun things that are alternatives to what you used to be able to do together. Figure out what your partner can reasonably do, then brainstorm away. Add to the list whenever you think of something new, and keep the list posted in an obvious place, like on the fridge or somewhere else in your kitchen. Try to do one of the activities on the list at least once a week. Shared activities are so important for maintaining the connection you have (or for reconnecting) and for building intimacy.

BEING IN A relationship with a partner who lives with chronic pain and illness can be challenging and frustrating. It can also be tremendously rewarding and fulfilling. You will need to make adjustments to accommodate your partner's condition and at the same time take additional care to ensure you continue to live healthily and happily. With some work and dedication, though, you can strengthen your bond, grow your intimacy, and become closer than ever before.

CHAPTER 13

Endings

MY STORY

SO MANY UNCOMFORTABLE and unwanted feelings came up for me when I sat down to write this chapter. I wish this discussion wasn't necessary, and I wish that for everyone with chronic pain and illness their relationships would work out the first time around. But, of course, relationships do end. They don't always work for otherwise healthy people, so why would our situation be any different?

I've gone through all kinds of break-ups: amicable, acrimonious, and just downright confusing. Some break-ups took less than an hour, and some took months. Some really hurt me, while others set me free. There are a few I would like to tell you about.

My relationship with my ex-husband, Rob, was very volatile and dysfunctional. I experienced considerable mental and emotional abuse while I was with him, and I was moody, reactive, and controlling. Nevertheless, I had tried very hard throughout the relationship to make it work—I saw counsellors, I read books on relationships, I sought advice from friends, but nothing seemed to help. One day, something just snapped in my head, and I was done. Just done. I had already spent years crying over what wasn't working. For example, I was used to waking up at 2am with Rob gone. When I would ask him later in the day where he had been, he would reply, "I went for a drive." At 2am? Who does that?! To this day, I still don't know what he was doing in the middle of the night, although I think I can make a pretty good guess.

When I finally decided it was over, I told him. At first, he was extremely upset and started to cry. Cry? I was incredibly confused because most of the time he was not at all present in the relationship and showed very little interest in me, let alone in making it work. He was more likely to ignore me for days or weeks than to express any sort of genuine emotion. I was the crier in this relationship! What was he doing crying? And boy did he cry. He cried and cried and cried and cried. I was so unused to seeing a grown man cry that I became extremely uncomfortable and had an overwhelming urge to laugh. I actually had to turn away so he wouldn't be able to see me struggling to rein in my mirth. After the crying, we talked for a bit, him pleading for me not to leave. But I made it clear that I had given him many chances that he hadn't taken, so I was leaving, period. I guess he realized that I was serious, so something shifted in him. Maybe he decided it was time to try a different approach, because this is what he said to me, referring to my pelvic pain:

"Who would ever want you? You should just stay with me."

I feel like that statement needs a moment of silence so all the implications have a chance to reverberate.

Rob uttered those words 14 years ago, and I still carry them around because, on some level, I believe them. Who *would* ever want me like this? My logical counsellor brain knows that this statement only carries the weight that I give it. It's not a truth. It's one person's opinion—the opinion of a person who had just been extremely hurt and was lashing out. Yet at the time I felt that it confirmed my doctor's prediction that my condition would prevent me from having a long-term relationship. I carried those two judgments around with me for so many years. They made me sad and afraid, and they stopped me from taking risks and possibly opening my heart to someone who would have accepted me just the way I was.

Rob wasn't the only one who had this kind of reaction. Many years later, when Jack and I broke up, he called after a few months to talk me into getting back together. I declined, gracefully I'd like to think. As much as I had loved Jack, I didn't want to end up back in that mentally and emotionally abusive relationship again (see the pattern here?). But he kept pushing. Finally, when he realized I was serious, he tried a different approach:

"We should stay together because you don't like sex, and I'm ok with that."

During the conversation he also implied that it would be hard for me to find anyone else who would be ok with my condition. My brain heard the same message from Jack that Rob had given me years before: *nobody is going to want you because you are defective.* I remember that my first thought at the time, after, "He's right," was, "But I love sex! It's just that it hurts." I had even told Jack this numerous times. I was confounded that after four years of being together, he still didn't understand.

Rob and Jack's words scraped over a raw spot in me, like a cheese grater on an open wound. My heart still hurts as I write about this, even though my brain knows that they were just words from men who were reacting out of fear and pain. And they weren't right about me. I've *had* relationships since them—better relationships, with caring and kind men who were willing to accept my physical condition. And you know what else? After each of my relationships with Rob and Jack ended, my physical pain decreased significantly. If that wasn't a clear sign from my body, I don't know what else could be.

Ok, one more break-up story, and this one's a little lighter. Last year I broke up with Antonio, whom I'd been dating for five or six months. The relationship was ok at first—he was kind, generous, chivalrous, attractive, and extremely intelligent—but as time went on, he started to withdraw. Antonio was going through a difficult time, questioning his life choices and generally unsure of where he was headed. The more he withdrew, the less fulfilled I felt in the relationship. By the end my emotional needs weren't even close to being met. While we were having our break-up talk he said, "I'm lost."

And I replied, "And I'm not lost."

In that moment, I felt the power of finally having stepped into myself, owned my feelings, stopped taking things personally, and taken responsibility for my emotions and actions. The last 20 years of pain, confusion, tears, frustration, anger, sadness, grief, trauma, exhaustion, struggle, abuse, and suffering—as well as all the years of therapy, personal growth work, introspection, reflection, medical appointments, researching, experimenting with endless therapies, hoping, reading, and fighting to over-come chronic pain and illness—all culminated in that one moment when I realized that for the first time in my life, I was not lost. I thought, *I know who I am. I love myself. I respect myself so much for what I have been through and what I have made of my life. I know what I want, and I'm not going to settle for anything less than I deserve because I have worked so damned hard to get here. I am not going anywhere but forward.*

"No, you're definitely not lost," he agreed.

LET'S DISCUSS

NOT ALL RELATIONSHIPS are strong enough to weather chronic pain and illness. And that can be really difficult to accept. It's extremely painful to realize that the relationship you're in isn't working and isn't supporting you at a time when you need it most.

Deciding to end a relationship can be incredibly tough. It may seem a lot easier to stay than to break up. But if the relationship is negatively affecting your health, is it worth it to stay? I mean *really* worth it?

Ending a Relationship

It takes courage to make the decision to end your relation-ship. You've got to be brave to recognize and acknowledge when something isn't working and it's time to end things.

The answer to whether a relationship is going to work cannot be found in how ill you are or how much pain you're in. Yes, chronic pain and illness seem to draw out and expose problems in relationships that might otherwise stay hidden a lot longer; but ultimately, it's all about whether you're with the right person for *you*. If you're in a relationship with someone incompatible, either the relationship is not going to last or it's going to be rocky and you're going to be unhappy. If you're solid, you're solid. If you're not, the cracks will start to show when the relationship is put under strain by something such as chronic pain or illness.

Here are three common reasons you might decide to step away from your relationship:

1. Couples counselling has not worked.
2. Your relationship isn't working, and your partner refuses to try couples counselling with you. As in any relationship, both of you have to be willing to dedicate time and energy to make it work; you can't do it all yourself.
3. You don't have the resilience to deal with your partner's unhelpful behaviour and personal issues.

A good sign that your partnership isn't working is increased pain and stress and decreased happiness. If you're waiting for him to change, to finally do what you've been asking him to do for the past few years—stop making excuses for him, stop waiting, and start packing. If your partner hasn't stepped up to the plate or changed his behaviour by now, it's not going to happen. And you don't need to know why he won't change, only that he hasn't. He may love you, but sometimes love isn't enough. Sometimes what's really needed is action. If any of this sounds familiar, it's time for you to move on and take care of *you*.

It might be harder to accept the break-up if your partner made the decision to end the relationship. You probably feel extremely hurt. You may be confused. You may be upset because you feel that, with a bit of effort, it really could have worked. But know that relationships that are healthy, solid, and heading in a positive direction generally don't end in break-ups. There was a reason for this, and if the relationship wasn't working, you will probably be better off in the long run without it. It's time to move on and look after yourself. Being rejected is never easy; if you're going through this, I would encourage you to go back to Chapter 6, on rejection and read through it again.

Regardless of who made the decision to end the relationship, more often than not you feel a lot of emotional pain when it ends. Your heart is aching and you feel like your life is over and nothing's ever going to be the same and you're never going to meet anyone ever again and this is the most tragic thing that has ever happened in your life and you're never going to get over it. And if you have a chronic condition, the voice in your head can get especially worked up. How will you ever again meet anyone who'll understand your condition, or who will be as patient and willing to be with you? How are you going to survive without his support and love? I can't tell you exactly how you will come through this, but I can tell you that *you will*.

For some of you, the opposite will be true in terms of emotions. You may experience very little pain when your relationship ends. You may instead feel tremendous relief, bittersweet feelings, freedom, and even happiness.

Whatever you feel when your relationship ends, the emotions will eventually pass, you will be able to move on, and life will continue. You may even find that your sense of well-being and happiness increase. But what do you do in the meantime? Read on.

Break-ups and Blame

Are you blaming yourself for your break-up? Do you feel that it happened because you did something wrong or because you're not good enough? If yes, then you're not alone. And you're also not alone in allowing your brain to twist itself into knots trying to find an explanation for why the relationship didn't work out. As humans our brains crave knowing the *why* of things, and when a clear answer isn't available we will create an imagined one. More often than not, we end up blaming ourselves in our imaginary world, without any basis for doing so.

Let me say this: there is nothing wrong with you. You didn't do anything wrong. You're not to blame. Your ex is not to blame. What happened was that the two of you were not the right match for a long-term relationship.

You might be tempted to blame your condition for the break-up. It can be easy to foist the entire relationship breakdown on your pain condition. It's just another way of blaming yourself. Putting all the blame on your condition is also a way of deflecting responsibility for your actual role in the break-up. In many cases, chronic pain and illness can be significant factors in a relationship ending, but they're not the only factors. There is so much more in play—your compatibility, communication style, values, schedules, and so on. Break-ups are complex, and it's rare (if not impossible) to be able to pin the blame on one issue.

Ultimately, blaming your pain or illness for the break-up of a relationship is futile and often inaccurate. Turning the blame for your condition inward is also really unhelpful, particularly as you need to be compassionate and caring with yourself, especially in difficult times. Your partner may blame your condition, and your condition may be one reason, but it's not the only reason, and if your partner blames your condition, his doing so says more about him than about you.

In a nutshell: blame is futile. Blaming someone or something for a relationship ending is not the answer. Taking responsibility for your role in the break-up, accepting that the relationship has ended, being as objective about the situation as you can, taking care of yourself with compassion, and forgiving yourself (and your partner, eventually)—those are the answers.

Surviving a Break-up

Suddenly you're alone. No partner to call or text with every day. He's not there to share meals with or enjoy a lazy cup of coffee on a Sunday. Maybe you're losing mutual friends and connections you made with his family. You're left to get on with your life, a life you had imagined would include him.

You and your old friends, chronic pain and illness, alone and together again. It can really be challenging to go through a break-up when you have chronic pain and illness. Because it's an extremely emotional time, and stress and depression can affect your condition, you may find that your symptoms increase. Your heart is aching, and so is the rest of your body. Hopefully, as your heart heals, the pain in your body will subside.

So how do you heal the pain in your heart? The only way out of difficult emotional situations is through them. This means allowing yourself to fully feel the sadness for the loss of your relationship. It's normal to go through the grieving process when a relationship ends. We talked about the grieving process earlier in the book: denial, anger, bargaining, depression, then acceptance. Expect these phases to come up in some form or another, and don't fight them.

If you allow yourself to really experience your emotions, you will likely feel them intensely. This is a good thing, even if it doesn't feel like it at the time. But the more you allow yourself to really experience the feelings, the more quickly they will pass. If you stuff them down, ignore them, or eat yourself numb, you are not going "through," you are going "around," which means those feelings will stay in your body, linger, and re-emerge throughout your life in the form of emotional and physical pain, fatigue, anger, resentment, and even loud outbursts. Being present with your emotions and going "through" them is difficult, yet it's faster, healthier, and less painful in the long run than avoiding them or stuffing them all back down.

Coping with emotions is one thing, but what about the empty gap that now exists where your partner used to be? How do you fill that void? Start by pulling out your Personal Foundation Sheet that you created in Chapter 3. Review your support system and what you need to do to take care of yourself, and then put your plan into action. Ask for help. Reach out to your friends, gain comfort from the people near and dear to you. Book an appointment with your counsellor. Talking about how you're feeling is a great way to start the healing process. Get in touch with those people who you feel will be able to support you best.

If you've been relying on your partner financially or to help with housework, errands, and driving, it might seem impossible for you to figure out how you're going to survive without him. But you *can* and you *will*. Go to your support network; ask for help. Talk to people and brainstorm how to deal with the gaps your partner used to fill.

You will survive this. And while it may seem utterly awful, painful, and defeating, and you may think you're never going to find another relationship and you're not going to be able to make it on your own, you may also find that in the long run, things turn out much better than you expected. You possess an incredible amount of strength that helps you get through every day of your pain and illness. You are probably stronger than most people you know. Use this strength to help you through this difficult time.

A Note on Reaching Out

When I used to go through break-ups, I believed that my friends should be the ones to reach out and get in touch with me. It was their job to contact me and check in regularly to see how I was doing—and when they didn't, I would become angry: "I'm the one who's hurting and in pain. Why should I be the one who reaches out to my friends? They should be reaching out to me!"

It took me a while to recognize how untrue this belief really was. I eventually realized that I was off track. My friends have no obligation to continuously check in with me, and they certainly can't read my mind as to what I need or when. You might think, "But they know I'm going through a break-up, so they should be here for me." The thing is, different people want different things during crises; some people like to be alone, while others need constant contact. Your friends won't know what you need without you telling them, and your expectations of what "being there" means may not match up with those of your friends.

When you start feeling resentful that your friends aren't getting in touch, pick up the phone and call (or text) them. You may not like it, and sometimes it may feel like you're swallowing your pride when you do it, but I'm pretty sure you'll feel a lot better after you do. It really works! Not only does you reaching out dissipate anger and resentment, but you will also receive comfort and companionship from your good friends who genuinely want to help. Your friends and family have their own lives; they get caught up in their own emotions, troubles, and day-to-day business. They're not going to be perfect with their timing or frequency of contact, and that's not their job anyway. So make a promise to yourself. Whenever you start to feel angry with a friend or family member in a situation like this, even if you logically understand that they have no obligation to call you, reach out to them. Make it a rule: don't let yourself wallow in the self-pity and anger that arises due to a twisted perspective. Take charge, empower yourself, and go get what you need!

Avoiding Self-Destruction

I find that in times of stress, I often want to engage in self-destructive behaviours. When I'm breaking up with someone, I usually have an overwhelming urge to smoke. I'm not a smoker, but I did smoke here and there in the past, and I just love the feeling of lighting up that cigarette and taking the first drag. Ooooooh yes! But now that both of my parents have died of cancer, I am unwilling to light up another cigarette ever again (not that that stops the cravings). I also want to go out and drink until I am obliterated. I want to party and do bad things. I want to get into trouble and be mischievous. I want a really hot, sexy, rebound man. Do I do any of these things anymore? No, but it doesn't stop me from wanting to.

What are your favourite post-break-up self-destructive behaviours?

Realistically, you probably know that if you were to act on these urges you would end up feeling utterly awful. So not worth it. The best thing to do when you have those self-destructive feelings is to surround yourself with friends, comfort, and lots of love. It may not satisfy your need to act out, but in the long run it's a lot better for you and will keep your pain and symptoms down rather than flare them up. Alcohol, cigarettes, drugs, unsafe sex, and food are not a good way to cope with emotions, and on top of that may well exacerbate your conditions.

Planning

After a break-up, aside from feeling sad, lost, and alone, it's common to feel scattered and directionless. This is a good time to make a plan. When you make a plan, you start to feel like your life has direction, purpose, and hope again. You'll begin to regain your strength and recognize your ability to be independent. A plan is often as simple as making a list of what you will do to take one step towards feeling better. When I'm going through a break-up, my plan might look something like this:

1. Have a warm bath when I feel sad.
2. E-mail with my friend Amanda at least once a day.
3. Spend time with two friends in person every week.

4. Do my restorative yoga practice at home three times a week.
5. Go for a daily walk, even if it is just once around the block.
6. Ask my stepmom to help me with the errands that my ex used to do for me.
7. Read uplifting books.
8. Cuddle with my dog, Molly.
9. Reconnect with my home environment and make it feel like it is strictly mine again.
10. Make a list of funny movies and stand-up comedy shows to watch when I need a pick-me-up.
11. Continue going to bed at the same time and waking up at the same time.

Your plan can be as short or as long as you like. If you can't do much, keep it simple. If you need your plan to be more medically oriented, then so be it. If you want your plan to include more interaction with people, great, write it down. Don't just leave your plan in your head, though: *write it down*. That way you can easily refer to it and remind yourself what you can do to make yourself feel better at any given moment. Creating a list of goals and plans will help take your mind off some of the pain that you're feeling in your heart and will start to allow you to move on.

Bits and Pieces

Here are a few more tips to help you get over your break-up:

- Stick to your routine; don't make any significant changes, as doing so can negatively affect your condition.

- If you had an exercise routine, stick with it, whether it was stretching, breathing, yoga, walking, swimming, or anything else. Moving your body is really helpful, so please don't give it up because you feel like your life has been derailed.
- Process your feelings more effectively by writing about them in a journal. If you don't have a journal, you can just take any old piece of paper and go for it. Writing about what you've been going through can be very cathartic.
- Note the difference between a normal reaction to a break-up and depression. If the sadness isn't going away after many months and you find yourself feeling continually depressed, unmotivated, and hopeless, seek help from your medical doctor.
- Remind yourself that you still have a future. It might be hard to picture right now, but you really don't know how things are going to turn out, and it's very possible that your biggest worries and fears aren't going to come true. In fact, things often turn out better than we think they will.
- Focus on the little things that make you happy. What can you do today to increase your happiness, even by just a little bit?
- Don't immediately dive into another relationship. You need time to grieve, heal, and reflect before you move on with someone else. Allow yourself the time and space you require to truly be ready to date again.
- Don't isolate; try to surround yourself with people as much as possible, whether that means virtually or in person. Consider making new friends. And of course,

please do respect your energy levels and physical abilities so you don't push yourself to do more than you are realistically able.

- As much as possible, stay present. Be in the moment. Try not to spend too much time in the past or in the future. The more you're able to stay in the present moment, feel what you are feeling right now, and focus on what is in front of you, the easier it will be to move on.
- Always remember that you are whole and complete just the way you are, and, like everyone else, you deserve to be loved.

TAKE ACTION!

1. Feel your emotions. Sit with them. Notice their physical sensation in your body. Allowing yourself to experience them fully will help you move forward and prevent you from becoming stuck in the past and/or depressed.

2. Don't blame the break-up on yourself or your condition. In fact, if you can take blame out of the equation completely, you'll have a greater sense of freedom and be less focused on feelings of resentment. And who doesn't want that?

3. Pull out your Personal Foundation Sheet and use it. Don't be afraid to reach out to the people on your list. You put them on there for a reason, and now is the time to rely on them.

4. Make a plan for yourself to help you gain a feeling of direction, purpose, and hope, and write it down.

5. Take excellent care of yourself and surround yourself with comfort and love. Comfort and love may come through any number of sources. I find warm baths and pets to be wonderfully nurturing. Perhaps there are certain people around whom you feel a great sense of love. Be around those who bring out positive feelings and give you energy, hope, and inspiration.

6. Check out resources on getting through break-ups, either online, from the library, or from a bookstore. If you know someone who gives really good advice, approach them, too. Refer to the Bits and Pieces section above.

ENDING A RELATIONSHIP. Breaking up. Separating. Splitting up. It's hard to do gracefully. I don't have a simple, pain-free solution, but what I do know is that this is something you *can* overcome. It takes time, patience, and faith, but you *will* get through it. And the more you take care of your body, mind, and spirit through the healing process, the less impact the break-up will have on your condition. So put yourself first, ask for what you need, and keep reminding yourself how strong you really are.

Hope

LIVING WITH CHRONIC pain and illness is hard. It's probably one of the most difficult challenges, if not *the* most difficult one, you will face in your life. Learning to live well and
joyfully in spite of your condition can significantly reduce
your burden. Finding a loving and mutually supportive relationship can provide you with comfort, energy, and purpose.
Navigating dating and relationships when you have chronic
pain and illness can be tricky, however. It is my hope that,
through this book, you have discovered that it is possible for
you to find and maintain a loving relationship, and you have
learned how to do that.

Along your path to change you'll be faced with numerous difficult decisions, frustrations, and disappointments. It
can be easy to focus on the challenges rather than the victories. When you're in pain, feeling defeated and discouraged
is tempting. Know that something you're doing *is* working.

Every day, you make it through another day. Appreciate yourself for this.

Acknowledge yourself for the work you're doing and for the progress you're making, however small or slow. Focus on what you *can* do. Don't wait for others to make you feel good about yourself. Give yourself a pat on the back whenever you have a good moment.

Living with chronic pain and illness requires refocusing on different accomplishments, kindnesses, and pleasures. There's absolutely nothing wrong with that. It doesn't make you any less of a person, you're simply living in a different way. Focus on yourself and your own happiness, because that's what really matters. Finding gratitude for the experiences you have in your day-to-day existence can be powerful. The more gratitude you feel and express, the more life will bring you to be grateful for, including people and relationships.

When you start putting yourself first, using new tools, and trying on new behaviours, it can feel awkward. This is normal but doesn't mean you should stop. It takes a while before new behaviour feels natural, so keep practicing. You might have to fake it until you make it, and that's just fine. You might have to work on the outside of you for a while before you really feel the results on the inside, in your heart.

You may sense a big void in your heart, a hole that the person you used to be used to fill. That void can feel like a vacuum—dark, infinite, and unfillable. But this void *can* be filled. It can be filled with self-love, self-care, and a sense of purpose. It can be a stretch to find purpose in your life when you are constantly fatigued, uncomfortable, and in pain, and yet it's not only possible but important to do so.

Your purpose may not be evident right away, but stay open to finding it. There were many times when I felt hopeless, useless, and worthless. I couldn't find a reason for my existence on this planet if I had to lie around on the couch for most of the day, every day. Finding my purpose was the antidote to these awful feelings.

My purpose is to help others—through my part-time work as a coach and counsellor, and through writing this book. I could not have written this book without enduring all the pain and suffering I've experienced in the last 20 years. My suffering gave me purpose. My suffering became my work, and now my work is giving me purpose. What gives *you* purpose? Recognizing your contribution to the world is uplifting and inspiring and brings deep comfort.

Relationships can also provide us with a sense of purpose. You may feel more purposeful simply because you are in a relationship, or because you develop a sense of purpose through the shared goals you and your partner set. It's critical, however, not to allow your partner to become your purpose for being. You are a separate and complete individual on your own, and it's important to retain a sense of self while in a relationship.

It's possible that you've read this book and decided that a relationship isn't going to work for you right now. And that's ok. Some of you may decide that having an intimate relationship on top of what you deal with every day will just be too much, ever. I get that. You may change your mind or you may not. Whatever you decide will be right for you. Please know, however, that it *is* possible for you to have a relationship that lasts, if that's what you want. Know that you are worthy of a relationship and of love. As human beings, one of our purposes is simply to love and be loved. Please don't deprive yourself of love because you feel unworthy, or you think it's too complicated, or you believe nobody will love you, or you think you're defective. There is nothing inherently wrong with you. You *are* lovable. If you're reading this and think that this applies to everyone else but you, think again. Every one of us is lovable, regardless of how messed up our bodies and minds may be at times. Our conditions don't make us any less human, any less worthy, or any less deserving of love.

This book covers some pretty serious stuff—lots of boundaries, limits, rules, communication, and work. I may have suggested having fun a few times, but perhaps not enough. So I want to remind you to have fun. Break your rules once in a while. For example, the other night I broke my strict in-bed-by-10 rule and stayed out until 2:30am— shocking, I know! I anticipated the consequences, and I paid them, but it was worth it. Once in a while, it *is* worth it. After all, you're not a robot!

What I haven't talked about much in this book is the idea of healing from chronic pain and illness. This doesn't mean that I don't believe it's possible. On the one hand, it's called chronic for a reason, and that means that it goes on and on and on and on—and on. Most of my doctors have told me that I can reasonably expect to have these conditions for the rest of my life. And that's their job because, for the most part, people don't recover from chronic conditions. On the other hand, I believe it's possible to recover fully and completely. I know that some people have, and therefore I know it's possible for the rest of us. The thing is, I don't know *how* to recover completely. I don't know what it will take for my body to shift into a different mode and be fully healed. I have tried a *lot* of different therapies. Some have helped, some have made things worse, and some have made absolutely no difference. I continue to try various therapies at my leisure without any major expectations. In the meantime, I accept the way things are right now. Acceptance doesn't mean I'm giving up. It means I'm being realistic about where I am right now and what I need in this moment. Acceptance gives me the space to take care of myself the way I need to.

Thank you for allowing me the opportunity to share a piece of my life that might in some way help others. I hope you have found it useful. For me, this book is all about hope. I wrote it for those who are in the midst of dealing with chronic pain and illness, to show that right now, even in this place of suffering, there is still the opportunity for love and joy in our lives, regardless of whether or not we recover from our condition. I wrote it for everyone with chronic pain and illness who has lost hope in the possibility of having a nurturing and loving relationship. And I wrote it for myself because I was one of those people. Today, I truly believe we can all have relationships that bring us love, joy, and healing, relationships that enrich our lives. Sure, it may take a considerable amount of work, and it will be more complicated than for those without chronic pain or illness, but it will be worth the effort.

Hope keeps me going. Hope gets me through the painful, exhausting days. Hope keeps me from getting discouraged. Hope is powerful. Hope itself raises me up and keeps me going. Without hope, life is pretty bleak. I would rather go through life with hope than without it. So, I keep hoping, because there is always a chance that things are going to work out just the way I want them to, or even better. And if they don't work out the way I want them to, I can trust that they will work out the way I need them to. I will be ok. You will be ok. All we have right now is the moment we are in, so let's make the most of this moment. Let's have hope in this moment.

Acknowledgements

THIS BOOK IS the result of many years of pain, illness, life experience, growth, learning and education. It would not have come to fruition without all the love and support I have received throughout my life from some very important people.

First, I would like to thank my incredible editor, Dania Sheldon. It was such a pleasure to work with her, not least because she really "got" me. I never thought the editing process would be enjoyable, but somehow, she managed to make it so.

Big props to my proofreader, Julia Caceres, for her exquisite attention to detail and enthusiastic support. It was a pleasure to work with her.

I'm thrilled with the book cover, and for that I thank Naomi MacDougall, who also worked her magic on the inside design.

Thank you to my team at Lucky Bat Books, Jessica Santina and Courtney Sermone, who helped me make this book a reality.

To Richard Dolmat of Digital Sound Magic Recording Studios Ltd., you are the best! I never thought I'd be able to record an audiobook myself, but you made it happen. Thank you.

I really lucked out when I put together my book team. Everyone has been so diligent, supportive, professional and fun to work with.

A big thank you to my medical team, who keeps me in one piece: Dr. Kaylani Chung, Dr. Ric Arseneau, Beverly Kosuljandic and Donna Topham.

Thank you to everyone else who helped make this book happen: Melanie Schroeder, Denise Stroude, Bea Rhodes, Amanda Chow, Morgyn Chandler and Sarah Keevil.

Two mentors have really stood out. Shea Hampton had a profound impact on my life from early on. I'm so grateful for everything that I have learned from her, especially those things that are not easily teachable. Denise Stroude has been the best role model and mentor I could have asked for in my "new life." I look forward to continuing to learn from her.

And last but certainly not least, thank you to my best friends who always have my back and are so incredibly patient and understanding: Julie Green, Jason Currell, Paula Becker, Amanda Chow, Gillian McKenzie and Stephanie Spacciante. I am the luckiest person to have them in my life!

Resources

Some of my favourite books:

Ansari, Aziz, and Eric Klinenberg. *Modern Romance.* New York: Penguin, 2015.

Beattie, Melody. *Codependent No More: How to Stop Controlling Others and Start Caring for Yourself.* Center City, MN: Hazelden, 1986.

Behrendt, Greg, and Liz Tuccillo. *He's Just Not That Into You: The No-Excuses Truth to Understanding Guys.* New York: Simon and Schuster, 2009.

Bernhard, Toni. *How to Be Sick: A Buddhist-Inspired Guide for the Chronically Ill and Their Caregivers.* Somerville, MA: Wisdom Publications, 2010.

Castillo, Brooke. *Self-Coaching 101: Use Your Mind – Don't Let it Use You.* USA: Brooke Castillo, 2009.

Chapman, Gary D. *The Five Love Languages: The Secret to Love that Lasts.* Chicago, IL: Moody Publishers, 2009.

Chapman, Gary D., and Jennifer Thomas. *The Five Languages of Apology: How to Experience Healing in All Your Relationships.* Chicago, IL: Northfield Publishing, 2006.

Hendrix, Harville. *Getting the Love You Want.* New York: St. Martin's Press, 1988.

Huber, Cheri. *There is Nothing Wrong With You.* Murphys, CA: Keep It Simple Books, 2001.

Frankl, Viktor E. *Man's Search for Meaning.* Boston: Beacon Press, 1959.

LaPorte, Danielle. *The Desire Map: A Guide to Creating Goals with Soul.* Louisville, CO: Sounds True Publishing, 2014.

Maté, Gabor. *When the Body Says No: The Cost of Hidden Stress.* Toronto: Vintage Canada, 2003.

Prophet, Elizabeth Clare. *Soul Mates and Twin Flames: The Spiritual Dimension of Love and Relationships.* Gardinar, MT: Summit University Press, 1999.

Ruiz, Don Miguel. *The Four Agreements: A Practical Guide to Personal Freedom.* San Rafael, CA: Amber-Allen Publishing, 1997.

Selak, Joy, and Steven S. Overman. *You Don't Look Sick! Living Well With Chronic Invisible Illness*. New York: Demos Medical Publishing, 2012.

Warner, Brad. *Hardcore Zen: Punk Rock, Monster Movies and the Truth About Reality*. Somerville, MA: Wisdom Publications, 2003.

My Favourite Website for Healing:

Abigail Steidley, Coach, Mentor, Healer: abigailsteidley.com

 **KIRA LYNNE** was born in Edmonton, Alberta, and has a Bachelor of Arts from the University of British Columbia as well as a Professional Counsellor Diploma from Rhodes Wellness College. Kira worked in law for many years before changing tracks to become a Life Coach, Professional Counsellor, and Registered Holistic Nutritionist. She has lived with chronic pain and illness for over 20 years, and it was her journey to find answers that led to this book. She lives in Vancouver, British Columbia.

54762615R00213

Made in the USA
Charleston, SC
13 April 2016